*Robert Frost*

Revised Edition

Twayne's United States Authors Series

Kenneth Eble, Editor
*University of Utah*

TUSAS 107

ROBERT FROST
(1874—1963)
*Photograph reprinted by permission of Dartmouth Library*

# *Robert Frost*

Revised Edition

By Philip L. Gerber

*State University of New York*
*College at Brockport*

*Twayne Publishers* • *Boston*

*Robert Frost*

Philip L. Gerber

First Edition Copyright © 1966 by
Twayne Publishers, Inc.
Revised Edition Copyright © 1982 by
G. K. Hall & Co.
Published by Twayne Publishers
A Division of G. K. Hall & Company
70 Lincoln Street
Boston, Massachusetts 02111

Book Production by Marne B. Sultz

Book Design by Barbara Anderson

Printed on permanent/durable acid-free
paper and bound in the United States of
America.


**Library of Congress Cataloging in
Publication Data**

Gerber, Philip L.
    Robert Frost.

    (Twayne's United States authors series :
    TUSAS 107)
    Bibliography: pp. 183–195
    Includes index.
    1. Frost, Robert, 1874–1963—
—Criticism and interpretation.
I. Title. II. Series.
PS3511.R94Z66    1982    811'.52    81-6976

    ISBN 0-8057-7348-7 (Hardcover)
    ISBN 0-8057-7426-2 (Paperback)

*Once Again, to Gene*

# Contents

## About the Author

Philip L. Gerber has taught American literature at universities in Texas, Utah, California, and South Dakota. He is currently Professor of English on the Brockport campus of the State University of New York. He also holds the rank of Faculty Exchange Scholar within the SUNY system. He has published books, articles, and interviews concerning a wide variety of modern figures, including Theodore Dreiser, Willa Cather, Amy Lowell, Harriet Monroe, William Carlos Williams, W. D. Snodgrass, Karl Shapiro, and Joyce Carol Oates. Two of his books, *Theodore Dreiser* and *Willa Cather,* have appeared in Twayne's United States Authors Series.

# Preface to the Revised Edition

When the first edition of this study was begun, Robert Frost was still with us, enjoying the final years of his immense and deserved popularity. His living presence offered the scholar of 1962 a precious sense of connection with the modern movement in American poetry which extended back to its earliest beginnings in 1912–13. That continuity has been broken almost totally today. The literary moment recedes further into history, with Archibald MacLeish now perhaps our sole surviving link with the early days. By the time the first edition was in print, Robert Frost had died, but the anticipated wave of material in print concerning him and his work had not yet gathered its full strength. During the years since Frost's death, much has been printed that has made a revision of this work not only desirable but mandatory.

By 1962 Frost's publication of *In the Clearing* had rendered his *Complete Poems* of 1949 obsolete. But the new book had not yet been incorporated into the body of his work. That task remained for Edward Connery Lathem, whose *The Poetry of Robert Frost* (1969) at once became the standard edition of Frost's complete verse. It is to this volume that the reader of the present revision is now sent for pertinent references concerning the texts of individual poems.

In the early 1960s the absence of Lawrance Thompson's award-winning biography of Robert Frost necessitated reliance for biographical data upon works such as Elizabeth Shepley Sergeant's *Robert Frost: The Trial by Existence*. Still an excellent and highly useful volume, the Sergeant biography was corrected and, of course, immeasurably superseded in scope by Thompson's three-volume life, the fruit of a quarter century of patient effort. I have relied upon Thompson particularly in evaluating my account of Robert Frost's life in Chapter One.

Fortunately, Louis Untermeyer had published his invaluable collection of Robert Frost's letters in time for me to mine them for unique personal opinions and statements before completing my original manuscript. Since 1963, however, these letters have been augmented by additional collections of correspondence, all of which have been of value in updating this study. Likewise, only the delightful memoir prepared by Daniel Smythe, *Robert Frost Speaks*, influenced my original text. Many other memoirs were to follow, notably in volumes by Cook, Francis, and Mertins. Memoirs of various types and lengths continue to appear, and I have consulted all that were accessible to me in preparing new copy.

While much valuable Frost criticism had appeared by 1964, the major studies of Frost's poetry by Kemp, Lentricchia, and Poirier were yet to see print, as were a plethora of critical articles. Whether published singly or in volumes of collected essays, these studies have enriched the body of criticism concerning Frost. The temptation has been to incorporate more from such works than befits an introductory survey. Reluctantly, I have remained content in most instances to point the reader in the direction of valuable essays intended for the specialist and of important critical volumes, where he may appreciate the critics' work in its full and original form.

But I have, at the same time, taken pains to keep the disclosures, opinions, analyses, and conclusions of other critics in mind as I examined my chapters concerning Robert Frost's craftsmanship, theories, and themes. In most instances, happily, I have found my original estimates to be sound and therefore have not altered my opinions radically. In certain instances I have enlarged my discussion in order to expand upon what was perhaps an inadequate treatment of an important issue. One such instance concerns the relationship of Robert Frost's thinking with that of his forebear Ralph Waldo Emerson. This is a significant connection, much depending upon how closely or loosely the minds and practices of these two American poets impinge upon one another. The issue has been hotly contested; much has been written comparing them, and much more undoubtedly will appear in the future.

Totally new to this edition is Chapter Six, concerning the body of criticism surrounding Robert Frost since 1913. In studying a major figure such as Frost, the student profits from having ready access to an overview of the critical activity which concerns the author, including an analysis of major trends within that activity and some indication of what the indispensable texts might be. In Chapter Six I have attempted to meet these needs.

*Preface to the Revised Edition*

That the bibliography attached to the second edition bears almost no resemblance to its original counterpart is but one indication of the immense strides that have been taken by scholars in filling gaps in the biographical, bibliographical, and critical areas important to an understanding of Robert Frost and his poetry. While the bibliography must of necessity be rather highly selective—more so than I would have wished, ideally—it does gather in one place representative titles from the most pertinent and valuable work published thus far. Finally, for the orientation of the reader, I have annotated each entry in the bibliography, pointing out, usually, the nature of its concern and its relative significance within the critical canon. For expansion of this selective list, the student is referred to the considerably more extensive bibliographical volumes on Robert Frost that now are readily available in most libraries.

Philip L. Gerber

*State University of New York, College at Brockport*

# *Acknowledgments*

I am indebted to Kenneth E. Eble, TUSAS Field Editor, for suggesting this revision of *Robert Frost* and for providing a valuable overview of needs and suggestions which have greatly aided me in writing it. At G. K. Hall, Caroline Birdsall and Christine Lamb have aided me during the two years in which the manuscript was in progress; and a special thanks is due Norma Fryatt, copyeditor, whose close eye for detail has saved me from any number of potential embarrassments. The State University of New York granted me a Sabbatical Leave during the school year 1979–80, and I am particularly grateful for the time which made it possible for this revision to be completed on schedule.

# Chronology

1874    March 26, Robert Lee Frost born in San Francisco, California, son of William Prescott Frost, Jr., and Isabelle Moodic Frost.

1874–1884    Early years in San Francisco.

1885    William Prescott Frost, Jr., dies. Robert Frost moves to Lawrence, Massachusetts, with mother and sister, Jeanie.

1892    Frost graduates from Lawrence High School, co-valedictorian with Elinor White, his high-school sweetheart. Enters Dartmouth College, remaining less than one semester.

1893    Teaches eighth grade in Methuen, Massachusetts; works in mill in Lawrence.

1894    November, "My Butterfly," Frost's first published poem, appears in *The Independent,* a New York City magazine.

1895    Works briefly as a newspaper reporter and teaches in a school managed by his mother. Marries Elinor Miriam White.

1896    September 25, birth of son Elliott.

1897–1899    September, attends Harvard College as a special student.

1899    April 28, birth of daughter Lesley.

1900    Elliott Frost dies. Frost family move to farm near Derry, New Hampshire. Isabelle Moodie Frost dies.

1902    Birth of son Carol.

1903    Birth of daughter Irma.

1905    Birth of daughter Marjorie. Composition of "The Black Cottage," "The Housekeeper," "The Death of the Hired Man."

1906 "The Tuft of Flowers" published in Derry *Enterprise.* Frost teaches at Pinkerton Academy, Derry. "The Trial by Existence" published in *The Independent.*

1907 Birth and death of daughter Elinor Bettina.

1909 "Into Mine Own" published in *New England Magazine.* Leaves the Derry farm.

1911 Ends teaching at Pinkerton Academy and begins teaching at New Hampshire State Normal School, Plymouth; sells Derry farm.

1912 Takes his family to England where he farms and writes poetry in Buckinghamshire.

1913 First book of poetry, *A Boy's Will,* published by David Nutt and Company, London.

1914 Outbreak of World War I. Frost family moves to Gloucestershire. David Nutt publishes Frost's *North of Boston.* Harriet Monroe publishes "The Code" in *Poetry* magazine.

1915 Frost family returns to America, settles on farm near Franconia, New Hampshire. Henry Holt and Company publishes *A Boy's Will* and *North of Boston.*

1916 June, reads "The Bonfire" at Phi Beta Kappa Day, Harvard. November, Henry Holt and Company publishes *Mountain Interval.* Frost elected to National Institute of Arts and Letters.

1917 Serves as Professor of English, Amherst College. *Poetry* awards "The Snow" a prize of $100.

1918 Awarded an honorary M.A. by Amherst.

1920 Leaves Amherst College and moves his family to a farm near South Shaftsbury, Vermont; aids in founding Bread Loaf School of English, Middlebury College.

1921–1923 Serves as Poet in Residence, University of Michigan, Ann Arbor. Returns as Fellow in Creative Arts until spring, 1923.

1923     Henry Holt and Company publishes *Selected Poems* and *New Hampshire.*

1923–1925     Serves as Professor of English, Amherst College.

1924     Receives Pulitzer Prize for *New Hampshire;* receives honorary Litt. D. from Middlebury and Yale.

1925–1926     Serves as Fellow in Letters, University of Michigan.

1926–1938     Serves as Professor of English, Amherst College.

1928     Henry Holt and Company publishes *West-Running Brook.*

1929     The Harbor Press publishes Frost's one-act play, *A Way Out.* Frost's sister, Jeanie, dies.

1930     Henry Holt and Company publishes *Collected Poems.* Frost elected to membership in American Academy of Arts and Letters.

1931     Receives Pulitzer Prize for *Collected Poems* and Russell Loines Poetry Prize of $1,000 from National Institute of Arts and Letters.

1934     Marjorie Frost Fraser dies. Robert and Elinor Frost make first visit to Florida.

1936     Henry Holt and Company publishes *A Further Range.* Frost serves as Charles Eliot Norton Professor of Poetry at Harvard.

1937     Receives his third Pulitzer Prize for *A Further Range.* Harvard awards Frost an honorary Litt. D. Elinor Frost operated on for cancer.

1938     Elinor White Frost dies. Frost resigns from Amherst.

1939     Henry Holt and Company publishes enlarged version of *Collected Poems.* The National Institute of Arts and Letters awards Frost its Gold Medal for Poetry. Frost purchases Homer Noble Farm in Ripton, Vermont.

1939–1942     Serves as Ralph Waldo Emerson Fellow in Poetry, Harvard.

1940    Carol Frost dies, a suicide. Tufts College invites Frost to read as Phi Beta Kappa poet on twenty-fifth anniversary of his first public reading.

1941    Receives Gold Medal from Poetry Society of America; buys home in Cambridge, Massachusetts.

1942    Henry Holt and Company publishes *A Witness Tree*.

1943    Receives his fourth Pulitzer Prize for *A Witness Tree*.

1943–1949    Serves as Ticknor Fellow in the Humanities at Dartmouth College.

1945    Henry Holt and Company publishes *A Masque of Reason*.

1947    Henry Holt and Company publishes *Steeple Bush* and *A Masque of Mercy*.

1948    Amherst College awards Frost an honorary Litt. D.

1949    Henry Holt and Company publishes *Complete Poems*. Amherst College appoints Frost as Simpson Lecturer in Literature. Gold Medal of Limited Editions Club.

1950    The United States Senate passes resolution commending Frost on event of his seventy-fifth birthday.

1953    Award to Frost from the Academy of American Poets.

1954    Publishers and friends honor Frost on his eightieth birthday, New York City and Amherst, Massachusetts. Serves as delegate to World Congress of Writers in São Paulo, Brazil.

1955    Awarded an honorary LL.D. by Dartmouth College.

1957    Trip to England. Oxford and Cambridge Universities and National University of Ireland award Frost honorary Litt. D.

1958    Serves as Consultant in Poetry to Library of Congress.

1959    Publishers and friends honor Frost on anniversary of his eighty-fifth birthday, New York City. United States Senate passes resolution honoring Frost.

1961    January 20, invited to read at inauguration of President John F. Kennedy; reads "The Gift Outright."

1962    Accompanied by Stewart L. Udall, Secretary of the Interior, visits Moscow, reads "Mending Wall," confers with Premier Khrushchev. Awarded an honorary LL.D. by University of Michigan. Holt, Rinehart and Winston publishes *In the Clearing*. December 3, Frost enters Peter Bent Brigham Hospital, Boston, for treatment.

1963    Awarded the Bollingen Prize in Poetry. January 29, dies in Boston, aged eighty-eight.

# Chapter One
# Man Into Myth: Frost's Life

Inappropriate as it may appear for a poet so solidly identified in the popular mind with New England, Robert Frost was born a continent away from the green hills and fields of the Atlantic seaboard. San Francisco in 1874 was a smallish city of wooden homes clustered hopefully below the hills, and its bay was crowded with the rigging of sailing vessels. Some ships had rested at anchor there, stranded, since the gold-rush days. Only now and then does Frost's writing remind one that he was Western-born. Sometimes the fact steals upon a reader with a wild shock of realization, as when in "A Peck of Gold" Frost includes himself as "one of the children told/Some of the blowing dust was gold."

Robert's father, William Prescott Frost, Jr., was something of a drifter. He was also, said his son, "a bad boy who never stopped being one." He worked usually as a newspaperman and sometimes squandered his wages in saloon and casino. Frost's mother, Isabelle Moodie Frost, had been courted by William on his way west from his native Lawrence, Massachusetts, during a time when both served as schoolteachers in a small private academy in Pennsylvania. Early in 1876, frightened by the violence that liquor kindled in her husband, Isabelle fled him and San Francisco. Packing two-year-old Robert with her, she crossed the continent to William's parents in Lawrence. But the elder Frosts reminded her that a woman's place was beside her husband. Besides, how could they believe their clever son undependable?

Belle Frost was pregnant when she left the Golden Gate. She was allowed to remain in Lawrence until the birth of Robert's sister, Jeanie; then the little family was packed on a westbound train. A few years later, William Frost was dead at the age of thirty-four. Belle's homing instinct—bulwarked this time by her husband's dying request to be buried at home—put the three on the road once more. By the time he was eleven, Robert Frost had crossed the United States three times. His memories of his father remained dim, and of San Francisco itself he was able to recall little except the unforgettable vision of the sea and the cliffs against which "the shattered water" broke. Although he seems to have gained little he could later put to literary use, Frost remained proud of the fact that he had "one foot in each great ocean."

Isabelle Frost went to work to support her children. She located a school in Salem, New Hampshire, at a stipend of nine dollars a week. Its paucity was mitigated by the fact that her son and daughter were included among her pupils. This day-long contact bound the family together into a closely knit group. When high school years came around, Robert entered school in Lawrence, his grandparents' home. He was fourteen and proved an excellent scholar.

Before long Robert formed an attachment with a girl whose mind matched his own, Elinor White. In 1892 Elinor served with him as co-valedictorian of their graduating class; and, when he was twenty-one, she married him. It was with Elinor's encouragement also that Robert first began to compose verse which he published in the Lawrence High School *Bulletin*. He gravitated naturally to the personal lyric, but his most ambitious neophyte work was based upon his reading of La Noche Triste in William Prescott's *The Conquest of Mexico*.

The poet's wings were sprouting but barely showed as yet, and he was far from being equipped for free flight. His high school valedictory concerned poetry. It included references to the poet's "varied heart beats and converse with nature" and spoke of a poet's grandest ideas coming after his last line was written. Frost's youthful mind was already occupied with what would eventually become both vocation and avocation, ideally blended.

Two years after graduation, his first commercially published poem, "My Butterfly," appeared in *The Independent,* a small magazine edited by William Hayes Ward, which came to his attention during the fall of 1892. "My Butterfly" was featured on the magazine's front page. Although it promised little in terms of future distinction for its author, the poem was at least a beginning. Its subject, the mutability of natural things, was of universal scope and would preoccupy later works. Its diction, not surprisingly, was "poetic" in the most stilted and imitative sense:

> Thine emulous fond flowers are dead, too,
> And the daft sun-assaulter, he
> That frighted thee so oft, is fled or dead:

The poem, Frost admitted in evaluating it much later, was not much, but "it was the beginning of *me.*" The editor of *The Independent* believed his young contributor to be under the beneficent influence of Sidney Lanier, and perhaps he was.

"I have but recently discovered my powers," wrote Frost in a note to *The Independent* when his verse was accepted.[1] What an adrenalin publication could be! The magazine's check for fifteen dollars caused him to walk on air. In the flush of enthusiasm, he was prompted to make the same sort of gesture many another young poet has made, before and since. At his own expense he rushed into print a slight volume of verse. Entitled *Twilight,* it contained five poems, among them "My Butterfly." The entire press run was two copies, one for himself, the other for Elinor White, then his fiancée. When Elinor seemed not to exhibit the proper appreciation of his tribute, he ripped his own copy impetuously and discarded it. That left a single copy extant, now among the genuine rarities of Frostiana.

Robert considered suicide, but instead he lost himself in an impulsive tramp through the Dismal Swamp of North Carolina, recovered his emotional balance, and returned home. Robert and Elinor soon patched up their spat. In the fall of 1895 Isabelle Frost launched a private school in Lawrence, and both young people served on her staff. Propinquity served its purpose. By late December the couple were married, a union which was to endure for more than forty years. For a time they continued with the school, Robert teaching arithmetic, Elinor instructing in French; but both were busy in other respects as well. Robert produced more poems and published them in *The Independent.* Elinor, in September, 1896, gave birth to a son, who was named Elliott.

Being a family man now, Frost began to lay plans for his future. How was he going to earn his bread and butter? Since poetry seemed to offer no practical possibilities as a vocation, he very naturally was led to consider a career in teaching. But then as now one needed college credits and a degree to get ahead. Young Frost had attended Dartmouth briefly upon completing high school, but he had withdrawn. It had not worked out well. Perhaps, though, he might be allowed to reenter college and gain a recognized teaching certificate. He wrote to Dean Briggs of Harvard, reminding him that five years earlier he had passed his examinations for admission. He felt secure, he assured the dean, in Latin, algebra, and geometry. He had certain abilities in French, physics, and astronomy also. And, he added with considerable under-statement, "If proficiency in English were any consideration," he believed he might qualify.

To Frost's admitted surprise, Harvard accepted his application. He entered in the fall of 1897, enrolling for courses in Latin, Greek, and philosophy. However, it seemed that his destiny frowned on the academic route. Although he did well in his studies, a college degree did not appear to be in the cards. First, a series of interruptions in his studies resulted from the overriding necessity to return to Lawrence and help his mother in her attempt to save her private school from failing. Then Robert became ill. Very possibly, psychosomatic symptoms were induced by stress; Frost was never quite free from such sieges of anxiety during his lifetime. At any rate, he left Harvard before his sophomore year was completed.

The Frosts soon were parents again, their daughter Lesley being born in 1899. But the following year gloom darkened the household when little Elliott died, not quite four years old—the first of several such blows that marred Frost's domestic happiness over the long span of his life. Within a few months the family took up residence on a farm near Derry, New Hampshire, with the aid of Robert's grandfather, who purchased the farm and who seemed, to his extremely sensitive grand-son, to be saying to him: "Go on out and die. Good riddance to you. You've been nothing except a bother to me, for years, and you're not worth anything except as a disappointment."[2] During the spring of 1899 Isabelle Moodie Frost had discovered that she had an incurable cancer. She died soon after her son moved to New Hampshire, and he was now forced to stand on his own two feet and make his family's way. Only two concerns occupied his mind—his poetry and his family's livelihood.

Frost lived on his farm for the next ten years. During these Derry years, three more children arrived: a son, Carol, and two daughters,

Irma and Marjorie. A sixth child, Elinor Bettina, died in infancy. Elizabeth Sergeant, a journalist who became a fan of Frost's during the 1920s and in 1960 published his biography, reports that during his first eight years on the farm Frost remained at home every night after eight o'clock in the evening. But the fears of his friends that in so isolating himself he was burying his brilliance were unfounded. Life was moving ahead, and Frost was moving with it. He was quite definitely active, in the most profound sense of the word. He was mastering his craft, learning as he was writing. Manuscripts were piling up. In the process of composition were poems which, when they saw print, would be called masterpieces.

Meanwhile, Frost returned to the classroom. He began teaching English in 1906 at the Pinkerton Academy in Derry. His duties occupied only two days a week and paid him two hundred dollars a year. In 1911, when Frost followed the principal of the academy to a new post at the State Normal School in Plymouth, it seemed evident that he was flirting with danger. Schoolteaching, after all, was his avocation, but it was also the way he earned his bread; and breadwinning had its way of insinuating itself into the center of attention.

There is evidence that Frost at this juncture awakened to an old but most crucial realization: No man can serve two masters. To the extent that his pledge to the classroom increased, his primary commitment to poetry was placed in jeopardy. It was increasingly plain that he was going to have to choose between the two. He solemnly promised himself that the new post in Plymouth would last for one year and no more.

Although Frost appears to have confided in no outsider, he must have recognized his own progress and, indeed, his achievement in the decade between 1900 and 1910. The entire countryside around Derry stimulated his creative faculties. Hills, valleys, farms, cabins, open sky, woods, fields, west-running brook, and rose pogonias became grist for his mill. And in the landscape inevitably stood the people, the lonely, introspective, self-reliant and sometimes self-destructive natives—the rural men and women whose tragedies, primarily, fill his poems. The best-known verses in *A Boy's Will*—"Storm Fear," "Mowing," "The Trial by Existence," "The Tuft of Flowers"—date from this period. Besides those that went into his first volume, others, such as "Design" and "The Death of the Hired Man," were already in his notebook.

Frost was quite literally stuffed with the materials of future books. At that moment in time, had the right publisher chanced to cross his path, two reputations might have been made simultaneously.

## Two Roads Diverged

In 1911 Robert Frost was thirty-seven years old, the sole support of a wife and four living children. For at least a decade he had been seriously committed to the writing of poetry, had published a reasonable amount of his apprentice verse without causing much notice, and also had been the recipient of enough rejection slips from the periodicals to be discouraged. Yet he continued to hope and plan, his spirits buoyed by the consistent acceptance of poems by *The Independent*. The assistant editor of the magazine, Miss Susan Hayes Ward, had become a regular correspondent. On numerous occasions he expressed to her his frustrations and indecisions.

As his thirties passed—crucial years to a creative artist—Frost became increasingly positive about his dedication to art. He dreamed big dreams, bulwarked by the backlog of verses he had "salted away." Ever more pressing became his determination to embark upon one big decisive push toward establishing himself with an achievement that would sweep him beyond the rank of a minor poet. In December, 1911, Frost wrote Miss Ward from the Normal School, sending her a booklet of manuscript verse for her consideration. He described the "grim stand" he had felt it essential to take in order to effect a clean break with his New Hampshire roots. "The forward movement," he concluded, "is to begin next year."[3]

The forward movement, as it eventually developed, involved a violent wrenching-away from the homeland, from friends and relatives. It looked toward a three-year stay in England where, in Elinor's delighted expectation, the family might "sleep under thatch!" "I had no letters of introduction," Frost afterward recalled; "I knew not one soul in England. But I felt impelled to lose myself among strangers, to write poetry without further scandal to friends or family."[4]

The emergence in England of Frost as a fresh, exciting, and major discovery happened so swiftly and dramatically that it made his decade at home seem even more slow and uneventful than it had in fact been.

Some have thought the trip itself made the difference, the change of climate and landscape suddenly triggering latent powers. Yet the metamorphosis was not of this nature at all. Actually, the poems that comprised Frost's first book were already written and stored in one of the trunks that went to England with the family. Frost himself reported that one night not long after his arrival and the family's establishment in Beaconsfield, he dug these poems out of the trunk and examined them.

Sifting the poems one by one and burning certain youthful experiments he wished to discard, Frost laid aside one pile of some thirty verses. These, he realized, would go together coherently as a volume. His daughter Lesley typed fresh copies for him; and, knowing next to nothing about English publishing houses, Frost set out to locate some venturesome firm that might see enough virtue in his work to publish it. On the chance advice of a new friend, he approached the offices of David Nutt, publisher of some of W. E. Henley's work. Mr. Nutt was dead, it turned out, but Mrs. Nutt received the manuscript, which Frost had entitled *A Boy's Will* after a line in Longfellow. Three days later it was accepted for publication.

This acceptance may be less fortuitous than it sounds, for nothing is clearer now than that Frost was ripe for publication. The pertinent question would appear to be: why had Frost's lode of poems not been tapped sooner? Immediately following the offer of a contract from the David Nutt firm, Frost wrote back to the United States for advice. To Thomas Bird Mosher, the New England publisher and anthologist, he explained that he had three other books nearing completion. At this time he referred to the nascent volumes as *Melanism, Villagers,* and *The Sense of Wrong.*

The poems intended for these books obviously appeared, if they were used at all, in volumes bearing other titles. But Frost's mention of enough poems for three books at this time is some indication of the literary trove he shipped across the Atlantic. And to demonstrate further his prescience, Frost expressed to Mosher genuine concern about his American reputation should all his first work be published abroad. "Won't it seem traitorously un-American?" he suggested.[5] Reflection evidently assured him that English publication would not be so un-American, after all. At least it was a hard offer, the only one he then had. He signed his contract with David Nutt, and the book went slowly to press.

While awaiting the appearance of *A Boy's Will* during that winter of 1913, Frost was introduced to Ezra Pound, then living in London. Impulsively, Pound suggested that the two of them walk to the offices of David Nutt, where the first copy of *A Boy's Will* had just been bound. They took it back to Pound's residence, where the red-haired expatriate read it, liked it, and offered then and there to write a review of it. Pound at once fulfilled his promise, wrote an extended appreciation of the volume, and sent it to his friend, Harriet Monroe, then spearheading the poetry revival in Chicago. In May, Miss Monroe printed Pound's review in *Poetry: A Magazine of Verse*. Pound was kind to his new "Amur'kn" discovery. Obviously he hoped to cultivate Frost as a member of his Imagist group. "This man has the good sense to speak naturally and to paint the thing, the thing as he sees it," Pound declared, adding, "he is without sham and without affectation."[6]

Frost was now hard at work perfecting his own brand of blank verse. Preferring to be his own man, he resisted the blandishments of Ezra Pound and *Les Imagistes*. He was not missed. Amy Lowell, recently arrived in London and afire with poetic ambition, sat at Pound's feet in his stead. Frost had a career to make, and he preferred not to make it as another's disciple. It was nearly twenty years now since he had published "My Butterfly" in *The Independent*. A good stretch of lost time had to be recouped.

By now a number of favorable reviews of *A Boy's Will* had appeared in England, and several of Frost's new poems were accepted by magazines, among them "The Housekeeper" and "The Code—Heroics," the latter scheduled to appear in Miss Monroe's *Poetry*. Soon, editors would be most happy to accept Frost's work. Not much later they would be clamoring for anything he might be so gracious as to release.

Frost continued meanwhile to scribble at a productive pace. Poems such as "Birches," a memory of New Hampshire which would be published much later, found their final form. Within a year after *A Boy's Will,* Frost had polished and arranged his second volume. David Nutt was again his publisher. As if to assert his American-ness, Frost called the book very simply *North of Boston,* to the understandable confusion of some Britishers as to its geographical designation. The book proved one of Frost's greatest successes and was probably the single most influential volume in establishing his career as a major poet.

Edward Thomas, the young British poet with whom Frost had become fast friends, reviewed *North of Boston* as "one of the most revolutionary books of modern times."[7] Other reviewers agreed upon the "poetic bonfire" Frost offered and the "memorable experience" he provided with verses such as "Mending Wall," "The Death of the Hired Man," "After Apple-Picking," and "The Wood-Pile." Ezra Pound, reviewing the book for *Poetry,* labeled Frost a Georgic, identifying him with that group of pastoral poets then popular in England. Amy Lowell attempted to interest American publishers in the volume. Amazingly, considering her militant powers, she experienced no success at all. Nevertheless, all that Frost's career needed was time and one significant push to start its climb to the pinnacle of fame.

## Home Again

As Frost savored the British success of *North of Boston,* Archduke Ferdinand was assassinated in Sarajevo. By August, less than two months later, Germany, Russia, France, and England were all at war. Frost recognized at once that the time had come for him to return home.

"The war is an ill wind to me," he wrote sadly to Sidney Cox. "It ends for the time being that thought of publishing any more books."[8] One of his deepest regrets was the deathblow he knew the war would deliver to the recent flowering of English verse, and he voiced his deep fears—all too soon to be realized—of what might become of the younger poets such as Rupert Brooke and Edward Thomas. Both subsequently died in battle.

The six Frosts sailed for America on February 13, 1915. Ten days later, when the *St. Paul* docked in Manhattan, no bands played and no crowd of fans waited with volumes to be autographed. Yet America stood ready to receive her new poet. On the newsstands were copies of the latest *New Republic,* in which Amy Lowell extolled the glories of *North of Boston.* And Henry Holt and Company had already arranged to bring out the first American editions of Frost's work.

Now affairs moved swiftly. "The Death of the Hired Man," composed in 1905 but withheld from magazine publication, had appeared in the *New Republic* for February 6. Henry Holt had issued *North of Boston* two days before the Frosts landed in New York, and the company would publish *A Boy's Will* in April. When Alfred Harcourt, then working for Holt, boasted that *North of Boston* would sell ten thousand copies, Harrison Smith and Sinclair Lewis raised a "hoot of disbelief" at such extravagant claims for a book of verse.[9] But the collection was universally acclaimed by the critics and became a best seller at once.

Fame came quickly and never left. From this point on Frost was sought out, entertained, lionized as intensely as he would allow. He met and formed a lasting acquaintance with Edwin Arlington Robinson, the forerunner of the poetic renaissance then flowering in Boston and Chicago. Robinson's poetic sketches of figures from Gardiner, Maine—his "children of the night," as he somberly referred to them—strongly resembled the New Hampshire hill people of Frost's poems. Later Frost would write an appreciative preface to Robinson's *King Jasper;* eventually he would outdistance the older man four-to-three in the winning of Pulitzer Prizes.

Ellery Sedgwick, editor of the influential *Atlantic Monthly,* entertained the poet at what Frost somewhat derisively referred to in his poems as a "cut-glass dinner." Soon Frost's poems would be making regular appearances in the pages that once could find no place for his vigorous verse. "Birches" and "The Road Not Taken" were published in the *Atlantic's* August issue. Both of these, along with "The Death of the Hired Man," were reprinted in William Braithwaite's *Anthology of Magazine Verse for 1915.* All three verses carried the star appended by Mr. Braithwaite for excellence. To Frost himself the anthologist conceded "absolute genius," finding Frost's "vigorous actuality of speech and meaning" particularly praiseworthy.[10]

The beginning of a lifelong friendship with Louis Untermeyer was among the pleasant events dating from this era. But as proof that the less pleasant concomitants of fame would make themselves felt also, Frost was requested to pay one hundred dollars over the going price, on the grounds that he was "somebody," when he purchased his farm near Franconia, New Hampshire.[11]

By the time *Mountain Interval* appeared in late 1916, Frost had conclusively severed his slight ties with England. He was "home" for good in the New England with which his countrymen would always afterwards identify him. His publisher now was Henry Holt and would be even beyond his death. Nutt of London, who had brought out his first work and given him his literary debut, but who had proven incommunicative—and much more serious, unremunerative—received no more of Frost's writing. *Mountain Interval,* whose title refers to the valley land between hills, contained "An Old Man's Winter Night," one of Frost's favorite poems—one nearly perfect in its form, he judged, but considerably less often anthologized than either "The Road Not Taken" or "Birches" from the same volume.

During the months preceding and following publication of *Mountain Interval,* Frost delivered the first of his famous campus lectures and readings. These began at colleges such as Bates in Maine, Tufts, Harvard, and Amherst in Massachusetts. For nearly fifty years these engagements carried him the length and breadth of the nation. Through them Frost became a familiar visitor to both smaller schools and large universities. Although the poet habitually assumed a cynical attitude toward colleges, this may have been no more than a pose he struck in keeping with his already established rural image. Traces of Emerson's scorn for "the education at college of fools" might seem apparent here. Yet Frost accepted his academic invitations gladly.

In addition, he formed semi-permanent associations with a number of schools in the capacity of teacher, lecturer, or consultant. Every evidence, including his reluctance to close off such associations after the temporal need for them was past, indicates that he relished his role as campus VIP. Among Frost's "interim" schools were the universities of Michigan and Harvard, and of course the Bread Loaf School in Vermont which he was instrumental in forming. But he had a fond spot in his heart for Amherst and kept returning always to the town in which Emily Dickinson had set high targets for him to aim for.

It was at Amherst that Frost began his several academic careers. Early in 1917, after a reading of his poems on campus, he was offered a full professorship. He would be given the opportunity to leave at will in order to deliver readings elsewhere and would be paid $1,500. He accepted. As it turned out, both the meager salary and the provision for leaves were fully appreciated because *Mountain Interval,* in contrast to the best-selling *North of Boston,* did poorly on the market. The experience taught Frost not to publish a book of poems simply because it seemed time for a new publication.

The year 1917 was a slow one. Only three of Frost's poems appeared in magazines. One of his reading trips took him to Chicago, then actively challenging the East for literary leadership. In Chicago he read under the sponsorship of the editors of *Poetry* magazine. The occasion brought him one hundred and fifty dollars. It also provided the influential Harriet Monroe and her associates an opportunity to compare him with their triumvirate of emerging bards: Vachel Lindsay, Edgar Lee Masters, and Carl Sandburg. Frost appears to have come off very well in the "competition." But all in all, he confided later to Elizabeth Sergeant, it was a "bad year."

### Poet in Residence

In 1919 Robert Frost had two decisions to make. His first involved his academic connections: should he remain at Amherst or leave? He chose to resign at the end of the first term and take his family back to Franconia, New Hampshire. There perhaps his writing would go faster and better, if he were removed from the distracting considerations of students and classes. His second decision was to make a choice between publishers. Although Henry Holt had first brought out his work in the United States, Frost's contact with the publisher had been primarily through his chief editor, Alfred Harcourt. Harcourt, enterprising and highly ambitious, saw immense possibilities in conducting business for himself. He planned to establish his own firm and had already rounded up a number of promising names in the literary arena, among them Carl Sandburg and Frost's friend Louis Untermeyer. But Frost, after considering carefully, decided to remain with Holt.

Perhaps these were minor decisions, relatively simple or even inevitable ones of the moment. Surely the poetry was the main thing. Frost continued to produce at a steady, unspectacular rate. His work found its way readily into periodicals. There was no trouble now about being accepted, only one of satisfying the increased demand. He was taken seriously by anyone pretending to write about the current state of verse. Amy Lowell's inclusion of him in her *Tendencies in Modern American Poetry* had set the pace, securely establishing his position in the vanguard. The anthologies also were reflecting his recognition. Louis Untermeyer, who then was establishing a reputation with the first of his many collections, saw to it that Frost was given a place of prominence. From 1917 it could be said that no anthology of modern

American verse could make even a pretense of completeness if it omitted Robert Frost.

Almost before he was aware of it, Frost was moving once again in academic circles. From Ann Arbor came an offer to preside as Poet in Residence at the University of Michigan, then a new and daring idea. The annual stipend of $5,000 was well over double what Amherst had paid him; besides, the university demanded nothing specific in the way of instruction. In fact, Frost would not be called upon to present any specific accomplishments whatever during his time in Ann Arbor; no progress reports, no summary of production need be filed to justify the stipend.

What was coveted was merely the poet's presence. It was felt that the ambience created simply by his being on campus, the stimulation this must be to creative thought and effort, was well worth the price. In return, Frost would be furnished with what was hoped would be favorable surroundings in which to continue his own composition. Obviously, however, the university anticipated great things of Frost and intended to bask in reflected glory.

The entire Frost family moved to Ann Arbor in the fall of 1921. Lesley Frost registered for her junior year there, and her father was wined and dined by faculty folk eager to rub shoulders with the up-and-coming poet. Frost referred to himself whimsically as the "Idle Fellow" because of his freedom from responsibilities. Yet he was far from wasting his time. Not only did he continue with his writing, including the composition of "The Witch of Coös," which the following fall won the $200 Levinson Prize awarded by *Poetry* magazine, but he was active also in lecturing to the many groups that requested a word from him. Frost delighted the campus literati by utilizing his growing prestige and wide personal connections to draw a number of practicing poets to Ann Arbor for readings. Carl Sandburg, Amy Lowell, and Vachel Lindsay were among those who answered Frost's summons to join him in Michigan as guests of the university.

Frost reveled in his life in Ann Arbor, where, as a central attraction, he was deferred to and honored. He hoped to be asked back for another year. But when commencement came, the university still had not completed any plans for continuation of the post. He received a friendly good-by, was presented with an honorary degree, but was given no definite word concerning future offers. But his lack of an invitation was of no great matter; there was much of his own work waiting to be done. The poetic cauldron simmered.

As if to prove that his year at Michigan had been gestatory, Frost upon reaching Vermont began writing rapidly. Two of his best poems were completed at this time, first the lengthy "New Hampshire," and then his most quoted and collected lyric, "Stopping by Woods on a Snowy Evening." Word from the West that funds had been allocated to finance his return to Michigan came too late to alter Frost's plans for writing and lecturing during the 1922–23 academic year. He did appear several times on the university campus at Ann Arbor, however. On at least one of these occasions he presented a reading of his own poetry, something he had not done the previous year. But the greater share of his time was occupied by a series of trips to the South and Southwest for major lectures.

Beyond this activity, Frost's energies were directed toward two forthcoming publications. Seven years had passed since he had published a new book of verse. Now his fourth collection, *New Hampshire,* was being readied for publication by Henry Holt. Before it appeared, he brought out his first résumé, *Selected Poems.* Both volumes were major works, and both sold well. Quite naturally, *Selected Poems,* culled as it was from all his work to date, became the volume any devotee must have. It remained indispensable until the appearance of the more definitive *Collected Poems* in 1930. *Selected Poems* is still of value for its implicit self-judgment of Frost's achievement to 1923 and for whatever insights are to be gained from observing Frost's method of grouping his major poems.

*New Hampshire,* which contained "Fire and Ice," "Stopping by Woods on a Snowy Evening," and "The Axe-Helve," in addition to the title poem, won Frost his first Pulitzer Prize. It was, in fact, the first collection of Frost poems to appear since the inception of such awards. The award was made at Columbia University in June, 1924, immediately prior to Frost's reception of his first honorary Doctorate in Letters, bestowed by Yale. From this date, both honorary degrees and literary prizes were to become regular events in Frost's career. By the time he died, he would be the most widely honored writer in the world, lacking only the Nobel award.

Previous to these particular honors, Frost had returned briefly to Amherst College in the fall of 1923 to assist the philosophy department. He was assigned a single course, to be centered around significant books not ordinarily studied by students surveying English literature. He trained his students to read deeply for the discernment of ideas and to write about their reading only when they found they had something pertinent to say. That he intended not to be a perfunctory reader of perfunctory writing was emphatically spelled out. But any spark of genuine interest or latent talent was to be encouraged. Again, as at Michigan, it was largely Frost's presence and obvious stature, rather than any series of brilliantly conceived or delivered lectures, that made his student contacts memorable.

Teaching made intense demands upon Frost's time and energy. Yet he had a definite, if unorthodox, gift for triggering communication. George F. Whicher, one of his colleagues at Amherst and famous for his work on Emily Dickinson, said of Frost that he was "a born teacher with a knack of charging dry subjects with intellectual excitement and a large patience for struggling learners." To Frost, Whicher added, teaching was "a natural extension of his unfeigned interest in people."[12]

Frost had agreed to remain at Amherst for two years. Yet he was doubtful, considering the extent to which teaching cut in upon his writing, whether he could manage to last it out. Nevertheless, before the two-year stint at Amherst had expired, Frost had agreed to return to Michigan where a Fellowship in the Creative Arts awaited him. The decision undoubtedly reflected Frost's awareness of his own enjoyment during previous appointments at the university and of the many friends he had made in Ann Arbor. But Michigan's promise of a $6,000 stipend should not be discounted; for, popular as he was proving to be, well known as his name had become, Frost was then far from affluent; and the poet's family had to eat and be shod like any other's.

It began to appear very much as if Frost were destined to vacillate between Michigan and Amherst like a fond lover indecisive as to which sweetheart claimed the larger portion of his heart. He remained at Michigan for only one year of the two expected of him. He resigned in order to return to Amherst, which finally—perhaps out of desperation—had arranged something considerably more tempting to him. He was to assume a professorship of English at a salary of $5,000. Though less than he had received from Michigan, it was far more than Amherst had been willing, or able, to offer in the past. He moved to the East again, and, settling now in Amherst for the next twelve years, Frost apparently found the place where he truly wanted to be. Conditions were arranged to keep him happy and working, at his own poetry if not teaching; for he was required to teach but three months in the year, periods often of his own choosing. The college felt it received its money's worth. Frost had the opportunity to continue his lecture and reading tours almost at will. It was an eminently workable plan.

Out of this arrangement the greatest profit came to the cause of poetry in America. Many across the land were enabled to hear Frost in person. He was respected, loved, admired—not yet venerated, but veneration would come in time; for the Frost mystique was beginning to take shape. The poet was in his fifties now, and his tousled, snow-thatched head set on his stocky shoulders was familiar everywhere through photographs reproduced in texts and periodicals. In 1928 Holt brought out his *West-Running Brook*. Containing "A Peck of Gold," "Once by the Pacific," and "Tree at My Window," the new volume stood up solidly in comparison to his earlier work and provided assurance that Frost remained at the height of his powers and would not soon burn out.

## A National Institution

The 1930s were troubled times for America. The aftermath of the stock market crash altered national ways and ideals, and the arts no less than economics were affected. Changing times dictated changing fashions. Among writers, many popular in the 1920s found themselves on the scrap heap in the 1930s. F. Scott Fitzgerald was one of these unfortunates. He died with his own tales of the Jazz Age, to be resuscitated much later as a nostalgic legend of an era whose glitter, seen from a distance, once again seemed golden.

Other writers, particularly the "proletarians," found themselves the rage. Especially popular were the socially conscious playwrights and the novelists who Frost remarked were producing "huge shapeless novels, huge gobs of raw sincerity."[13] Art for art's sake was in for bad days. Propaganda for socio-politico-economic reform carried the new times. For Frost himself the 1930s were times of both triumph and tragedy. He was fifty-five years of age when the decade began, old enough perhaps to be closing out his career—older, in fact, than many American writers were when they laid down their pens. Yet 1930 itself appeared to augur well for the future. Frost published his most comprehensive book, *Collected Poems.* In one sense, he thereby delivered himself over to the critics by presenting them with a sizable body of work to be appraised. It was a fate he protested as being similar to handing over a corpse to scientists for autopsy. He most emphatically did not want to be "analyzed." While there is every indication that Frost was highly flattered by all the talk his work engendered, his protest against the critics and explicators was in character. The myth he had encouraged from the start, that of Frost as good, gray poet, "country boy" from New Hampshire, had flourished. This myth presupposed simple verses that need not be pulled apart to satisfy the curious.

Also in 1930 Frost was elected to the American Academy of Arts and Letters, an honor surely, but one from a group whose own arrogance and cliquishness had led them to snub many writers of top rank. Frost's election is an example of the good taste this group at times demonstrated. Moreover, two serious studies of the poet and his work had appeared. Gorham Munson in 1927 published *Robert Frost: A Study in Sensibility and Common Sense;* and in 1929 appeared Sidney Cox's *Robert Frost: Original "Ordinary Man."* The titles of both studies were indicative of the popular appraisal of Frost. They also helped define the gulf that lay between him and the poets then emerging into prominence: T. S. Eliot and his followers.

Frost's personal life had been comparatively harmonious and without tremendous disruption, but he suffered hugely during the 1930s when three of his closest and dearest were lost. The first, in 1934, was his daughter Marjorie. For some time she had been a source of concern to her parents, having contracted tuberculosis and been sent for treatment in the mountain air of Boulder, Colorado, where the Frosts had visited her in 1932. She recovered her health and married, only to die of an infection following childbirth. The elder Frosts had done everything possible to save Marjorie, including flying her to the Mayo Clinic in Rochester, Minnesota, for treatment. They took this blow hard, but after a normal period of recuperation they seemed to be reconciled.

Each winter the Frosts traveled south or southwest to escape the hard snowbound winters of the northeast. Apparently Frost preferred writing about snow to tramping through it. In 1938 they were settled in Gainesville, Florida, accompanied by Carol Frost and his family. There, on March 20, Elinor Frost suffered a sudden heart attack. Without warning, the poet's greatest and most dependable bulwark was gone.

Less than two years later, Elinor's death was followed by that of her son. Carol Frost had always been a bit unstable. He had not adapted well to any formal education and as a result had no profession. He fancied himself a poet, but his verses were rejected by the journals to which he submitted them. Probably the most devastating fact of Carol's life was his own father, by whose shadow he was dwarfed continually. The steady growth of the elder Frost's fame made Carol's own feeble efforts appear more and more hopeless. Although his father thought he had dissuaded him from suicide, Carol ended his life with a gun.

Through all this disruption, Frost's own career as a poet proceeded as if unmarked by personal difficulty. Honorary degrees became a regular feature of his way of life, almost a bore: Harvard's was awarded in 1937. A new book of verse, issued by Henry Holt, was called *A Further Range;* it was Frost's sixth volume. It contained some of his best-known poems, including "Two Tramps in Mud Time" and the delightful satire "Departmental." As a result of Holt's furnishing him with a regular monthly stipend of $250, Frost had remained comparatively unaffected by the national financial plunge; but any incipient money problems were taken care of when *A Further Range* was given the Book-of-the-Month Award in the summer of 1936. The next spring this collection of poems brought him his third Pulitzer Prize.

In 1938 criticism of Frost began to lose its air of mere appreciation and to take a more serious tone, one first evidenced in the collection of diverse materials edited by Richard Thornton under the title: *Recognition of Robert Frost.* By the end of the decade, Frost had published an updated edition of *Collected Poems,* and the National Institute of Arts and Letters had awarded him its Gold Medal for Poetry.

When a person reaches age sixty-five, established almost by fiat as the national retirement year, he may look backward over his career and accomplishments, with a view to respite and perhaps the rocking chair. But Frost's career had a quarter of a century to run; the poet had many miles to go before he slept. Even so, one would not be mistaken to surmise that the solid establishment of Robert Frost as national legend dates from this period.

Already solidly anchored in the modern mythology of the United States was the mental portrait of Frost which would remain secure. A sampling of descriptions supplied impromptu by a college poetry class some time after the poet's death is representative of the basic features included in that picture. According to these young people, Robert Frost was variously "a kindly old rural farmer"; "a sensitive person who sees what others don't notice, but when he puts it down, then they see"; and "a New Englander who shows what that part of the country is like, the quality of the people." In short, to his great "public" Frost was the epitome of the benevolent farmer-sage, a type of ideal regional figure whose communion with nature purified him and raised him to the status of a seer, but whose total humility rendered him approachable to all.

He represented in many important respects the ideal American leader, combining sharpness of mind with the indispensable common touch, regional identity with national appeal. Contributory to this image of rural genius was the fortuitous Frost face and figure, now jelled into outlines that would not change much except to become broader, more clearly defined as the man aged. Reginald Cook, who knew him well, has depicted Frost with rare precision as he appeared in these years:

Physically, Frost has the solidity of the close-sodded native soil. He stands about five feet nine, and you are aware at once of his strong-armed, full-chested, rugged build. In his old clothes he looks bigger than he actually is. When approached in the garden, he appears to loom; but when dressed up, he shrinks to medium height. Close up you notice the full, thick, muscular, workmanlike hands, the backs of them rough, the thumb large, the fingers long, the tips blunt, the nails wide and thick—firm fingers to grasp an ax, strong shoulders to start the swing, muscular forearms to follow through. His practical truths are the tougher, you think, recalling Thoreau, for the calluses on the broad, well-lined palms. His blue eyes, which are rarely measuring, nevertheless take you in. He looks, listens, appraises. And he sizes up memorably, saying, "I see what I see." His nose is strong and aggressive. His lips are full but not sensual; the chin is firm.[14]

So far there was nothing to clash with the prevailing image; and one could ask any American who knows Frost at all for his picture of the poet. Invariably, Cook's is the portrait he will pull out of his wallet, so to speak, and show; for it is the only snapshot of Frost that most Americans possess: the wise old farmer with workman's hands. If one opens an illustrated anthology of American literature, he sees the frank, open face with just the right amount of smile playing at the edge of the lips.

Yet Cook's description continues, including traits not commonly a part of the image: the manner "not unurban," the carriage which is that of a city dweller, the speech "not identifiable with rustic voices." This is another Frost, clearly, unpublicized and therefore unknown to most; but he is the only Frost who could claim authorship of *Complete Poems*.

Frost began the 1940s already burdened by the most dire tragedies possible for the head of a family. Looked at another way, his troubles were a release; for the various family deaths at least assured him that these particular blows could not fall again. Once past and survived, they were over. He was beginning now to emerge again from the darkness. He began teaching at Harvard—quite a vindication for the man who had tried Harvard so many years earlier and withdrawn. Now he became the Ralph Waldo Emerson Fellow in Poetry at the university, a role he would continue for three years. In 1941 the Harvard Phi Beta Kappa chapter invited Frost to read a new poem. He selected "The Lesson for Today." The occasion marked the twenty-fifth anniversary of his first public reading.

In Ripton, Vermont, Frost at this time acquired the Homer Noble Farm, which was to become his "homestead." Until his death he would find peace there. He was visited at Ripton in 1962 by an old friend, Daniel Smythe, who recalls that Frost, living his farmer's part to the end, interrupted the conversation to scratch in his garden for potatoes with the same hands that had just autographed a thousand copies of his books.[15]

The fresh surge of activity and optimism which seemed to characterize Frost's activities was reinforced by publication in 1942 of *A Witness Tree.* The next year this volume made its author the only four-time winner of the Pulitzer Prize for Poetry. *A Witness Tree,* while not studded as heavily as some previous collections with sure-fire anthology pieces, did confirm Frost's ability to continue his lyrical output. In all justice, no volume containing the beautifully conceived and wrought "A Considerable Speck" could be termed undistinguished, particularly when that book offered also "Come In" and "The Quest of the Purple-Fringed." It was to *A Witness Tree* that Frost returned in 1961 for "The Gift Outright," used at the inauguration of President John F. Kennedy.

As his three-year stint at Harvard drew to a close, Frost lacked the enthusiasm to continue in Cambridge. He loved to teach; he had felt drawn magnetically to the classroom for decades, ever since his youthful days when he had aided his mother in her small school. Writing can be a most lonely vocation, and poets probably need more reflective solitude than other authors. It is easy to imagine Frost's need of the classroom as a balance wheel against the loneliness. Another reason had kept him there as well. He possessed, as Emerson put it, the "fury to impart" his knowledge to receptive ears. He was a born communicator, burning to tell the new fact. When others burned to hear it, he was content.

Frost felt with considerable justification that Harvard did not appreciate either his stature in the world of letters or the prestige his presence lent to the campus. Incredible as it may seem, he was, by and large, taken for granted—an attitude he keenly resented. In part, this apparent nonchalance seems to have resulted from the general turmoil into which World War II had thrown the nation's entire educational system. Emphasis was all upon the practical, the scientific, the immediately useful. In sad contrast, the arts and humanities generally were either ignored or tolerated for the peripheral service they might render to wartime concerns. Despite Frost's awareness of military exigencies, he could not bring himself to accept wholly the ignominious position to which the situation relegated him.

Dartmouth College, becoming aware of Frost's restiveness, bid for him. In the summer of 1943 he accepted Dartmouth's offer of the George Ticknor Fellowship in the Humanities. He remained in Hanover until the end of the 1940s, when he resigned to return—this time finally and permanently—to his favorite campus, Amherst.

Meanwhile, for the remaining war years, he dealt primarily with young soldiers attending Dartmouth on the Army Specialized Training Program assignment. He took particular delight in leading these sharp young minds to his own awareness of the ultimate limitations of science.

Frost used a special technique for leading his soldier-students to a face-to-face confrontation with the larger questions. For example, he might quote from Shakespeare's sonnet, "Let Me Not to the Marriage of True Minds." When he reached the description of the star "whose worth's unknown, although his height be taken," he would pause knowingly. "Science measures height, but can't measure worth," he would tell his boys. "Science will never know."[16] It was in Frost's nature to be cynical of science and particularly of the material progress which for too many was synonymous with improvement of the race. There was enough of the Transcendentalist in Frost to bring out real fire on this issue. Science, he argued, was earthbound. It could never discern value. It could measure weight, height, speed and mass, yes. But how could it ever expect to provide a satisfactory approach to the measurement of friendship? Or of love?

As if the pump were never going to run dry, Frost's books continued to tumble forth. In 1945 and 1947 Frost's two volume-length dramatic dialogues, *A Masque of Reason* and *A Masque of Mercy,* appeared. With their sophisticated air, the masques seemed atypical of what people expected from Frost. Perhaps the old man had a few surprises in him yet. A group of new poems, *Steeple Bush,* came out also in 1947. Immediately recognized in this book was the impact of the war, and particularly its aftermath, on Frost. "Sarcastic Science" was portrayed as reaching its nadir in the nuclear explosions which ended the war. The Frankenstein overtones of man's overreaching were not lost on the poet, who in verses like "The Planners," "Bursting Rapture," and "U. S. 1946 King's X" drew upon the nightmare of nuclear holocaust and The Bomb.

## On to Olympus

In 1949, somewhat prematurely as it turned out, appeared a thick volume of over six hundred pages called *Complete Poems.* It contained all that Frost cared to save, and it went back a long distance, even to "My Butterfly"; but great strides had been taken since that simple lyric graced the cover of *The Independent* in 1894. With the appearance of this stout volume carrying more than a hint of valedictory in its title, one might reasonably anticipate that Frost would rest his case once and for all. He had reached the age of seventy-five. In a sense he did sit back and survey what he had wrought. This was a time when honors and awards snowed in upon him in blizzard proportions. It was almost embarrassing. At every turn some group or another presented a medal or a scroll, a college bestowed a degree. Only the more significant honors stood out above the deluge.

Upon the occasion of his seventy-fifth birthday, Frost was honored by a Resolution of the United States Senate. The resolution called attention to the poet's significant achievement in writing poems "which are enjoyed, repeated, and thought about by people of all ages and callings," and which "have helped to guide American thought with humor and wisdom." Affirming that Frost's position in American literature was secure, the resolution closed with "felicitations of the Nation which he has served so well."[17]

The Senate was tardy by a year. But no one knew, and Frost was not telling, not until he surprised everyone by celebrating his eightieth birthday a scant four years later. Then it became known that the date (1875) commonly assumed to mark his birth was in fact erroneous. He had actually entered the world a year previously. In celebration of the eightieth birthday, Henry Holt and Company honored Frost at a gala dinner at the Waldorf Astoria. Amherst College, the campus where Frost declared he had "belonged longest, nearly twenty-five of the last thirty-five, and belong now," also arranged a festive occasion to which one hundred of Frost's friends and colleagues were invited. Sadly, he had already outlived some of his special favorites; but, even so, tickets to the banquet had to be distributed on a highly selective basis.

When Frost was appointed Consultant in Poetry to the Library of Congress in 1958, he might without criticism have stayed in Ripton with his potatoes and pumpkins. His somewhat unspecified duties could easily have been carried out in the manner of an absentee landlord. But Frost elected to travel to Washington and go to work. He relished being placed at the heart of national affairs and apparently thrived on his new experience. It was as if this opportunity to mingle with the active, ambitious personalities that characterize the capital endowed Frost himself with another touch of youth. At the drop of a hat he would consent to give a reading to a local group, although many a college now clamored in vain for a lecture date.

Congressmen were made well aware that "their librarian" was on the job. Frost demonstrated to them that a poet, even one well into his eighties, need not be a recluse. If poets by tradition are thought to write in garrets, Frost proved that he could operate in the agora as well. So successful was his tenure as librarian that, upon the conclusion of his year, he was asked to remain in Washington as Consultant in the Humanities.

Very early in Robert Frost's career, not long after the publication of *A Boy's Will* and *North of Boston,* the widow of William Vaughn Moody made a prediction to Frost. Her husband's poetry had constituted one of the few genuine voices in the long poetic drought that followed the deaths of the nineteenth-century titans, and that continued until the dramatic emergence of the "new" poets after 1910. Harriet Moody guarded her husband's reputation jealously, which may be one reason why she said what she did. Frost, she remarked, might very well become the best poet in America. Even so, she added, he could not hope to approach the stature of the worst England could produce.[18]

The statement itself was impulsive, and one need not be an Anglophobe to bristle at hearing it. If Frost recalled Mrs. Moody's words—and with his ambition he was not the kind to forget such an affront—he must have taken even greater satisfaction in receiving honorary degrees from both Oxford and Cambridge universities during the summer of 1957. The fact that he traveled to England for these occasions is indicative of the value he assigned the honors. He must have known by this time that he was the best poet produced in the twentieth century by either America or England, for this is what critics of both countries were saying in loud, clear voices.

## The Last Years

By the time the 1950s gave way to a new decade, Frost's position in America was unmistakably that of elder statesman. In any age, poetry must be caviar. In the twentieth century, a time dominated by prose writers, relatively few read poetry for its own sake. Yet from coast to coast, persons who read no other poet or who read no poet at all knew of Robert Frost and his work. He had, of course, never shirked self-advertisement. The phenomenon resulted from far more than puffery. Sheer age and Frost's remarkable staying-power had something to do with it. Imagine, eighty-six and still going like a top!

Like the glaciers of Everest, Frost's snow-crowned head was simply *there* marking the horizon. He soared above all others. He had been there since well before the majority of his fellow citizens could recall. Something hinted of eternity. He had outlasted all of his contemporaries, except perhaps Carl Sandburg, who failed to grow. But the others—Amy Lowell, Edgar Lee Masters, Vachel Lindsay, and the rest—were dim figures from the past or else curios of a previous age. With others of his stamp, such as Herbert Hoover, General Douglas MacArthur, and above all, Mrs. Eleanor Roosevelt, Frost was venerated. He could do no wrong. One would have needed to be as ready to stamp on the colors or to hate apple pie as to denigrate the author of "Birches" and "Mending Wall." It may not be too extreme to suggest that liking Robert Frost came near to being an ultimate test of one's Americanism, almost in the nature of a loyalty oath. And this was not bad. A nation could do worse than be a worshipper of poets.

Of all the honors the world seemed anxious to bestow, most of which came Frost's way with such seeming ease and inevitability, only one eluded him. American literature had been given significant recognition by the Swedish Academy since 1930 when Sinclair Lewis became the first native winner of the Nobel Prize for Literature. During Frost's lifetime Pearl Buck, Eugene O'Neill, William Faulkner, and then Ernest Hemingway were given the prize, but never Robert Frost. The poet's admirers began to get edgy as their man advanced in years. It seemed a national disgrace that Frost should be passed over time and again while poets of other countries, many of minor stature, were honored. Frost's champions—the poet John Ciardi was one—began to write essays in open rebellion against this state of affairs. Neglect was one thing, but the Nobel awards to T. S. Eliot and Albert Camus were taken by Frost as a "personal affront," says Louis Untermeyer, whose long friendship with the poet came near the breaking point over a misunderstanding regarding Untermeyer's backing of Frost.[19] The last opportunity came in 1962, and then the award to a fellow American,

John Steinbeck, must have seemed the Swedish Academy's way of deliberately informing Frost that he did not qualify.

After Frost was dead, Dr. Anders Oesterling, the Secretary of the Swedish Academy, broke a long-standing rule of silence on candidates to explain that Frost had been considered on a number of occasions. The reasons for his rejection may be complex, and probably we will never know precisely what they might have been; but we can imagine that the difficulty of translation may have had something to do with it. Other poets, it is true, have been awarded the Nobel Prize. Yet Frost's idiom, the simple voice so unmistakably American, probably suffers considerably more in translation than would the works of a writer who depends less upon the authenticity of common, almost vernacular speech. Frost had said himself that poetry could be defined as that which was lost altogether in translation. The answer could be as simple as that.

Frost never spoke publicly in regard to the Nobel Prize. But he had plenty to say on other topics. At his age—not that he had ever been known for reticence—he was quite capable of saying what was on his mind. He rather enjoyed having the public hang upon his every word as he spoke to group after group, disparaging the "beatnik" poets as shooting "wide of the mark," or remarking that the works of Shakespeare and Henry James contain more psychology than all of Freud, or describing his own rapid-reading process as one of contemplating the title of a book for a year and then glancing at the last chapter to see how closely he had guessed its content and import. These are the remarks of a man who knows he is being listened to.

In 1960, at a time when he was supporting a movement that would have created a National Academy of Culture aimed at providing poets official "equality" with scientists and businessmen, Frost spoke of his hopes for the Presidency. The next occupant of the White House, he urged, should be a literate individual, one who read books and quoted poetry. "Especially mine," he added with a grin. He was willing to name a pair of possible candidates who met the test. One was Adlai Stevenson. The other was John F. Kennedy, who as the campaign progressed often used the final lines of "Stopping by Woods on a Snowy Evening" to close his speeches. When in November Kennedy was elected over Richard Nixon, the President-Elect responded by inviting Frost to compose a special poem for the inaugural occasion and read it at the ceremony in Washington.

"I have never taken the view that the world of politics and the world of Poetry are so far apart," said Kennedy.[20] Frost could have responded wholeheartedly with a couplet from his first book published half a century earlier:

> "Men work together," I told him from the heart,
> "Whether they work together or apart."

Many were amazed to realize that this was the first occasion upon which a representative of the literary arts had been included in the formal inaugural program. It was indicative of the "style" with which the incoming administration reached out a welcoming hand to art and to intellect.

January 30, 1961, was a cold blustery day in Washington, despite a blinding winter sun whose rays made one squint. Frost, bundled in a heavy overcoat with a voluminous muffler wrapped around his neck, was ready, manuscript in hand. He sat with the mighty that day. The Eisenhowers, Lyndon Johnson, Jacqueline Kennedy, and her triumphant husband watched apprehensively as the eighty-eight-year-old poet slipped on his eyeglasses and rose to perform. But the blowing wind twisted his papers. The sun, even with the loan of a hat held so that it shaded the podium, glanced off the papers so that he could not see. Millions of his countrymen, watching on television, held their breaths. Frost, unable to read, hesitated only so long as it took to make his audience aware of his predicament and wonder which might be more politic—to sit it out or rise and help. But Frost was faster than any of those surrounding him. He put away "The Preface," the poem he had composed for the day. He had intended—or so he afterward claimed—to follow the new poem with a reading of his "The Gift Outright." Be that as it may, he recited the older poem from memory and sat down. In one sense this recital was the very peak of his long career. It was surely the single most dramatic moment of his latter years.

Later Frost revised "The Preface" and called it "For John F. Kennedy His Inauguration." It was included in his new—and last—book of poems, *In the Clearing*. "The Gift Outright" serves as its coda. *In the Clearing*, published in 1962, contained little that would challenge the ranking of previous Frost favorites. Those who might have hoped for another "Mending Wall" or "Tree at my Window" hoped in vain. Yet the volume reaffirmed Frost's strength in his ninth decade. It was offered by the Book of the Month Club and received generous reviews. Publicity made it one of Frost's most widely purchased and read volumes.

As the summer of his last year waned, Frost undertook another trip abroad. Hobnobbing with Washington officials had appealed to him immensely, and had even influenced his verses. He had become a celebrity through the back door, so to speak; and it was generally understood that he was "in favor" with the Democratic administration. His reputation added lustre to the environment which was desired but difficult to develop from the bog of anti-intellectualism which had prevailed for so long. Then too, Frost's white head added a needed note of sobriety to the cluster of bright young men whom John Kennedy had gathered around him.

Now Frost was off for, of all places, Russia. Accompanying him was the young Secretary of the Interior, Stewart Udall of Arizona. Frost was not in good physical condition, but his immense international prestige made him seem logical for this role in the program of cultural exchange. Stanley Kauffmann describes Frost at this period as being "a kind of portable Roman ruin," not useful except in a symbolic sense.[21] In Russia, Frost fell ill, and Premier Khrushchev visited him in the hospital. The two spoke for an hour and a half. Little was accomplished other than a "dramatic confrontation of two irreverent and much-honored men," but Frost was quick to discern the cleverness and intelligence of the Russian politician. "He's not afraid of us," Frost remarked; but he at once added: "We're not afraid of him either."[22]

Although Russian-American relations at the time were relatively good, considerably improved over the cold-war strain of a few years before, one bone of contention between the two powers was serving as grist for the propaganda mills. The city of Berlin had been in dispute ever since the German surrender of 1945, and multitudes of refugees had found easy escape from the eastern portion of Berlin, controlled by Russia, to the western sector, under Allied supervision. Finally the Russians had erected an ugly but most effective wall between the two sectors to put an end to this leakage.

Howls of disapproval were heard throughout the Western nations at this action; and those few refugees who managed to slip past the wall, or who on occasion challenged it in armored trucks, were welcomed by cheering crowds of West Berliners. At a literary evening in Moscow, Robert Frost chose to recite his poem "Mending Wall," which begins "Something there is that doesn't love a wall,/That wants it down." The poem goes on to speak of the danger by which a wall, in preventing communication, fosters misunderstanding and belligerence. As he read in English, it is doubtful that Frost's point came across to his Russian listeners. Indeed, reports of this evening's reading would indicate that his message was lost. But it was understood at once in the West, where it was taken to be the poet's personal reprimand to the Russians.[23]

This was Robert Frost's last public gesture. Back home again as winter set in, he fell ill. On December 3, 1962, he entered Peter Bent Brigham hospital in Boston for treatment of a urinary obstruction. Surgery followed on December 10; and for a time it seemed as if the poet, who was now going on eighty-nine, might recover. Shortly afterwards, he suffered a heart attack which medical efforts failed to counteract. He lingered for a month while his tough old body fought back and doctors tried what they could to relieve him, including surgery on the veins of his legs. On January 29, 1963, the news went out that Robert Frost was dead.

Radio and television news commentators, who had kept the public informed as to Frost's condition, employed valuable network time to speak of his death in the somber tones reserved for figures of state. Across the land people felt the loss personally, although many of these lacked any full idea of what that loss entailed. Messages of condolence poured into the national news media, not only from fellow writers and citizens but from the world's capitals: London, Paris, Stockholm, Moscow. In Washington, the man who within a few months was to follow Frost as an assassin's bullet tore his brain apart said to his people: "His death impoverishes us all; but he has bequeathed his nation a body of imperishable verse from which Americans will forever gain joy and understanding. He had promises to keep and miles to go, and now he sleeps."[24]

## Chapter Two
# Poet in a Landscape: Frost's Career

Beneath the deafening chorus of praise for Robert Frost which began with the publication of *A Boy's Will* and *North of Boston* and deepened as the poet grew older, lone voices can be heard chanting their own tune, one of discord with the general eulogy. These nay-sayers, if indeed they are noticed at all, are not often heeded; but what they have to say merits an ear. Frost, they protest, was not of the modern age. Rather than looking forward, blazing fresh trails, and indicating new paths between reality and the soul, he leaned to the past, peered back longingly to an older, more idyllic time and place. A fair case can be made for accepting this view of the poet. Even more truth would be contained in a portrait of Frost facing both ways, backward as well as forward.

The vital impression created by Frost as a topical figure in the 1950s and in the early 1960s may cause one to forget that of course he *does* belong with an earlier era. One who recalls Frost visiting Soviet Russia and conferring with Premier Khrushchev must stop for a second to reflect. It comes as something of a jolt to realize that when Frost was born in 1874 William Cullen Bryant was still writing; Longfellow, Whittier, James Russell Lowell, and Oliver Wendell Holmes still had the better portion of two active decades yet before them. So did Walt Whitman, who had broken ground for new times to come but was still misunderstood and unappreciated. Emily Dickinson, another modern rebuffed by her own day, was adding to her secret lode of verse in an upstairs bedroom in Amherst.

Most of the writers whose works one considers as constituting the mainstream of modern American literature were not even born until Robert Frost had entered young manhood. In fact, some of the most prominent writers were born after Frost had already begun to publish his verses in *The Independent* (he started two years after Whitman's death). And not a few of these "moderns" had died—Wolfe, Faulkner, Hemingway, and Fitzgerald—well before Frost's own days on earth ended.

Admittedly, it was not altogether inevitable that Robert Frost should reflect traits of the old school. At the same time, it is not surprising to meet these connections in his work. Nor is it particularly unusual that two of the chief influences upon his career should be those giant figures of the previous century, Emerson and Thoreau. Placing Frost in chronological perspective helps explain why he consistently defended Henry Wadsworth Longfellow at a time when that poet was scorned in the academies, as he still is, though recent reappraisal tends to provide him with greater justice. For years Frost actively championed the "miracle play" of Longfellow's achievement; and it is an interesting footnote that, when Frost died, he was described as the nation's best-loved poet since Longfellow.

A considerable debt is also owed to William Cullen Bryant. Bryant and Frost were more alike than has generally been noted. Perhaps few read beyond "Thanatopsis" anymore, but in both his themes and his verse forms Bryant is Robert Frost's natural ancestor. For many of his briefer lyrics—"The Yellow Violet" or "To the Fringed Gentian," among others—Bryant selected the same subject matter and verse form later chosen by Frost. Bryant's blank verse pieces, which helped unbend that form considerably, bear strong resemblances to Frost's later work. It must be granted that Bryant's verse is overly freighted with diction smacking of the eighteenth-century: the plenitude of *thee's* and *shalt thou's* falls ponderously on the modern ear. Yet Frost's poems in *A Boy's Will*, with their noticeable overuse of *e'er, o'er,* and *'tis,* also look backward to an earlier poetic fashion.

If Bryant's language sounds outmoded, Frost's "My Butterfly" should be reread. It was a poem for which Frost felt a special fondness because it was his first commercially printed verse, but it contains lines hardly less archaic than those found in Bryant. Can the following be the voice of the Robert Frost that the modern age claims as its own?

> And I was glad for thee,
> And glad for me, I wist.

Thou didst not know, who tottered, wandering on high,
That fate had made thee for the pleasure of the wind.

Above all, their mutual concentration upon nature, their deep reverence for it, and their similar use of natural things as a springboard for
poetry link Bryant and Frost most closely. Bryant looked upon nature
with typical nineteenth-century romantic eyes, discerning in woods
and sky an authentic healing power, a spiritual inspiration. This view
remained true whether he was considering nature as a totally encom-
passing force for good or whether he was searching out small natural
objects to extract from them the human lessons they contained. Much
of the same is evident in Frost's lyrics from "Rose Pogonias" in his early
work to "Unharvested" in his later.

As an illustration of the close relationship between Bryant and Frost,
one may place examples of their blank verse side by side. Here is the ice
storm, first seen by Bryant, then recorded by Frost:

Come when the rains
Have glazed the snow, and clothed the trees with ice;
While the slant sun of February pours
Into the bowers a flood of light. . . .
Look! the massy trunks
Are cased in pure crystal, each light spray,
Nodding and tinkling in the breath of heaven,
Is studded with its trembling water-drops,
That stream with rainbow radiance as they move.
But round the parent stem the long low boughs
Bend, in a glittering ring, and arbors hide
The grassy floor. Oh! you might deem the spot
The spacious cavern of the virgin mine,
Deep in the womb of earth—where the gems grow,
And diamonds put forth radiant rods and bud
With amethyst and topaz. . . .
But all shall pass away
With the next sun. From numberless vast trunks,
Loosened, the crashing ice shall make a sound
Like the far roar of rivers, and the eve
Shall close o'er the brown woods as it was wont.
—From "A Winter Piece"

> Often you must have seen them
> Loaded with ice on a sunny winter morning
> After a rain. They click upon themselves
> As the breeze rises, and turn many-colored
> As the stir cracks and crazes their enamel.
> Soon the sun's warmth makes them shed crystal shells
> Shattering and avalanching on the snow-crust—
> Such heaps of broken glass to sweep away
> You'd think the inner dome of heaven had fallen.
> They are dragged to the withered bracken by the load,
> And they seem not to break; though once they are bowed
> So low for long, they never right themselves:
> You may see their trunks arching in the woods
> Years afterwards, trailing their leaves on the ground
> Like girls on hands and knees that throw their hair
> Before them over their heads to dry in the sun.
>
> —From "Birches"

These verses speak for themselves; yet one might point out the identity of subject matter, the similarity of treatment, with its mixture of realism and imagination, and the evocation in some instances of parallel imagery.

## Emerson and Thoreau

In the nineteenth century the principal champions of nature and interpreters of things natural were Emerson and Thoreau. Both were discernible influences upon Robert Frost, probably at firsthand but at least through the tradition they dominated. Along with *Robinson Crusoe*, Thoreau's *Walden* was Frost's favorite book. Well that it should be, with its traveling much in Concord and its dogged search for elementals. Thoreau's subjects are Frost's subjects, become familiar to the reader through his poems: snow piled deep against a lake and woods, an army of ants on the march, broad patches of blueberries ripening on burnt-over hills, forests of birch trees, skittering woodchucks and squirrels, woodcutters slogging through isolated tracts, ice breaking up in the spring thaw.

From every event and image Thoreau manages to extract its core of significance. He had withdrawn to Walden Pond in response to the beat

of his different drummer, determined to drive life into a corner and
taste of it "near the bone where it is sweetest." Thoreau uncovered an
entire world within the circumference of Walden. He endowed this
world with metaphor and wrote it as poetry, even though the result is
published in paragraphs and chapters like any ordinary book:

White Pond and Walden are great crystals on the surface of the earth, Lakes
of Light. If they were permanently congealed, and small enough to be
clutched, they would, perchance, be carried off by slaves, like precious
stones, to adorn the heads of emperors.[1]

Time is but the stream I go a-fishing in; but while I drink I see the sandy
bottom and detect how shallow it is. Its thin current slides away, but eternity
remains. I would drink deeper; fish in the sky, whose bottom is pebbly with
stars.[2]

Within a circle not so very much broader in diameter than Walden,
Robert Frost discovered the world with which one typically associates
him. Most of what he created from its materials had been suggested by
Thoreau long before: compare Thoreau's description of the thaw in
"Spring" with Frost's "A Hillside Thaw." The subjects are the same; so
also are the authors' approaches. Each man is stimulated poetically to
conjure up the image of organisms assuming life shapes as the snow
sinks, melts, and trickles down the slopes. Thoreau perceives various
shapes, both vegetable and animal: ". . . it takes the forms of sappy
leaves or vines, making heaps of pulpy sprays a foot or more in depth,
and resembling, as you look down on them, the lacinated, lobed, and
imbricated thalluses of some lichens; or you are reminded of coral, of
leopards' paws or birds' feet."[3] The kinetics of the thaw captivated
Thoreau. In *Walden* he dwelt on it for pages. His mind, inspired to
flights of fancy, sparked like fireworks, shooting off enough comparisons to serve a dozen poets as points of departure.

Frost, less the scientist and more the conscious artist, eschewed the
technical terms. In his thaw he had a vision of the sun releasing "ten
million silver lizards out of snow" and very wisely developed this figure
to the exclusion of any others suggested by the spectacle. Yet both men
are transfixed by the same scene and describe it from the moment the
noonday sun brings it pulsing to life until the sudden approach of dusk

immobilizes, literally freezes, the action into a living photograph.

Thoreau's hegira to Walden Pond occurred under the stimulus of Emerson, whose *Nature* and other essays had become the stars by which the young man navigated. The two friends were related as teacher and student: Emerson the theorizer, Thoreau the practitioner. As disciple, Thoreau tested the ideas of his master and found them viable. "The Stars," declared Emerson, "awaken a certain reverence, because though always present, they are inaccessible; but all natural objects make a kindred impression, when the mind is open to their influence."[4] Nature is the Bible in which man may read all things, providing his mind is attuned to the tongue nature employs. Nature serves man for Commodity, for Beauty, for Language, and for Discipline. To the receptive man, Nature speaks at all times and in all places. The poet possesses antennae superior to those of the man in the street; the country life provides advantages "over the artificial and curtailed life of cities." All things are symbolic, the seasons providing analogies with human life. "Parts of speech are metaphors," and every individual item, no matter how huge or trifling, preaches to man. "The moral influence of nature upon every individual is that amount of truth which it illustrates to him."[5] Those familiar with the writing of Thoreau will hear echoes of these principles resounding everywhere in his books. Those familiar with the poems of Frost will hear the same echoes ringing loud and clear in his poetry. This comparison is not to insist that Frost was a disciple in the Thoreauvian sense, or even to suggest that he was a conscious Emersonian, although that is not beyond possibility. At the same time, however, in reading Frost one may expect at any moment to be brought up suddenly by a passage strongly reminiscent of Emerson, who has been called Frost's "intellectual and spiritual godfather."[6]

Establishing the precise relationship of Frost to the great writers of New England and to Emerson in particular has been of increasing importance to recent critics, and there has been anything but unanimity among them. Although Frost pledged his allegiance to Emerson on more than one occasion, not all agree that the two men are similar. In assessing the New England tradition, Hayden Carruth correctly asserts, for instance, that to Emerson "every tree, every tree frog, and every philosopher was a teleological event, whose end was bound by its very existence to the immanent unity of a spiritual world." In Frost's poetry, however, Carruth finds no more than a tissue of evidence to establish this kind of stance. He offers "For Once, Then, Something" as a poem which does reveal something of "the persistent trace of Emersonian spiritual aspiration," but as told by Frost, the "temptation to hope" which always vitalized Emerson's writing becomes more properly the "temptation to non-despair," a lesser thing by far.[7]

Alvan S. Ryan goes further in suggesting that the similarities which so many have noted between Emerson and Frost are mostly superficial, that in neither their concepts of the role of poet nor in their practice of poetry itself do the personalities of the two writers coincide.[8] Critics too easily assume that the use of nature imagery must be tied to transcendental doctrines in which natural objects correspond to states of mind, writes Nina Baym. For her, this assumption, which were it true would bind Frost to Emerson, is mere wishful thinking. For what the two poets do share is really little more than the notion that an observation of nature may be useful in disclosing the underlying laws that govern the working of the natural universe. But Frost always remains earthbound, never takes Emerson's characteristic leap into the clouds of spiritual meaning. For Frost there resides in physical nature no "transcendental unity or an assurance of rebirth, but rather the grim laws of change and decay."[9] For Malcolm Cowley, to compare Frost with Emerson is only to discover the second-rate quality of Frost's performance. The ideal that Frost sets before his readers is "not of charity or brotherhood, but of separateness"—a quality which Frost never seems able to distinguish from self-centeredness. Cowley sees him as teetering on the brink of narcissism, lacking altogether the crusading vigor of the great Transcendentalists. It is not possible for Cowley ever to imagine Frost "thundering against the Fugitive Slave Law, like Emerson."[10]

Allied with Cowley in this respect is Frank Lentricchia, for whom the chief difference between Frost and Emerson is Frost's lack of his predecessor's zeal for reforming the individual and society. Their basic approaches to nature differ widely, Emerson seeing man "eternally young and integrated" with the natural world, and Frost seeing the two as separate and immutably divided. In Frost's poems, man remains alienated from the often barren and inhospitable world that is his home. Lentricchia reminds his reader that in "Tree at My Window," even while the poet's curtain is not drawn against the tree at night, his window sash is lowered, protectively. Frost's poems seem to lead toward isolation more often than they lead toward unity.[11] Above all, adds Roy Harvey Pearce, Emerson wished to be thought "contemporary," whereas Robert Frost is a thoroughgoing traditionalist, "our greatest stock-taker"; he has no wish to be a leader, much less a culture hero.[12] And John Kemp, who has devoted an entire volume to Frost's relationship to New England, finds that, while Frost does share with Emerson a basic assumption that the country is better off for its separation from the city, his similarity to Emerson never extends much beyond that point.[13]

At the same time, it is becoming commonplace to suggest that Robert Frost resembles Emerson less than he resembles Emerson's disciple, Thoreau. This is the firm opinion of Alvan Ryan, and also of S.P.C. Duvall, who has said, "Both the particularity of his imagery and its extension into metaphor align Frost with Thoreau rather than Emerson, just as do his wit, his verbal precision, and his command of the ironic mode."[14]

## Heritage from the Nineteenth Century

Besides his acute response to the analogies that nature strews so abundantly to enrich the poetic inclination, Robert Frost can be credited with inheriting at least four vital attributes from the age that was fading as he was born.

First, a strong realization of the necessity for "an original relation to the universe," as Emerson put it, meaning direct and firsthand perception. This relationship would not exclude awareness of the beneficial results of physical labor, the least of which would involve good coming to the body from activity. More important was psychical release or a sense of communion with one's environment. "Two Tramps in Mud Time," with its poet out of doors at the first whistle of spring chopping good solid chunks of maple, shows what is meant. Walt Whitman, with whom Frost has more affinity than appears on the surface, expressed the original-relation concept well (he also was an Emersonian) in his brief poem describing the boredom engendered by the learned astronomer's lecture, contrasted with the exultation of gazing with naked eye at the star-studded heavens.

Second, a glad acceptance of intuition and a forthright reliance upon it. Frost seldom proceeded from reasoning or thinking. If in practice he may have slipped, in theory he never admitted its legitimacy. He would quickly join Herman Melville in his expostulation: "I stand for the heart. To the dogs with the head! I had rather be a fool with a heart, than Jupiter Olympus with his head.[15] For Frost it was heart over head, all the way, even to a seeming distrust of the human mental process. He knew he was a Romantic, and he gloried in it. "A poem is never a put-up job," he declared to Louis Untermeyer soon after *North of Boston* was published. "It begins as a lump in the throat, a sense of wrong, a homesickness, a lovesickness. It is never a thought to begin with. . . . A poem particularly must not begin with thought first."[16]

Third, an ineradicable sense of his own national identity in literature. Emerson had demanded *American* poets, not imitators of foreign models, as he touched off this continent's literary declaration of independence. Frost for years after his return from his successful British launching was touchy on the subject of what influence those brief years abroad may have had upon him and his work.[17] It was very difficult to displace in the popular mind the notion that because his first books had been taken by an English publisher it naturally followed that they had also been written in England. Actually, as he tried to make clear, the materials were pretty well completed before his voyage; but they were assembled in book form after he arrived in England. It may be that his effort to establish his complete Americanism explains to some degree his own rapid self-identification with the regional New England scene upon his return from abroad and the insistent use of the adjective *American* in early reviews written by friends and admirers. The United States has no other poet, with the possible exception of Whitman, who seems to have thought of himself as so thoroughly American; and yet Karl Shapiro disclaims Frost as an American poet at all and labels him the last of the great Britishers. Frost's intuition may have told him this classification was something he was going to have to contend with.

Fourth, steady confirmation of his own integrity as a self-reliant individual. The complete mental and spiritual independence and the self-sufficiency of each human being were enthroned by Emerson. Thoreau did what he could to make the meaning of Emerson's "self-reliance" literal, even to declaring himself independent of the state.

Frost's individualism announces itself in two directions: positively, in his self-reliant immersion in the daily activities of country life (seldom in his poems is Frost accompanied or aided by any other person); and negatively, in his total aversion to anything that smacked of the "tenderer than thou collectivism" which he satirized in a series of didactic political verses. Group-thought was not for Frost, as many have pointed out.

The import of this backward look is to suggest that the past is genuinely prelude. Much more went into the making of this poet than is discernible to the casual eye. Frost emerged from what went before him, gathered his forces, and then struck forward as far as he was able. In so doing, any man will be limited by what he is and cannot help being: Frost's limitations included his own view of himself and the extent of his psychological and emotional bondage to previous times.

One evidence of Frost's inability or unwillingness, whichever it was, to break conclusively with the total ambience created by Bryant and Longfellow, Emerson and Thoreau, is apparent in his reluctance to innovate. His works never take the breath away by their daring. He was a stranger to the *avant-garde*. What new paths he does indicate, such as his increase of fluidity in blank verse and his moderate experimentation with the sonnet form, are quite minor breaches of established convention. They are considerably less venturesome, for instance, than the departures taken so freely by Emily Dickinson in her stately isolation. Frost is almost wholly traditional. Beside the flamboyant influences of the Imagist group, the brazen advances made by Sandburg in free-verse form, the "explosion" of language and poetic structure by E. E. Cummings, or the esoteric but bold symbol- and allusion-complexes of T. S. Eliot and his followers, Frost indeed seems in many respects a relic of the previous century.

Frost himself was not deceived as to how little of the trailblazer was in him: "Do or say my damndest I can't be other than orthodox in politics love and religion: I can't escape salvation: I can't burn if I was born into this world to shine without heat."[18] Apparently this realization came early. Once it was accepted, Frost set out to make the most of what he might be. He knew that his orthodoxy had its own advantages; one of the most important was that it released him from the danger of following fads past their crests into oblivion. "The one thing I boast I

can't be, is disillusioned," he told Elizabeth Shepley Sergeant.[19]
Commitment to the established ways, however, did impose obvious
limitations upon Frost as a poet. To cite the most obvious, he changed
amazingly little in his long career. Critics find this a point of genuine
and debilitating weakness, yet it must be granted that within his
natural boundaries Frost managed to perform brilliantly and to sustain
that performance for half a century.

Frost was not unaware that he appeared to be rooted to one spot while
others moved. Movement, of course, is not a synonym for progress nor
does it guarantee achievement. Again it seemed best simply to admit he
was traditional, then go ahead to more profitable topics. His self-
description comes with remarkable candor: "Anything I ever thought I
still think. Any poet I ever liked I still like. It is noticeable, I go back on
no one. It is merely that others go back on me. I take nothing back. I
don't even grow."[20] In accepting as fact what many writers—perhaps
the majority—would go to equal lengths to camouflage, Frost
theorized that each individual is endowed with a specified "speed"
either for racing forward or for "standing still like a water beetle." To
make a world takes all kinds, as Emerson had said; and therefore the
mountain need not call the squirrel little prig.

Frost has always stood somewhat alone among American poets.
Largely unaffected by movements to the right or left, he was equally
free of association with coteries and cabals. His work has most in
common with that of Edwin Arlington Robinson, at least with Robinson's earlier poems; and in personal relationships Frost appears to have
gotten on with that poet more congenially than with any other of his
major contemporaries. Robinson's dark portraits in *Children of the Night*
(1897) are in tune with those in *North of Boston*. It was fitting that Frost
should suggest that "Mr. Flood's Party" was Robinson's best single
poem; in subject, theme, and form, it could be mistaken for Frost's
own. To Frost's chagrin, Robinson was sidetracked from his true
material into writing verse narratives inspired by history and myth,
what Frost called "Arthurian twaddle"; but Frost continued to work
the same garden in which he began.

If he had little in common with the newer poets, he was more nearly
like Willa Cather, the Nebraska novelist, who was born just a year
before him. Both of these writers put in a long apprenticeship while
they learned their craft so thoroughly that each, at last beginning to

publish in earnest, was able to burst almost fully formed upon a waiting public. Each made an impressive debut at the age of thirty-nine; indeed, Miss Cather's *Alexander's Bridge* appeared the year prior to *A Boy's Will*. Then, within a year, both published books more solid and more typical of their mature powers: in Frost's case, *North of Boston;* in Miss Cather's, *O Pioneers!*

Neither of these writers experienced significant change during the long, successful careers that ensued. They published regularly, were highly praised, earned the respect of readers and critics alike, and with justice won most of the literary prizes to be had. But their new books as they came from press resembled those that had gone before. Better crafted perhaps, and burnished with a higher control, they rarely took new directions. Within their limits, both writers were perfectionists who strongly affirmed the esthetic virtues of form and diction. Readers knew what to expect from them; the public was rarely disappointed even if critics sometimes were unkind enough to notice. Cather, like Frost, was a regionalist. For her wide Nebraska plains, so different from New England in climate and topography yet so similar in effect upon human lives, she achieved the same degree of universality the poet achieved. She too was inclined to gaze nostalgically backward to a more idyllic time, to retreat simultaneously from the awkward present and from a future she grew to dread.

Frost was capable of great unkindness when discussing his contemporaries' works and personalities. But he and Willa Cather remained good friends, full of admiration for each other's integrity. Her story "Coming, Aphrodite!" he described as "sheer perfection."[21] Today Miss Cather is less widely appreciated than she was once. Her stature in literary history has been measured; if she is not always credited with standing in the first rank, it is undoubtedly due in part to her concentration upon regional themes. And Frost himself had great fears of going down to posterity eventually as a minor figure because of his dedication to the New England scene.

## The Renaissance in Poetry

Frost's overnight success in England, his propitious return to the United States upon the outbreak of World War I, and his subsequent acclaim here, all combined to establish him prominently in a literary scene startlingly altered from that which had existed when he sailed for England in 1912. Rarely has America seen a literary flowering to compare with the outpouring of verse which began in that year. When Frost sailed for England, "he left a country apparently deaf to his work," according to Amy Lowell. When he returned two-and-a-half years later, it was to a land hailing him as one of the brightest promises in a renaissance.

Even before Frost's embarkation for Europe, strong undercurrents were stirring the American literary scene. Operating from her home base in Chicago, Harriet Monroe was busily writing letters to individuals at home and abroad calculated to stir up the most intense interest possible in a new magazine. To make her plans workable, she was soliciting manuscripts. She needed verses. Even more so she wanted names. Who were the young, the new, the forward-looking poets? Where were they working? What manner of poetry were they interested in writing?

Miss Monroe was well enough in tune with her times to sense what few others realized: the poetic kettle was seething and would soon begin to bubble. The immediate response to her appeals convinced her that she was on the right track. In October, 1912, the first issue of her magazine appeared. Its title was straight from the shoulder: *Poetry: A Magazine of Verse*. A first printing of a thousand copies was snatched up at once and a reprinting was hastily arranged.[22] Foresightedly, Miss Monroe, now on her way to becoming a genuine force in the land, had arranged for the plates to be kept intact. At that moment Robert Frost was less than one month gone from America.

Overnight, the floodgates opened. As magazine editors awakened to the knowledge that a revolution was under way, that the populace would actually read—and what is more, discuss—the work of the new poets, the stranglehold held on periodicals by writers of trite, sentimental verse was abruptly broken. From all parts of the nation authentic new voices rose clamoring to be heard.

Traditionally, the broad and nondescript American mid-region had been considered worthy only of being ignored. Occasionally, Eastern attention was forced to acknowledge the existence of these "outlands" because from time to time, inexplicably, as if by an embarrassing quirk of destiny, an acceptable writer emerged from the prairie. However, if he was alert in discovering his geographical blunder, he lost no time going East. Now it became apparent that the barren midland was in fact populated by poets. Many of these purported bards were exceedingly youthful; others were reaching maturity, but all seemed to join together in a common determination to reject a tradition grown sterile and to drive instead toward new forms, new subjects.

Free verse was welcomed as befitting the genuine American expression. Prose writers, casting off the shackles of sweetness and light inherited from the genteel tradition and rejecting the "smiling aspects of life" as an exclusive guide to acceptability, had opened heretofore closed areas of experience to penetrating examination. Could not poets do the same? In 1910 the dominant atmosphere could only cause most of these new writers to resign themselves to laboring in silence and obscurity and with scant hope for recognition. By the close of 1912 all had changed.

Most amazingly, the Midwestern poets appeared proud of their homeland, its stark landscapes, raw cities, and plain inhabitants. In fact, they championed their native states as being eminently worthy of serious literary treatment. With an influential organ ready to amplify their voices, Edgar Lee Masters, Carl Sandburg, Vachel Lindsay, and a battalion of others leaped forward to challenge the Easterners' literary supremacy. Chicago, it was boasted, would soon supplant Boston as the nation's writing capital. Although this faded hope seems very distant now, America may wait a long time for a happier conjunction of forces than was represented by this sudden flowering of new writers, the means to publish them, and the audience to receive them.

Less than a month after the debut of *Poetry,* Ferdinand Earle completed work on an anthology that provided further evidence that a rebirth of American poetry was imminent. Earle's projected book was aimed at collecting the work of one hundred poets who would be "representative, as much as possible, of the work done to-day in America."[23] To achieve this ambition, Earle called for entries in a competition through which selections for the book would be made. The two thousand writers who answered his summons flooded him with ten thousand poems. These submissions were culled by a trio of judges, and the anthology *The Lyric Year* was published before the year's end. In his editor's preface Earle pridefully noted evidence of a new masculinity in

American verse, attributable he believed to a "decline of Latin and Grecian influence." He particularly called attention to the independent attitudes of his writers. Their verse, he affirmed, was brushed by "the liberating touch of Walt Whitman"; it reflected the "exhilarating trend" already sensed in continental art.[24]

*The Lyric Year,* a landmark in the twentieth-century literary resurgence, is most famous perhaps for its inclusion of "Renascence" by Edna St. Vincent Millay, at that time a schoolgirl of barely twenty. Her poem, by all odds the best-known, most enduring one in the volume, did not win a prize in the competition, although the vote which Ferdinand Earle cast for it assured its being singled out for individual praise. Among the hundred poets represented in *The Lyric Year,* aside from Edna Millay, were many who would soon make their reputations either in verse or in allied fields: Zoë Akins, William Rose Benét, Witter Bynner, Donn Byrne, Joyce Kilmer, Ludwig Lewisohn, Vachel Lindsay (who was then using his first name, Nicholas), George Sterling, Sara Teasdale, and Louis Untermeyer.

The poetic renaissance gained swift momentum. *Poetry,* its prestige rising with each issue, undertook to publish one new poet after another. As a result, editors of other periodicals caught fire and opened their pages to work that earlier would have been rejected as too blunt, too realistic, or too experimental. From a country considered imitative and essentially unpoetic, poets emerged seemingly all at once, like moths in season shedding their cocoons and spreading their wings for flight.

No precedent existed for comparison. The incessant, month-to-month touting of successive new discoveries went on without stop. It all seemed far too good to be true. A critic might easily be forgiven if the unending claims roused by the revival made him cynical, for Parnassus indeed seemed crowded. Edwin Arlington Robinson, who had waited long, was at last acclaimed as a trailblazer. Stephen Crane's poems were rediscovered and his experimental forms emulated. Schools, groups, and movements abounded, springing up as fast as foliage under the summer sun.

Inside a five-year span, books of substance and durability appeared from the pens of at least seven new major figures: Vachel Lindsay, Amy Lowell, Robert Frost, Edgar Lee Masters, Carl Sandburg, T. S. Eliot, and Edna Millay. The list of other poets who were either to fill minor roles or to rise eventually to first-level rank was staggering. Suddenly the nation had Ezra Pound, Sara Teasdale, Stephen Vincent Benét,

Hilda Doolittle (H.D.), Wallace Stevens, William Carlos Williams, Robinson Jeffers, Marianne Moore, Hart Crane, and the arch-experimentalist who preferred to sign himself "ee cummings." All seemed to be scribbling at top speed to deliver verses generally robust, sometimes shocking, often dazzling, and always buoyantly youthful. The mirror was held up deliberately to the modern age. Diction was consciously updated, even the vernacular being explored by such as Sandburg for that it might contribute to the communication of fresh, native materials. *Vers libre,* of course, was in with a vengeance.

Louis Untermeyer, acting in dual roles of participator in the revival and observer of the phenomenon, supplies an accurate summary of all that was occurring:

> By 1917, the "new" poetry was ranked as "America's first national art"; its success was sweeping, its sales unprecedented. People who never before had read verse, turned to it and found they could not only read but relish it. They discovered that for the enjoyment of poetry it was not necessary to have at their elbows a dictionary of rare words and classical references; they no longer were required to be acquainted with Latin legendry and the minor love-affairs of the major Greek divinities. Life was their glossary, not literature. The new product spoke to them in their own language.[25]

Without difficulty one could imagine that the great audiences begged for by Whitman finally had arrived.

The true impact of this flood of new verse can be measured by the durability enjoyed by such a high percentage of it. One might dramatize by conjecturing that the Pulitzer Prize for Poetry had been established during the poetic renaissance; the hypothetical Pulitzer Committee for 1915 might have selected from a host which included Arthur Guiterman's *The Laughing Muse,* Masters' *Spoon River Anthology,* Robinson's revision of *Captain Craig,* Amy Lowell's anthology *Some Imagist Poets,* Sara Teasdale's *Rivers to the Sea,* and Frost's two volumes, *A Boy's Will* and *North of Boston.* In succeeding years, decisions would have been no simpler to make. Contenders for the 1916 prize would have included Sandburg's *Chicago Poems,* Robinson's *The Man Against the Sky,* and Frost's *A Mountain Interval.* And in 1917 the committee might easily have vacillated between Lindsay's *The Chinese Nightingale* and Millay's *Renascence.* Had young T. S. Eliot not expatriated himself, his *Prufrock and Other Observations* would have complicated the decision further. These were not years in which the prize could have gone by default or could have been, as it was in 1964, withheld entirely for lack of substantial candidates. Riches were truly an embarrassment. Clearly, the revival provided Robert Frost with more than an opportunity for immediate publication. This opportunity was important, of course; but even more crucial to his future was the already-stimulated audience created by the renaissance—and of greatest consequence was the chance for his poems to be assessed in competition with a dozen peer contenders.

### "Don't Join Too Many Gangs"

In England Frost had chanced upon a literary life whose activity contrasted with the dormancy he had left at home. The Georgian poets, with their emphasis upon the pastoral, were popular; and they received Frost in a friendly embrace. He became relatively close to Wilfrid Wilson Gibson and Lascelles Abercrombie and to a number of younger poets, particularly Edward Thomas. In London, Stephen Phillips's *Poetry Review* provided ready outlet for verse, as did *Poetry and Drama,* whose editors encouraged more experimental styles. Ezra Pound was in town, acting as unpaid foreign correspondent for *Poetry* at the invitation of Harriet Monroe. Pound and Frost became acquainted, and soon excited letters arrived in America expressing incredulity as to why Frost had not been published there and demanding that Harriet Monroe reserve space at once in *Poetry* for this native singer.

Miss Monroe was not overly responsive, but she did print the review of *North of Boston* which Pound wrote for her; and Frost gave Pound credit for "bullying" her into printing "The Code," his first poem to appear in the United States after he took up residence in England. In London also was the redoubtable Amy Lowell, whose fortune allowed her to travel everywhere—and who did precisely that—hotly pursuing undisputed leadership of the "new poetry." During the summer of 1914 she purchased Frost's *North of Boston* at The Poetry Book Shop and at once enlisted as one of his champions. Amy did her level best to lasso Frost and bring him into her corral of Imagists (or "Amygists," as Pound called them); but she had no more influence upon him than had Pound or Abercrombie or Gibson.

Amy Lowell's description of the British literary situation in 1914 provides a valid summary of Frost's ability to resist the blandishments of the famous and the influential:

London was full of poets, and, what is better, the beliefs, and protests, and hates of poets. They made a lively buzzing which meant that the art was in a vigorous condition. . . . here, there, and everywhere, if you happened to be a poet, was talk of forms and directions, technique and substance, the thousand and one things which, if taken in small doses, do so much to keep the poet's craft sound and sane. . . . To anyone less firmly set on his own artistic feet than Mr. Frost, the situation was intoxicating, but it is characteristic of the man that he lost neither his head nor his originality. He changed no whit in poetry, speech, or appearance. He talked and listened, and went home and did the same thing right over again only better. . . . He went his own way, grew his vegetables, and wrote "North of Boston."[26]

Miss Lowell praised *North of Boston* generously. But she found it a sad book, revelatory of the disease which she herself observed destroying the legendary vitality of New England. She was quick to notice that Frost dealt less with the New England of his own day than with "left-overs of the old stock, morbid, pursued by phantoms, slowly sinking to insanity."[27] Thus she became the first to point out specifically what later critics have made much of: Frost's conservatism, his tendency to glance longingly back over his shoulder to previous times. Even Frost's later attempts to deal with "modern" topics such as the hydrogen bomb did little to counteract this deficiency.

If his conservatism, including his insistence upon being his own self and detached from various "movements" which characterized the poetic renaissance, held Frost back and prevented him perhaps from making a greater contribution than he did, it at the same time proved to be his poetic salvation. It preserved him as a unique figure and added to his stature, just as anything truly fine remains fine so long as it remains itself—in the same manner as an edifice of genuine Greek pattern is grand while it resists the innovations surrounding it, and looks even finer against the decaying remnants of gingerbread among which it may eventually stand.

"Robert Frost has never been in fashion," says his close friend Sidney Cox.[28] If one reads this correctly, not as a complaint but a boast, Cox is saying that Frost has never been the current fad, the poet whose book one must have tucked under his arm. If so, this situation has proved fortunate. Fads, while they may roar in with the power of a cyclone, die not with a bang but a whimper. If Frost has never been in fashion, neither has he been out of fashion.

In sum, Frost remained aside from, and above, fashion. His resistance to identification with insurgent groups, while perhaps denying him whatever sudden notoriety the groups may have garnered under the spotlight, simultaneously preserved him from consignment to the junk heap with these same groups as they became passé. Amy Lowell's Imagists, for instance, shone brightly for a time. To a large extent, the limelight in which they basked was self-generated. Then they became outmoded, superseded, finally antiquated, and then extinct. Meanwhile, Frost continued to trudge ahead, his old reliable self, doing what was expected of him, much less a comet than a fixed star.

Frost has made his own comments upon what he considered the misguided and wild-headed "quest of new ways to be new":

Science put it into our heads that there must be new ways to be new. Those tried were largely by subtraction—elimination. Poetry for example was tried without punctuation. It was tried without capital letters. It was tried without metric frame on which to measure the rhythm. It was tried without any images but those to the eye. . . . It was tried without content under the trade name of poesie pure. It was tried without phrase, epigram, coherence, logic, and consistency. It was tried without ability. . . . It was tried premature like the delicacy of unborn calf in Asia. It was tried without feeling or sentiment like murder for small pay in the underworld. These many things it was tried without, and what had we left? Still something.[29]

Few concessions were made to the new ways of others. Frost's highest praise for Edwin Arlington Robinson was that his fellow poet had also resisted the popular impulse and remained content with the old-fashioned way. Both stepped back as the roman candles of innovation flared out; then they proceeded on their way.

Frost's innate Emersonianism never showed as plainly as when he observed Emerson's directive to "feel all confidence in himself, and never to defer to the popular cry." When some act of government, or fashion, or personality was being cried up by half the populace and cried down by the rest, and the impression was left that all history depended upon the moment, the resultant crisis provided the test of the self-reliant individual. "Let him not quit his belief," advised Emerson, "that a popgun is a popgun, though the ancient and honorable of the earth affirm it to be the crack of doom."[30] Thus it was for Frost with the Imagism of the World War I years, the art-for-art's sake of the 1920s, the social consciousness of the 1930s, the superpatriotism of the forties. In none of these seductive pools did Frost more than wet his toes.

Yet he did not stand entirely aloof from the pervasive excitement hovering over the poetic scene of his day. He was skeptical of the radically new, and his natural impulse was to withdraw from involvement. But where personalities were concerned, it was an entirely different matter. This was so particularly when he saw new poets—often mistakenly—as rivals whose sole aim was to dethrone him. He was not averse to lending an occasional helping hand to a young and unestablished writer, but his kindnesses to published poets were chiefly reserved for those he considered no direct personal threat, like Vachel Lindsay, or for obviously minor figures, like Louis Untermeyer, who could be praised with safety. Frost had a reputation to establish. His career demanded priority above any other considerations. When he returned from England, he was forty years old, mature, and fully formed as a writer. His plan for the future did not include the gratuitous puffing of poets whose accomplishments might in any way detract from his own.

## "My Own Salesman"

The popular myth that inclines to see Frost as a simple New England fellow who happens to think in stanzas is well removed from reality. It is not a myth totally invented by the poet himself, but he did lend a hand to its promulgation from an early date. In some ways the picture seems to have resulted from as calculated a campaign as any press agent ever dreamed. Essentially it is a pose, but not an overly dishonest one. It possesses enough truth to lend it substance, enough artificiality to set it in the same class with the pseudo-primitive attitude assumed by Ernest Hemingway and William Faulkner. His pose is characterized by the same pretended disdain of critical analysis and interpretation of literary works.

One indication of this disdain is Frost's pretense of impatience with "professors" (he was one himself for most of his mature life) and with the subtleties they found in his poems. Frost's popular image, from its earliest days, was that he was a poet well versed in country things. This image had popular appeal, and he did nothing to contradict the notion that he was a farmer who had stumbled into a bookstore. Even when he described his own brand of moderate realism, he used the homely phrases expected of him, saying that he was like the painter who preferred to sketch a washed potato, not one with the dirt of the field still clinging to it.

As early as 1916 Robert Frost told Louis Untermeyer that he had already passed through "several phases, four to be exact" as a poet and considered himself permanently shaped. He knew what it was that he could do well. He intended to go ahead and do it, and along the way make certain that everyone who counted knew what he was doing and appreciated him. "I have myself all in a strong box where I can unfold as a personality at discretion,"[31] he said matter-of-factly, but with justifiable elation.

No one was going to hurry Robert Frost. He could wait; like Whitman, he contained amplitudes of time. The dangers flirted with by rushing too soon and too often into print were known intuitively. A book a year had been the ruin of Edwin Arlington Robinson—mortal self-depletion to accommodate a publisher.[32] It was not for him. Were an interested party to inquire as to the progress of a certain poem Frost had casually mentioned that he intended to write, he would answer that he had not yet composed it; but he was not uneasy since he knew where the poem was coming from. Such answers produced, he felt, "great effect of strength and mastery!"[33]

"I am become my own salesman," Frost could admit candidly as he launched his plan to sell himself simultaneously to the populace and to the critics.[34] It was quality goods he had to sell. Inevitably he was led to consider all other poets as salesmen like himself, and therefore as very real rivals for acclaim. During the early years in which his reputation was being established, his "rivals" were Vachel Lindsay, Carl Sandburg, Edgar Lee Masters, and Amy Lowell. Each was a strong personality, and all were prolific and highly active when Frost returned from England.

Vachel Lindsay, the disorganized Midwestern troubadour, the neurotic chanter of American songs, was killing himself with strenuous reading tours and nightmares of the mind long before he swallowed Lysol in 1931. Frost treated him gently and seems to have been genuinely fond of the impractical dreamer from Springfield, Illinois, since he invariably spoke of him with affection. Upon Lindsay's death, Frost expressed himself clearly: "I feel more as if I had lost a child (with all sorts of foolish little ways) than a brother and fellow-artist. It comes near me."[35]

Carl Sandburg was twitted by Frost for the "set routine" he followed in presenting the program on his tours. First came the set of definitions of poetry, then the recitation of favorite verses, then the twanging on the guitar. By now many people must have heard the story of Sandburg's reading at Michigan University upon Frost's invitation: how, when Sandburg proved tardy coming downstairs at the Frosts, someone inquired whether he was in his room preparing his program. "No," replied the host, "he's standing by his mirror fixing his hair so it will look as if a comb had never touched it."[36] Frost may have had special insight, for he himself always dressed the suitably casual part for his own lectures and often mussed his own white hair with a deliberate sweep of the hand.

On the lecture circuit Sandburg remained Frost's greatest competitor. Although the two men, very close in age, grew old together as a pair of unofficial poets-laureate, they were never close. The strain of those early competitive years endured to the end. Only now and then did Frost have kind words to say of Sandburg. And although Sandburg was generous upon the event of Frost's death, it was obvious that each was happier when not commenting upon the other.

For Edgar Lee Masters and Amy Lowell, Frost reserved his real pettiness. Masters truly alarmed him. *The Spoon River Anthology* came out in the spring of 1915 almost simultaneously with *North of Boston*. Frost was in terror lest this very impressive, extremely popular collection of mordant Midwestern portraits overshadow his own book. The *Spoon River* poems exposed the downstate Illinois village in the same manner that the *North of Boston* poems penetrated back of the scenes in upstate New England. Both books were immensely popular and sold far more copies than any volume of poetry is generally supposed to sell. But of the two, *Spoon River* aroused the greater controversy, was more talked up, more highly praised, more widely read. This success hurt Frost, and he described the book as "false-realistic" and commented curtly, "I think Spoon River is perfectly all right for them as likes it."[37]

As for Masters himself, he became to Frost at once "my hated rival."[38] "There is a Masters Mountain and right beside it a Frost Hollow hereabouts. What can be done to bring the mountain low and cast up the hollow?" he wanted to know.[39] As fate would have it, Masters in time eroded his own mountain; his work declined steadily after *Spoon River*. He became less and less a man to be reckoned with, but Frost could not forget the early threat. More than twenty years after *Spoon River*, at a time when Masters's writing and following had deteriorated so badly that he was almost in oblivion, Frost still referred to him as "the megacephalus Masters" and worried that Robert P. Tristram Coffin, a younger poet, might be "snuggling" up to him. "I am very sensitive to political shifts like this. We are choosing up sides, balancing our powers for the next world war in art," he explained.[40] If it ever had been a war, it had long since been won by Frost. Yet he seemed unable to rest until the vanquished Masters had been obliterated.

The other rival most keenly felt was Amy Lowell, whose "wealth, social position, and the influence she has been able to purchase and cozen"[41] made Frost's hackles rise. Amy was overpowering, one must admit; and her money was a constant affront to those fighting desperate odds in the hope of gleaning a living from verse. Frost complained that she told him and Robinson they had no right to be poets because they were not wealthy enough to afford that luxury. In actuality Amy Lowell was never an authentic rival in the sense Frost felt her to be. She was devoted totally to her school of Imagists. She first encountered Frost's work in England and then did her best to find an American publisher for it. Even though she did attempt to snare him into her Imagist movement, she apparently had a genuine interest in Frost as a fellow poet, was anxious to see him recognized, and was not at all ambitious to dominate him in the public eye.

Perhaps what really rankled was her personality. She was an inveterate limelighter and a scene-stealer. She had a way of playing the empress—it came naturally to her—and of summoning her admirers and fellow poets to the throne room. Frost objected. He cared even less for her habit of traveling everywhere, always being on the spot for whatever publicity came her way. Of course, the famous Lowell name also irritated him. And her notorious cigar-smoking was a stupendous bit of stage magic in retaliation against which mussed hair seemed a feeble gimmick. With burning Corona in hand, Amy Lowell could easily upstage any rival, if she cared to.

Two years after Frost's books appeared in America, she generously included him as one of six American poets in her *Tendencies in Modern American Poetry.* Only he and Edwin Arlington Robinson appeared in chapters devoted solely to themselves. She was practically unstinting in her praise; and the book, considering its author's prestige and the fact that it was the first extended evaluation of Frost's work, gave an enormous boost to Frost's early career.

Despite her generosity, Frost chose to carp at small errors of fact and judgment allegedly contained in her appraisal. He found fault with what he took to be her assertion that his poems had been inspired solely by New England (actually, her point was that, with New England, Frost had located his ideal subject matter). Especially was he infuriated with her portrait of Elinor Frost as "the conventional helpmeet of genius."[42] This description of his wife seemed in some manner to deprecate Frost's own achievement. "Unpardonable," he called it in 1917, although after Elinor's death, he evaluated her aid in even more glowing terms than Amy Lowell had used. But these reactions were, for the most part, private—shared only with intimates. On the surface, Frost did his utmost to remain friends with Amy Lowell. She was, after all, a most excellent individual to have on one's side in those days, one nearly indispensable to an ambitious poet. Frost, who reserved his remarks for private letters, publicly placated her, using her reputation for whatever glow it might be able to cast on his own.

When Amy Lowell's poetry became the topic of open conversation, Frost donned what he called a "light mask" of hypocrisy. When closeted with friends, he ridiculed her work unmercifully. "I don't believe she is anything but a fake," he confided to Louis Untermeyer. Hopefully, he spoke of a time when he might afford to expose her "for a fool as well as fraud." Wouldn't it, he mused, be more honest if he were simply and flatly to refuse to allow his poems to be bound between the same covers with those of such a charlatan as she?[43] When he had reached this extreme, Frost was in genuine danger of hauling out a sixteen-inch gun to shoot a sparrow. No doubt he realized it himself, for he never pursued the matter further. His poems continued to appear in the anthologies side by side with Lowell poems.

Frost's pettiness in dealing with his contemporaries was never demonstrated more clearly than when, in deference to Amy Lowell's reputation and acknowledged "power" in the literary world, he invited her to read at the University of Michigan in 1922, while he was Poet in Residence. Amy came. The audience clamored for a glimpse of her engaged in smoking her cigar. She pooh-poohed the notion. The audience's interest only increased. At the speaker's podium, Amy joggled a pitcher of water and a lamp. Both upset. It took ten minutes to disentangle the lamp cord. Gleefully Frost wrote Untermeyer, "I never heard such spontaneous shouts of laughter." But Amy Lowell proved as poised a showman as any. Throughout this comedy of errors she quipped with the audience, winning them to her side, forcing Frost to admit grudgingly, "As a show she was more or less successful."[44]

So strong was his aversion to Amy Lowell that Frost could find fault automatically with whomever she thought well of. John Gould Fletcher, one of the six poets whose work she had extolled in *Tendencies in Modern American Poetry*, was also commonly known to be her protégé. In 1919 the *Dial* published a Fletcher contribution Frost disapproved. "Look," he snickered, "what Amy's pig-eyed young bear-cat done all over the Dial for want of a little historical sense. Amy ought to be ashamed of him. Right through his diapers!"[45] But Fletcher was a better writer than Frost might intimate, and Frost later was big enough to admit, "I have mixed him up too much with Amy to be fair to him."[46]

Even the mighty were likely to be stung when their achievements loomed too large. William Butler Yeats, author of "Byzantium" and winner of the Nobel Prize, was one of these. One must be careful, Frost insisted, not to grant Yeats more than his due: "He's disposed to crowd the rest of us as it is." Having rechecked Yeats's work, Frost was convinced that "even where all is contrived to look so choice and so chosen there are whole pages that are nothing."[47]

Unhappily and despite his huge popularity as a poet, a success which dwarfed all of his competitors, Frost seems never to have overcome his early fears that he might be counted as no more than one among many. Lawrance Thompson tells the story of Frost's fury at discovering in 1937 that Henry Holt and Company intended to publish a collection of critical essays whose editor had not included any piece regarding himself and his work. Richard Thornton, then the president of Holt, tried to persuade Frost that the book *Recognition of Robert Frost,* then about to be published and totally devoted to his poetry, would more than compensate for the oversight. But Frost persisted to storm, with the upshot that Holt sold the plates of the critical anthology to another publisher and mollified its editor by absorbing all of his permission costs.[48] Twenty years after this, when Alfred Kazin and Robert Frost were both on the campus of Amherst College, Kazin found Frost to be "a raging battlefield of ambition, competitiveness, guilt" who "could not stop talking about *them,* early enemies."[49]

This side of Robert Frost may appear harsh and discordant to many who revere his memory. It has dismayed a good many to learn that he was human after all. But even in Frost's poems, all is not sweetness and light, even though selective reading and reprinting of his works has lodged that belief in the popular mind. So ingrained is the image of the good gray poet, which Frost himself in word, dress, and action fostered, that the spectacle of poet as cantankerous old curmudgeon is perhaps painful to accept.

## "The Demolition of Our Masters"

During the decade 1910–1920, with the poetic renaissance reaching its height and Frost's reputation taking permanent shape, he was aided not only by Amy Lowell's influential volume but by a number of other literary persons, the anthologists. These were the editors who determined which authors were to be represented in collections printed for popular consumption and for classroom study. Recognition of a new and modern poetry flowering after long drought years stimulated collections of verse for which a ready audience was waiting. The editors of these books had no difficulty in spotting Robert Frost as a poet of outstanding ability.

One of the anthologists, William Stanley Braithwaite, capitalized on
the flood of verse by editing each year a collection of poems that had
appeared in periodicals. His *Anthology of Magazine Verse for 1915* contained high praise of Frost. The praise was appreciated; but, in discussing Frost, Braithwaite invariably linked him with Edgar Lee Masters.
Evidently the struggle for supremacy which so upset Frost himself was
apparent also to others. "The two great successes of the year up to the
writing of these paragraphs have been the American poets Frost and
Masters," wrote Braithwaite.[50]

Even Braithwaite's laudatory review of *A Boy's Will* and *North of
Boston* contained less pleasure than it might had it not stated that "With
Mr. Masters Robert Frost has contributed the most valuable additions
to American poetry of the year." Conversely, in discussing *Spoon River,*
the anthologist declared, "It comes out of the West to meet Mr. Frost's
achievement in the East."[51] His concentration upon the Frost-Masters
rivalry must have seemed to border on the perverse to those concerned.
In all, Braithwaite evaluated Masters above Frost, calling *Spoon River*
not only the most widely discussed book of poetry for the year, but also
the most original literary work produced in America for a considerable
time. Such bracketing of himself with his rival, the critical edge going
to the Westerner, undoubtedly contributed to Frost's identification of
Masters as the rival to be brought down.

In his 1915 volume Braithwaite included three Frost poems:
"Birches," "The Road Not Taken," and "The Death of the Hired
Man"—well-known Frost "standards" to the present day. The competition that year was indeed fierce. The anthology included, among
others, Amy Lowell's "Patterns" and Masters's "Washington
McNeeley" and "Hannah Armstrong." Edwin Arlington Robinson had
three entries: "Flammonde," "Old King Cole," and "Cassandra."
Wallace Stevens, whom the editors of *Poetry* had introduced as a new
poet, was represented by "Peter Quince at the Clavier." Most of these
poems are still anthologized regularly in histories of American literature. In his succeeding anthologies Braithwaite continued to include
Frost; but Masters, who published more profusely, was consistently
more highly praised as "the most typical American poet of to-day."[52]

Harriet Monroe and Alice Corbin Henderson, whose joint work on
*Poetry* magazine had proved so influential, began editing in 1917 *The*

*New Poetry.* Frost was represented by seven poems, including "Mending Wall," "After Apple-picking," and "Storm Fear." Masters, by way of comparison, had twenty-one poems in the book, mostly from *Spoon River.* Carl Sandburg had eighteen, and Amy Lowell eleven. In this and other ways, the editors indicated their preference for *vers libre.* However, Frost proved the best long-distance runner. By 1917 he was just beginning to hit his stride; the others mentioned here, although no one had then a crystal ball which would tell, had expended their major effort and would soon begin to wane.

While in England Frost had contributed two poems, "The Fear" and "A Hundred Collars," to the British quarterly *Poetry and Drama.* These aroused the curiosity of a youthful American fieldworker for the magazine, Louis Untermeyer, himself a hopeful poet. Upon inquiry he learned that the poems were, as he had suspected, the product of a fellow countryman. Immediately upon Frost's return to the United States, Untermeyer, having just reviewed *North of Boston* for the *Chicago Evening Post,* wrote Frost a congratulatory note and suggested a personal interview. The two met in April, 1915, and at once became fast friends, carrying on a regular correspondence until Frost's death.

Untermeyer, already enjoying a mild success as a poet, turned to anthologizing and won his widest reputation in this field. His first collection, *Modern American Poetry,* appeared in 1919. In it Frost was preeminent, his range illustrated by eight selections. Only Carl Sandburg was allowed as many poems; Amy Lowell and Edwin Arlington Robinson were restricted to seven; and Masters was represented by only four. The youthful Untermeyer became, and remained, one of Frost's greatest boosters. Frost took every opportunity for encouraging Untermeyer to act as his "hatchet man" against Masters, writing him in 1917: "Vision of you whirling me terribly by the ankle round and round your head (never stopping to recover your derby which you have knocked off) as you advance to the demolition of our masters. Hit 'im with me! I suppose it mayn't do me as much good as it does him harm; but it has to be."[53] That Untermeyer responded, or appeared to, is evident from his comparison of the two poets in his anthology: "Frost and Masters were the bright particular planets of 1915, although the star of the latter waned while the light of the former grew in magnitude,"[54] This appraisal must have been immensely gratifying to

Frost, even if it did not permanently stifle his concern. Untermeyer's service in promoting Frost's career was repaid with praise of the anthologist's poems, which at times seemed disproportionate to their merit. This flattery extended also to the work of Jean Starr Untermeyer, like her husband a poet of considerable promise but modest achievement.

### Spirits Grown Eliotic

After the first decade following his American debut, Robert Frost had less reason to feel threatened by his contemporary "rivals." Sandburg turned to history and his monumental work on Lincoln. Masters suffered a steady, agonizing decline in quality and reputation. Lindsay committed suicide in a fit of despondency. Amy Lowell died suddenly of a stroke in 1925. The momentum of the poetic renaissance, once past its zenith, slowed down considerably. As it faded, so also did the intense competition of the war years, dissipating the need to bring down Masters and raise Frost.

One genuine rival remained, T. S. Eliot. His "Love Song of J. Alfred Prufrock" had provoked so much discussion and interest when it appeared in *Poetry* that Eliot might easily have become an adversary in a duel-of-titans with Frost. But Eliot's residence in England and his subsequent avowal of British citizenship removed him from the immediate scene. He emerged less as a rival than as the guidon of a truly new poetic movement far removed from that in which Frost prevailed.

The tremendous impact of Eliot's *The Waste Land* in 1922 stimulated the popularity of an entirely original trend. Eliot became the spokesman for the disillusionment rampant in the wake of the Great War. During the 1920s with that decade's pervading ambience of nihilism, his wasteland motif was a natural rallying point for the lost generation. The defeatism of Eliot's verse matched what Ernest Hemingway and others were producing in prose; *The Sun Also Rises,* bearing down hard on the sterility theme, is only one case in point. A "winner-take-nothing" philosophy prevailed, and poets such as Edna Millay caught the bittersweet cynicism of the trend.

The poetry of Eliot and his followers could not have resembled less the qualities for which the Imagists had gone to battle and for which

Frost was still praised. The natural, the simple, and the idiomatic were rejected by Eliot in favor of a much more highly intellectualized, erudite, esoteric verse. Obscurity, whether intended or not, became enshrined as virtue. To read *The Waste Land* with intelligence—not to speak of comprehending it—one needed to be conversant with Latin, Greek, German, Italian, and French. One must know his history and be well acquainted with legend and myth. A working knowledge of Elizabethan drama was helpful as well. Dante was indispensable—and the Bible, or Wagnerian opera. In fact, what was required was a literary background of the widest possible scope and depth; for at any moment the reader might be expected to respond spontaneously to obscure literary allusions, or indeed to phrases and lines plucked from the contexts of old, neglected works by writers long removed from the mainstream.

Yet in 1921 Louis Untermeyer could still characterize the modern verse movement as one of "simplification," reminding his readers that "as the speech of the modern poet has grown less elaborate, so have the patterns that embody it."[55] After 1922, however, such a summary was not possible. Ignored was the first dictum of the Imagists: *To use the language of common speech.* Without a good dictionary, what were those who championed the simple and natural to make of verse with the vocabulary employed in *Burnt Norton?*

> Internal darkness, deprivation
> And destitution of all property,
> Desiccation of the world of sense,
> Evacuation of the world of fancy,
> Inoperancy of the world of spirit;
> This is the one way, and the other
> Is not the same, not in movement
> But abstention from movement; while the world moves
> In appetency, on its metalled ways
> Of time past and time future.[56]

In vogue were the symbols—private sometimes, ambivalent, plucked from myth, religion, geography, and subconscious, but rarely from the Nature of Emerson. With the symbols and the new, abstract diction and the impressionism of the poetry came a new breed of readers. Most of those who had patronized the poetic renaissance in its first phases were unequipped to deal with Eliotic verse. What was needed was clarification, interpretation. To fill the vacuum, an army of explicators moved in on the new poetry, men who might provide the marginalia that would solve its puzzles and untwist its riddles. Students were needed, not readers. Eliot had provided his own set of footnotes for *The Waste Land,* but their incompleteness only whetted the appetites of scholars for more. The audience for this breed of poetry gravitated quite naturally to the college campus, where the necessary specialists resided and where there were both the talent and the facilities for researching the poems.

Before long, colleges came to be dominated by the New Critics, who accepted the challenge of the new poets. The text was the thing: reading the text, line for line, word for word. Hours were spent unraveling the varied nuances of a single phrase. Volumes were written unearthing the buried sources, hence implications, of a stanza. Frost's reputation with this new audience suffered. Where was the challenge in his work? One could really work at an Eliot poem. Eliot was of the immediate hour, and Frost in contrast seemed more than ever rooted in a bankrupt past.

For his part, Frost remained cold to Eliot. The two met from time to time, but had little that was meaningful to say to one another. Eliot was the converse of Frost. His poems were drenched in sophistication, their elaborately conceived metaphors and esoteric allusions constituting only a fraction of the machinery that made them turn. Furthermore, Eliot used his verse to convey chronologically his evolving philosophy: he was a thinker, or portrayed himself as one. From the bankruptcy of the wasteland world he peered ahead to better times and to a world peopled not by hollow men but by worshippers suffused with grace. It was a great and dramatic concept, despondency evaporating under the sun of hope as Eliot discovered spiritual values.

This pattern of "growth" provided the academies with new corners in which to probe, and Eliot became more popular than ever on the campuses, where academic poets and critics-in-residence were increasing. As Eliot went on to become a reasonably successful playwright, and winner of the Nobel Prize, Frost must have recalled that the same Ezra Pound who inspired *The Waste Land,* invented its forms and guided it line-by-line to completion had once long ago offered to act as father *manqué* to the unknown author of *A Boy's Will*. It was a road not taken—but one not, I think, regretted, regardless of Frost's unfulfilled hope of being tapped by the Swedish Academy.

The Great Depression dominated the 1930s, sparking in writers a latent social consciousness which, once released, came swiftly to the front. On the stage, but particularly in the novels of John Dos Passos, James T. Farrell, and John Steinbeck, the message of these authors was preeminent. Before long the reformers carried their crusades into fashionable verse as well. Archibald MacLeish was only one of the many who became so concerned about the plight of the Forgotten Man that, Frost may have thought, these poets lost all idea of what poetry was about.

MacLeish's argument that poets must descend from the ivory tower and become active forces in urging social and economic reform made little sense to Frost. He was totally out of sympathy with the attempt "to use poetry as a vehicle of grievances against the un-Utopian state."[57] MacLeish's obsession with topical problems only proved to the older poet that "a man doesn't have to think to be a poet." "Before I get through I'm going to drive these social servitors back to the social settlements or to concentration camps where I can starve their sympathies to death," Frost insisted.[58] For Franklin D. Roosevelt and his New Deal, Frost had nothing but contempt. What was all this fuss about poor people, anyway? He had been writing about poor people for as long as he could remember, only he thought of them as people first, and poor second. "A Considerable Speck" provides a good insight into his attitude. He loved humanity, but he was determined not to be *told* who and how to love.

With the new decade came World War II. Out went poverty, at least on the scale that typified the depression decade; in came war-boom prosperity, a grim type of well-being. Suddenly the socioeconomic polemics of the 1930s appeared very dated. As a substitute, writers enlisted their pens in the service of their country. For war now was the only thing worth considering, the single theme large enough to warrant speaking of. Walt Whitman had committed the same error eighty years before, believing that his sole responsibility was to act as propagandist for the North against the Confederate States: "Would the talkers be talking? Would the singer attempt to sing?" Even Allen

Tate, a leader in the new critical school of explicators, was moved to observe, not altogether happily, that "Spirits grown Eliotic/Now Patriotic/Are."[59]

Robert Frost wanted none of this new topicality. He was by no means unaware of the misery in the world about him, nor were his sympathies in any way suspect; but he felt it would be all wrong to squeeze himself into the rigid role of propagandist. It seemed too artificial, too highly contrived. "I am no Lawrence of Arabia," he explained to Untermeyer, who had joined the Office of War Information.

Untermeyer attempted to enlist Frost's aid in the direct attack upon fascism, but to no avail. For one thing, Frost deeply mistrusted America's sudden friendship with her wartime allies, particularly with Russia. In a lengthy poem of explanation he said as much:

> I'm bad at politics.
> I was born blind to faults in those I love,
> But I refuse to blind myself on purpose
> To the faults of my mere confederates.
> Great are the communistic Soviets!
> If nothing more were asked of me to say
> I could pass muster with the State Department.
> Hull may be right about their being good
> As well as great. He may be also right
> About their interests lying close enough
> To ours for us to help them run the world.
> I'm waiting to see where their interests lie.[60]

Those who awaited the publication in 1942 of *A Witness Tree,* Frost's first new book of poems since 1936, were disappointed if they hoped for any sign that Frost had enlisted in the great crusade. Other poets might, if they chose, squander their powers on propaganda verse, as Edna Millay surely did in "Lidice"; but Frost was Frost. Nor did the poems in *Steeple Bush,* appearing shortly after the armistice, deal any more directly with the conflict's topical nature than is indicated in the half-handful of brief verses satirizing the Frankenstein achievement of nuclear science.

## "A Terrifying Poet"

All this long time, this half century, between *A Boy's Will* and *In The Clearing,* Robert Frost tilled essentially the same garden spot. He was an expert; he produced better verses of the home-grown variety than anyone else. Seldom did he put a toe outside his established lot-line. Readers did not look to Frost for the new or startling; they looked to him for more of the same. Generally they got what they looked for: polished verses with the master's hallmark clearly stamped on them, poems with a good share of Frostian wit, natural references, here and there a genuine bite of irony. His was work that was new and not new. He played endless varieties of the same tune. Seemingly he had himself followed the philosophy of the minister in "The Black Cottage" who held to his traditional creed for the perfectly defensible reason that it made no sense to "abandon a belief merely because it ceases to be true."

Like fashions of the moment, a belief need only be clung to long enough, clutched tightly enough, to provide the natural cycles a chance to demonstrate its validity:

> It will turn true again, for so it goes.
> Most of the change we think we see in life
> Is due to truths being in and out of favour.

In this concept, one again finds a reflection of Emerson—with his image of society as a wave which never advances or alters, even though surface motion provides that illusion. Change is not *ipso facto* ameliora-tion. One leaves Frost at the end of *A Boy's Will,* returns to him in *In The Clearing,* and finds the same man, same spot, same thoughts.

Whatever damage Frost's hewing to his main line may have done to the degree of greatness critics might assign to him, it had one tremen-dous advantage, at least in his own lifetime. It was of incalculable aid in imprinting the indelible Frost "image" on the national consciousness. Walt Whitman had provided the objective, in declaring that "the proof of a poet is that his country absorbs him as affectionately as he has absorbed it."[61] The mass of citizens thought of Frost as a kindly old soul, wise, bucolic and pastoral, who never grumbled about anything or anybody. This view may be an oversimplification, but it does not do serious violence to the vision of the good gray poet with which people equated Frost.

If any change characterized Robert Frost during his lifetime, it was a long subtle alteration of his image from national critic to national hero. At the beginning of his public career he was known for his grim approach to life, his facing up to the unpleasant realities which were destroying New England and its people. On many fronts he was

accepted as another grim modern realist, verging on the morbid. Louis
Untermeyer felt it his duty to inject a corrective. Admitting the reality
and power of Frost's dramatic narratives, Untermeyer feared that the
stark terror they evoked had been emphasized beyond proportion;
readers should consider another aspect: "Frost is by no means the dark
naturalist that many suspect. Behind the mask of 'grimness' which
many of his critics have fastened upon him, there is a continual elfin
pucker; a whimsical smile, a half-disclosed raillery glints beneath his
most somber monologues. His most concrete facts are symbols of
spiritual values."[62] This is the portrait that gradually won the field
from that grim poet who published "Home Burial" and "The Hill
Wife."

That this "new" image had become a thoroughly ingrained bit of
American folklore was dramatized in 1959 at Frost's eighty-fifth birthday dinner. Lionel Trilling, the principal speaker at this testimonial
affair, expressed the compelling need to bring balance into the currently
popular view of Frost. Americans, he was certain, found Robert Frost
representative of an ideal somewhat removed from the realities both of
actual life and of Frost's own poetry. "The manifest America of Mr.
Frost's poems is . . . rural in a highly moralized way, in an aggressively
moralized way."[63] It was the America of an idyllic past that readers
found in the man's work, a past which had never really existed, but
which men desperately needed to believe had existed—and still did
exist. From Frost's poems they took those elements that tallied comfortably with their need to escape from an overly complex, overly
anxious, overly urbanized society.

Trilling's Frost was not at all the Frost of his many admirers. Not for
him the Frost who reassured the masses by "affirmation of old virtues,
simplicities, pieties, and ways of feeling." "I think of Robert Frost as a
terrifying poet. Call him, if it makes things any easier, a tragic poet,
but it might be useful every now and then to come out from under the
shelter of that literary word. The universe that he conceives is a
terrifying universe."[64] Doubters might read the poem "Design." Trilling advised them to try it, to see if it in any way induced a more
tranquil sleep. Or they might study another verse, "Neither Out Far
Nor In Deep," and see whether terrors were thereby laid to rest. One
could read, Trilling might well have added, "Desert Places" or "Once
by the Pacific" to find out whether Frost was the confident American
poet he was commonly thought to be.

Trilling forced attention to the unsettling tragic vision which had so mightily impressed Frost's earliest critics. The storm broke at once. Was nothing sacred and inviolate? One might as easily have proposed the demolition of the White House as the de-mythicizing of America's beloved white-headed poet. Letters of dismay flooded in upon the editors of the literary reviews. Imagine comparing Robert Frost, already canonized the patron saint of American tradition, with Sophocles. Imagine so much as intimating that only a poet who would anatomize the terrifying aspects of life could then provide comfort from them. "Holy mackerel!" exclaimed J. Donald Adams in the *New York Times Book Review,* "Frost simply sees the universe as it is and accepts it. He isn't terrified by what he sees, and neither should we be."[65]

Readers gave their unstinted support to Adams's view. Trilling must have lost his way in the tangled briar-forests of Freudianism, wrote one. He had better wake up before it was too late. Another letter-writer, responding in white-heat to Adams's indictment of Trilling, provided the phrase-perfect. He hoped, he said fervently, that, as Frost followed the thrusts and parries of this controversy, he was enjoying "a nice plate of buckwheat cakes and Vermont maple syrup":[66] What could better epitomize the popular vision of Frost as national hand-holder?

Robert Frost himself declared that his ultimate goal was that of any serious poet: "to lodge a few poems where they will be hard to get rid of."[67] This he had already done long before he died. Whether in making the great effort his salesmanship had also lodged a reputation that would be hard to get rid of is yet to be seen. There seems little doubt that Frost will be remembered. But only time will tell whether he is to be recalled as a physician who distributed placebos to his troubled age, or as a good Greek out of New England who drew back the dark curtain of eternity and directed men's eyes into the realm of final mysteries.

# Chapter Three

# The Appropriate Tool: Frost's Craftsmanship

While a fruitful debate might ensue from questioning whether Robert Frost has looked out far or in deep sufficiently to warrant his position as major poet, praise for his craftsmanship has been almost universal. His range may be doubted, but his skill within it is generally granted. Poetry being a house with many doors, poets are not expected to be duplicates of one another: entering by the same portals or viewing the world from identical casements. Poetry might also be described as a workshop whose walls are lined with pegs holding tools of the craft. Few can master every implement, but a man is expected to select the tools appropriate to the artifices he wishes to create and to excel at wielding these with some measure of dexterity. A close look at the techniques Frost selects from the multitude available promises hope of arriving at a meaningful definition of the poet as craftsman.

## Commitment to Convention

At least part of Robert Frost's reputation as a poet of "simplicity" derives from the metrical tools he selects. Opening a copy of *The Poetry of Robert Frost* at random pages, the average reader gains two solid impressions. The poems are preponderantly short, seldom running over from one page to another. Also, the verses are composed in brief forms, the quatrain appearing repeatedly, along with numerous stanzas only slightly longer. Exceptions appear, of course, notably in the longer blank-verse pieces, but they do not alter the dominant impression of brevity, hence simplicity.

This casual impression, while not altogether incorrect, does deceive. The simpler English metrics are admirably suited to the subjects and themes Frost presents, and Frost does select them for the majority of his poems. At the same time, within these limits, he brings to his verses an unending variety, the mark not of a primitive but of a true sophisticate. To employ the more complicated French forms—the rondeau or villanelle, for example—might prove a greater virtuosity, but these would be foreign to the simple subjects that are his strength. The requirements of their rhymes would conflict with the natural speech he strived for. He did attempt once to work in terza rima. The result, "Acquainted with the Night," shows that he was able to handle more intricate forms if he wished. The form he "invented" for "Stopping by Woods on a Snowy Evening" actually owes a considerable debt to conventional terza rima, with its interlocking rhymes holding the stanzas together and its method of closing off the final stanza with uniform rhymes.

"What we have in English is mostly iambic"[1] was Frost's way of expressing the natural pattern of his native speech. He rarely strayed far from this meter. He appears to do so at times, but then he is merely exercising a poet's privilege to allow speech patterns to triumph over imposed forms. Here and there a genuine exception can be noted, as in "The Demiurge's Laugh," with its admission of an occasional anapestic line: "The sound was behind me instead of before." Yet the line following reverts to the more typical iambic: "A sleepy sound, but mocking half."

In *North of Boston* Frost included one of his rare exceptions to the iambic pattern. "Blueberries" is uniformly anapestic:

> It must be on charcoal they fatten their fruit.
> I taste in them sometimes the flavour of soot.
> And after all really they're ebony skinned:
> The blue's but a mist from the breath of the wind.

Ferreting out these deviations is like tearing apart a haystack for the proverbial needle. He was explicit concerning the range of available forms: "The poet goes in like a rope skipper to make the most of his opportunities. If he trips himself, he stops the rope. He is of our stock and has been brought up by ear to choice of two metres, strict iambic and loose iambic (not to count varieties of the latter)."[2]

Strict iambic and *loose* iambic. It was characteristic of Frost to leave himself a generous loophole in the rule—and to take full advantage of it.

The iambic rhythm, as Frost uses it, may range from lines of metronomic regularity to lines in which the pattern is all but extinguished. "Birches" is one piece that begins without any appreciable variation:

> When I see birches bend to left and right
> Across the lines of straighter darker trees,
> I like to think some boy's been swinging them.
> But swinging doesn't bend them down to stay.

But "An Old Man's Winter Night" begins as it must, allowing the speech pattern to dominate without regard for mechanical uniformity:

> All out of doors looked darkly in at him
> Through the thin frost, almost in separate stars,
> That gathers on the pane in empty rooms.
> What kept his eyes from giving back the gaze
> Was the lamp tilted near them in his hand.

Knowing from study, or observation, or intuition, that the iambic best approximates the rhythm of the English language, Frost recognized also that within this limitation the four- or five-stress line would work out most happily. The majority of his lines extend to tetrameter or pentameter, although here again he maintains his freedom to vary the length of his lines whenever he chooses. Not too infrequently one comes upon the dimeter, as in "Dust of Snow":

> The way a crow
> Shook down on me
> The dust of snow
> From a hemlock tree

Or the trimeter:

> Nature's first green is gold,
> Her hardest hue to hold.
> Her early leaf's a flower;
> But only so an hour.

While Frost's poems are built upon two- and three-stress lines often enough so that those lines might be called typical, lines which exceed the pentameter are much rarer. The poet "may have any length of line up to six feet," Frost said.[3] He usually held himself well within that self-imposed limitation. One could easily tally on the fingers of one hand the poems that exceed the six-foot prescription. An example is "A Leaf Treader" from *A Further Range,* written in heptameters:

> All summer long they were overhead, more lifted up than I
> To come to their final place in earth they had to pass me by.
> All summer long I thought I heard them threatening under their
>     breath.
> And when they came it seemed with a will to carry me with
>     them to death . . .

A glance at two other verses will suggest a generalization containing some truth about the poet's choices of stanzas:

> I'm going out to clean the pasture spring;
> I'll only stop to rake the leaves away
> (And wait to watch the water clear, I may):
> I sha'n't be gone long.—You come too.

> In winter in the woods alone
> Against the trees I go.
> I mark a maple for my own
> And lay the maple low.

These verses—similar in subject, remarking as each does upon a homely, natural act—are related metrically also. Yet the first of this pair of simple quatrains was used to preface *A Boy's Will* (1913), and the second concluded the last volume *In The Clearing* (1962). Half a century apart, both hew to the same convention.

## Frost's Stanza Forms

The quatrain stands out as Frost's favorite form. Not only does he use it again and again, but he provides it with an infinite variety of rhyme, ranging from the traditional ballad to interlocking schemes of his own devising. Occasionally he writes in the familiar *abab* pattern, as in "Pea Brush":

> The sun in the new-cut narrow gap
> Was hot enough for the first of May,
> And stifling hot with the odor of sap
> From stumps still bleeding their life away.

He may turn also to the *abba* quatrain, as in "Fragmentary Blue":

> Why make so much of fragmentary blue
> In here and there a bird, or butterfly,
> Or flower, or wearing-stone, or open eye,
> When heaven presents in sheets the solid hue?

In "Desert Places" he employs another variant, *aaba:*

> Snow falling and night falling fast oh fast
> In a field I looked into going past,
> And the ground almost covered smooth in snow,
> But a few weeds and stubble showing last.

This same form is used in his most ingeniously devised lyric, "Stopping by Woods on a Snowy Evening." In that poem, each third-line rhyme becomes a commitment as major rhyme for the stanza following, linking stanzas together in a chain. The double similarity between the quatrain above and "Stopping by Woods," a similarity that embraces both image and form, raises speculation as to whether the two poems are not more closely related than has been thought.

At times he concocts a pseudo-quatrain out of a pair of couplets; for the couplet appears, next to the four-line stanza, to be his workhorse. He employs these paired rhymes separately, in quatrains, in six- and eight-line stanzas, or he binds them together into longer poems like "The Thatch." In one instance, "Into My Own," he composes an experimental sonnet entirely of couplets. The couplet is his favorite form for light verse. "Departmental," "A Considerable Speck," and other poems with a touch of whimsy are rhymed in this manner.

Sometimes his couplet-poems surprise the reader with the inclusion of a tercet. This happens in the middle of "The Thatch" in which one suddenly finds three rhymes in place of the expected pair. The frequency with which he uses tercets is arresting, considering the increased difficulty of continuing rhymes by threes instead of by twos. He is fond of closing a chain of couplets with a tercet, but he is also skilled at continuing them throughout a work. "Provide, Provide" is typical. Always the conscious artist, he was not unaware of the difficulty the tercet imposes: "To the right person it will seem lucky. . . . Does anyone believe I would have committed myself to the treason-reason-season rhyme-set in my "Reluctance" if I had been blasé enough to know that these three words about exhausted the possibilities?"[4]

As Frost enlarges his quatrains into the five- and six-line stanzas that occur so often among his collected works, he manages to continue the same pattern of variety. The third poem of *A Boy's Will*, "Ghost House," is his first five-line stanza. It is formed from couplets to which is added a repetition of the *a* rhyme:

> I dwell in a lonely house I know
> That vanished many a summer ago,
> And left no trace but the cellar walls,
> And a cellar in which the daylight falls,
> And the purple-stemmed wild raspberries grow.

As his work proceeds, he locates new and more ingenious ways of forming these verses. Representative examples, followed by their rhyme schemes, are found throughout his volumes: "My November Guest," *abaab;* "Pan With Us," *aaabb;* "The Road Not Taken," *abbab;* "Bond and Free," *abbaa;* "After-flakes," *abccb;* and "Clear and Colder," *ababb*.

A similar variety is found in his use of the six-line stanza, many of which are extensions of the quatrain or combinations of quatrain and couplet. "The Demiurge's Laugh" follows a traditional alternately rhyming quatrain with a new couplet, for a pattern of *ababcc:*

> It was far in the sameness of the wood;
> I was running with joy on the Demon's trail,
> Though I knew what I hunted was no true god.
> It was just as the light was beginning to fail
> That I suddenly heard—all I needed to hear:
> It has lasted me many and many a year.

This particular design was not used again until fifteen years later, when it reappeared in *West-Running Brook* in "The Freedom of the Moon."

But other patterns, similar yet significantly altered, appeared in the interim: "Reluctance," *abcbdb;* "Innate Helium," *abbaba;* "Spring Pools," *aabcbc;* and "Acceptance," *ababaa.*

A poet already known for his work in couplets, tercets, and quatrains does not surprise if he eventually produces the sonnet. The smaller forms combine together naturally, adhering like building blocks to produce the longer poem. Frost offers polished sonnets in both the conventionally popular forms: Shakespearean ("Putting in the Seed," "On a Tree Fallen Across the Road") and Italian ("Meeting and Passing," "Range-Finding"). Yet as often as he held to the prescribed pattern, he released himself from that commitment, producing sonnets that "resemble" one or another of the conventional forms or that appear to be contrived by a conscious mixture of the two. Thus a sonnet beginning with the *abba* rhymes of the Italian form may well end in a Shakespearean couplet. Again, couplets may comprise the octave of an otherwise conventional Italian sonnet. A string of four tercets may terminate in a couplet. He experimented also with sonnets of thirteen and fifteen lines. A reading of "Why Wait for Science," "The Flood," or "The Vantage Point" is instructive. Apparently he was more inclined to freedom in the sonnet as he grew older. "Etherealizing" from *Steeple Bush* (1947) is representative of his later work:

> A theory if you hold it hard enough
> And long enough gets rated as a creed:
> Such as that flesh is something we can slough
> So that the mind can be entirely freed.
> Then when the arms and legs have atrophied,
> And brain is all that's left of mortal stuff,
> We can lie on the beach with the seaweed
> And take our daily tide baths smooth and rough.
> There once we lay as blobs of jellyfish
> At evolution's opposite extreme.
> But now as blobs of brain we'll lie and dream,
> With only one vestigial creature wish:
> Oh may the tide be soon enough at high
> To keep our abstract verse from being dry.

"Etherealizing" blends the traditional forms until they are indistinguishable from one another, producing a true hybrid. The thought divides between the eighth and ninth lines, suggesting the Italian model. The "octave" limits itself to the two rhymes allowed in the Italian form—but these rhymes are arranged in the Shakespearean manner. The sestet contains three rhymes, also traditional. But again the arrangement startles. The first two rhymes fall into the pattern of an Italian-sonnet quatrain, but the third pair of rhymes concludes the sonnet with an English ending.

For the dramatic narratives, a type at which he not only excelled but is accepted as the modern master, Frost used blank verse. It is not the blank verse of Milton nor that of Wordsworth but his own. He used it first in *North of Boston,* subtitled *This Book of People.* The subtitle is crucial. In the numerous and well-known monologues and dialogues, blank verse provides the flavor of idiomatic American speech as it is spoken. If blank verse had not existed, he would have needed to invent it for these poems; and to some extent it could be argued that he did so. For his blank verse, free and unhampered, is no more inhibited by previous models than his sonnets are impeded by established forms. Accents are transposed apparently at will; feet are added and subtracted whenever the occasion demands. Frost's blank verse reads quickly, easily, above all naturally; and at every turn it exhibits the "careful casualness" with which Paul Engle credits it.[5]

The ease with which blank verse must read to be good engenders a corresponding impression that it must be relatively easy to write. The complete absence of rhyme probably contributes to this illusion. But poets know it as one of the most difficult patterns to produce.[6] To produce *well,* one might add, for the illusion of ease and simplicity conceals art. Only two American poets have felt completely at home with blank verse: in the nineteenth century, William Cullen Bryant; in the twentieth, Robert Frost. England cannot boast a higher percentage: Shakespeare and Milton; then in the last century Wordsworth and Tennyson. Other figures are minor, surely, where blank verse is concerned.

The craft in composing blank verse is to produce regularity without the appearance of it. The metronome must be well concealed. End-stopped lines, rhymes, quatrains, and other standard paraphernalia for impressing readers with the obligatory demarcation of equal units and balanced structure are eliminated. Blank verse, like prose, must be composed in paragraphs. Yet it cannot be prose; if so, it fails.

Not everyone agrees that Frost avoids failure in his blank verse. Yvor Winters, who believes that Frost generally is overrated as a poet, takes him to task on this very point:

Frost early began his endeavor to make his style approximate as closely as possible the style of conversation, and his endeavor has added to his reputation: it has helped to make him seem "natural." But poetry is not conversation, and I see no reason why poetry should be called upon to imitate conversation. Conversation is the most careless and formless of human utterance; it is spontaneous and unrevised, and its vocabulary is commonly limited. . . . [He] is extremely inept in managing blank verse; in blank verse his theory of conversational style shows itself at its worst—the rhythms are undistinguished and are repetitious to the point of deadly monotony.[7]

But the majority of critics have thought Winters wrong. They have pointed out that, while conversation is what Frost aims for—and must aim for—in his dialogues, it is not conversation *per se* that results from his efforts, but the *appearance* of it. There is a world of difference between the two. Any close examination of the dramatic narratives reveals an artist beneath the easy, casual texture which is a chief glory of blank verse. It is a texture "apparently loose yet actually cunningly woven."[8] Behind the scenes the poet is actively editing, realigning, compressing. The result is that the reader is given, not what the average man might have spoken into a concealed tape recorder, but a heightened version, taut and direct, with fumblings, blind-alleys, and nonessentials excised.

Blank verse poems predominate in Frost's second book, and that form was one of the first he mastered. Edward Garnett recognized the difference of Frost's blank verse from historical models and appreciated that difference as a modification essential for capturing the modern temper. Garnett described the verse: "So extraordinarily close to normal everyday speech . . . that I anticipate some academic person may test its metre with a metronome, and declare that the verse is often awkward in its scansion. No doubt. But so also is the blank verse of many a master hard to scan, if the academic foot-rule be not applied with a nice comprehension of where to give and when to take."[9] Two years after the American edition of *North of Boston* appeared, Amy Lowell discussed Frost's blank verse at some length, allowing that it "does not hesitate to leave out a syllable or put one in, whenever it feels like it."[10] Admitting that the verse might disturb purists, she extracted individual lines which, isolated, illustrate the extent to which Frost violated his iambic pentameter:

> Mary sat musing on the lamp-flame at the table
> . . . . . . . . . . . . . .
> I crossed the river and swung round the mountain
> . . . . . . . . . . . . . .
> She withdrew shrinking from beneath his arm
> That rested on the banister and slid downstairs.
> . . . . . . . . . . . . . .
> Call her Nausicaa, the unafraid

Yet one might isolate lines from past masters and experience the same freedom of movement. Ever since its innovation by the Earl of Surrey, blank verse has been growing away from end-stopped lines and metronomic pace. Christopher Marlowe's mighty lines are by no means mechanically regular, and Milton's sublime cadences show many evidences of adaptation for his purposes and his era. The blank verse of *Paradise Lost* varies considerably, not only in regularity but in the number of accents per line:

> For cold, hot, moist, and dry, four champions fierce
> . . . . . . . . . . . . . .
> Save what the glimmering of these livid flames
> . . . . . . . . . . . . . .
> His mighty stature; on each hand the flames
> Driven backward slope their pointing spires, and rolled[11]

Particularly:

> Rocks, caves, lakes, fens, bogs, dens, and shades of death.[12]

Amy Lowell suggested that Frost's method of writing blank verse had advantages: it produced lines with the hardness of New England granite: "It is halting and maimed like the life it portrays, unyielding in substance and broken in effect." To others' praise of Frost's work, she added: "I agree . . . that these lapses from strict blank verse vary the lines delightfully, and give a rich and tonic effect."[13] Her judgment has been in accord with the consensus.

## A New Free Form

A good portion of Robert Frost's poetry is composed in a form very different from the couplets, quatrains, sonnets, and blank verse so far described. This form bears a strong resemblance to free verse, yet it is hardly that. Free verse, in Frost's opinion, made far too little commitment to convention. He described it once as being somewhat like playing tennis with the net down. Another time he expressed the opinion that free-verse poems read as if they had been composed from uncorrected proof sheets. The challenge of established rules was, he thought, a good share of the fun in any game.

The "free form" used by Frost is not, in any event, the free verse championed by the "new poets"; and it is a far cry from Whitman and even farther from Sandburg. With its characteristic variety in line lengths and its unpatterned rhymes, it resembles some of the work of T. S. Eliot, notably "The love Song of J. Alfred Prufrock," more than any others. Frost himself described this form in affirming that the poet "may use an assortment of line lengths for any shape of stanza, like Herrick in 'To Daffodils.' Not that he is running wild. His intention is of course a particular mood that won't be satisfied with anything less than its own fulfillment."[14] Rhyme pairs may be broken up and distributed at will, as long as they are placed not more than five lines apart, this distance evidently indicating, to Frost at least, the reader's limitation of ability to discern pattern.

His way of saying that new free form was not to be held in abject bondage to convention was to explain that it "shrinks shyly from anticipatory expression."[15] This statement—no more than another way of expressing the organic theory of Emerson and Whitman— reasserts the primacy of thought over form. The verse retains surprises for the reader, who approaches it sensing that he will find conventional pattern, but who finds instead a design which, even as it appears to establish itself in one dimension, alters itself in another. In application the form is highly successful, and possibly embodies Frost's rapprochement with the new poetic trends and the influence of the *vers libre* movement.

This statement is not to imply capitulation. Frost was too firmly set in bedrock orthodoxy for that. The "new" ways to be new—the radical experiments proceeding on all fronts—were not for him. The innate distrust of form appeared both blatant and injustifiable. The same held for the coining of new words; this was not called for, it would not serve: "We play the words as we find them. We make them do."[16] It is not, for instance, conceivable to imagine his ever writing of a grasshopper, though by itself this might be a typical subject for him, in the manner of E. E. Cummings's "r-p-o-p-h-e-s-s-a-g-r."[17] To illustrate, this is Cummings's insect, a blur of motion in mid-air:

upnowgath

PPEGORHRASS

eringint(o-

aThe):l

eA

!p:

The case of Cummings would be furthered very little by explaining to Frost that the poet feels challenged to produce things yet unattempted in prose or rhyme—to reproduce linguistically the leap of a grasshopper from stem to stem. Of course, the seventeenth-century writers tried something in the same vein: to mold their poems in the physical shape of the object portrayed, as George Herbert did in "Easter Wings" and "The Altar." But Cummings goes far enough beyond to make Herbert's pictographs seem tame indeed.

"r-p-o-p-h-e-s-s-a-g-r" literally explodes the language, then reassembles the fragments into an arresting, wholly original concept. Cummings's kinetic poetry employs typography as a medium for blending language with motion picture film—a true "talking picture." Whether Frost ever had reason to comment publicly upon this Cummings poem is not known, but, if he had, he would have branded it not only as gibberish but as completely uncalled-for gibberish. Frost, who always gave serious consideration to posterity, was unwilling to take unnecessary risks where his future reputation was at stake. In one sense this diffidence limited him; in another, his commitment to convention acted as a stabilizing keel.

Frost's style is quite opposite to Cummings's. When he sets out to describe an object or to convey the impression of a natural action, he goes at it straightforwardly. The eyes see, the mind discerns, the alchemy of art transforms, the hand transcribes. All remains within the essential bounds of proven tradition. Frost also wrote poems describing natural motion, but the difference is profound. For Cummings, the poem must be the motion even as it portrays the motion. He demands that his verse perform beyond the scope of verse—and at times he is exhilaratingly successful.

Frost is more relaxed. He is just as anxious to capture the sensation of motion as it occurs—but within his commitment to convention. This is not to say that his self-imposed bounds are an insuperable handicap; for, relieved of the burden of reshaping the language, he is free to bring all his considerable power of precise observation to bear upon the task. For instance, one may consider the accuracy in portraying the motion involved as a seed germinates and sprouts from the soil:

> How Love burns through the Putting in the Seed
> On through the watching for that early birth
> When, just as the soil tarnishes with weed,
> The sturdy seedling with arched body comes
> Shouldering its way and shedding the earth crumbs[18]

For anyone who has observed this phenomenon—and he need not be versed in country ways to have been captivated by the mystery of resurrection from a seed—the description provides a thrill of recognition: the sprouting, exactly and precisely. Nothing, not a syllable, is extraneous as the act is caught and held for its instant—and just long enough to be seen and recognized, on the spot, as it were, as it occurs. What comes to mind is the remarkable stop-photography system developed in recent years for nature films and widely used to capture the growth of organisms or the glorious burst of a rose from bud to bloom.

The free-form orthodox poem is as far as Frost is willing to go in adapting convention. Throughout his long career he employed this looser pattern in writing some of his most highly regarded verses. "Fire and Ice" and "After Apple-Picking" are two of the better known. Yet it was not something that "developed" or that he grew into at a stage of his poetic maturation. The free form appears already full-blown in his earliest work, being used in 1913 in *A Boy's Will* where it serves the poem "Storm Fear":

> When the wind works against us in the dark,
> And pelts with snow
> The lower chamber window on the east,
> And whispers with a sort of stifled bark,
> The beast,
> "Come out! Come out!"—
> It costs no inward struggle not to go,
> Ah, no!
> I count our strength,
> Two and a child,
> Those of us not asleep subdued to mark
> How the cold creeps as the fire dies at length,—
> How drifts are piled,
> Dooryard and road ungraded,
> Till even the comforting barn grows far away,
> And my heart owns a doubt
> Whether 'tis in us to arise with day
> And save ourselves unaided.

"Storm Fear" is fully representative of the freer manner. Its eighteen lines range from monometer to pentameter. The eight pairs of rhymes are scattered apparently at random, the *a* and *b* rhymes each returning for a third appearance. One notes, however, that, notwithstanding the casualness deliberately induced by this arrangement, the poem is subject at all points to regulation. In conformance with his own ruling, no rhyme but one is separated from its mate by more than five lines. He worked with a good deal of ease in the more loosely confined verse, yet not more than a tiny minority of his verses are structured in this mode. And it is symptomatic that he felt obligated to justify himself by pointing to the seventeenth century where he could lean upon the historical precedent of Herrick and others.

## The Playfully Objected Rhyme

Frost's commitment to convention appears also in his dogged adherence to rhyme at a time when the strongest currents in modern poetry ran counter to tradition. Except in the blank verse, where unrhymed lines stemmed from a noble lineage, he did not care much for poetry that abandoned this value of sound. His references to tennis with the nets down and to writing from uncorrected proof pages make this clear. On the other hand, his continued insistence upon the excellence of Henry Wadsworth Longfellow no doubt resulted to a large extent from that poet's artistic stewardship: his infinite pains not only with meter but with perfection of rhyme. Longfellow, thought Frost, "was a true poet for anyone with the ears to judge poetry by ear."[19]

The influence of Emerson again comes through. In "Merlin," Emerson, although he elsewhere extolled purely organic verse and insisted upon the primacy of thought over form, spoke of another concept of rhyme. To him the repetition of similar sounds in verse became an artistic acknowledgment of "balance-loving Nature" which "made all things in pairs." Thus hand matches hand and foot matches foot; thus earth and sky, nature and spirit, man and woman. Robert Frost, besides sharing this same love of balance, saw rhyme also as an integral part of the challenge which faced a poet. From the moment a new thought cries to be written, it raises the question of form. Every new poem sets up new hurdles to be gotten over without stumbling, if possible. Is it feasible to write a sonnet, to pile everything neatly into that single-sized basket, without falling two lines short or needing to extend fourteen lines to fifteen? Is it possible, once committed to a rhyme pattern, to continue the scheme without doing violence to thought or syntax?

In the larger sense, Frost's delight in rhyme is indicative of his alertness to the potential of language itself. Having restricted himself to the existing dictionary and, basically, to standard and idiomatic modes of expression—in short, to the *old*—he searched always for the old ways to be new. The coining of words was not called for: "We play the words as we find them."[20] But, just as he played with blank verse to stretch its conventional limits to produce the more casual line while remaining at least in the broad sense within established boundaries, he continually played with language. Its potentialities within convention fascinated him. He was interested in hitting upon unforeseen possibilities for new and arresting uses of everyday words. His playfulness is evident in some of the published verse, particularly in the satiric poems; but it can be seen best in his letters and in certain unpublished verses which circulated only among his intimate circle. His obvious delight in the lowly pun is a case in point.

*The Poetry* only hints at the games he played with puns, but in his letters he employed them more freely. "The frosts come and the Frosts go," he wrote one autumn as he thought ahead to the annual winter migration from the New England cold.[21] Of his foreword to Edwin Arlington Robinson's *King Jasper,* he confided, "There is some high, some low, and some Jack (Frost) in it."[22] To Louis Untermeyer he wrote, "It would be descent of you to acknowledge the resent scent I cent you."[23] In private he toyed with the language, but he withstood the temptation to include the results in his public pronouncements, perhaps in deference to his image as a "serious" poet.

Frost's punning appears regularly in private remarks directed at his rivals and the rising generation of poets, MacLeish, Jeffers, and company—"my rising contemptuaries" as he slightingly referred to them. While living in Ann Arbor, Frost was unwillingly connected with the homespun and extremely popular "Edgar Guessed." By virtue of present residence, both writers were considered "Michigan poets"—a prime example of the perils of departmentalization. The author of *Spoon River* becomes "our edgarly masters," and Conrad Aiken, in acknowledgment of his poetic laments, is transmuted into "Comrad Aching." Frost's own signature on letters is likely to turn up as "Robbered Frossed."[24]

Only traces of this playfulness can be found in the published work. There it makes itself felt in feminine rhymes, some of which upon examination turn out to be repetitions: "A Loose Mountain" admits the pairs *apparatus–at us* and *orbit–absorb it*. Something of the same note is struck by the *love–evil of* rhymes in "A Considerable Speck" and by *divinity–femininity* in Two Leading Lights." But more typical are standard feminine rhymes like the *blow it–know it* combination of "The Cocoon." These become increasingly numerous in later poems; "Kitty Hawk," for instance, is peppered with them. And he knows precisely when and how to use these pairs to contribute to the reader's enjoyment of a verse. Consider the part played by the rhymes in this couplet from *In the Clearing:*

> It takes all sorts of in and outdoor schooling
> To get adapted to my kind of fooling.

"All the fun's in how you say a thing," wrote Frost in *North of Boston:* the couplet quoted above gives assurance that he followed his aphorism throughout his career. One presumes he was thinking of it when he allowed *flint* to pair off with *in't* in "A Missive Missile," or when in *Steeple Bush* he began "An Importer" with this couplet: "Mrs. Someone's been to Asia/What she brought back 'would amaze ye."

He knew also that, besides rhyming together as many syllables as possible, a poet could inject "fun" into a verse by suddenly extending a rhyme-series well beyond the single pair ordinarily anticipated. To create the unexpected from which so much humor springs, he might continue rhyming for three, four, or—as in the case of "The Hardship of Accounting"—for even five lines:

> Never ask of money spent
> Where the spender thinks it went.
> Nobody was every meant
> To remember or invent
> What he did with every cent.

When he sets out consciously to be amusing, he brings into calculated play all of his knowledge of rhyming effects. A poem, for instance, like "Departmental," one of the best known of its type, is a genuine *tour de force* of his craftsmanship. Taking as his subject a slightly forced view of human society suggested by analogy with the highly regimented existence of a colony of ants, the poet is in command at all times; he makes certain that it is the *way* the poem conveys its idea that wins the field. Frost once defined style as the way a poet "carries himself toward his ideas and deeds. . . . It is the mind skating circles round itself as it moves forward."[25] The mind skating circles round itself: what better way to describe the style, the flourish, of "Departmental."

The poem explodes its rhymes in a brilliant display of fireworks whose sparkle creates half or more of the impact. Frost was proud of "Departmental" and always called attention to the rhyming pairs. Few readers fail to register the anticipated tremor of astonishment at the unexpected alignment of *people* with *sepal, petal* with *nettle;* but there is no time for adjustment. In rapid succession these are conjoined with the cleverness of feminine pairs like *Formic–McCormic, mortician–position, middle–atwiddle,* culminating in the perfectly attuned understatement of the concluding couplet:

> It couldn't be called ungentle.
> But how thoroughly departmental.

Accompanying the feminine rhyme pairs as an additional flourish is the extended series through which the linguistic figure-skater flashes his skill:

> Our selfless forager Jerry.
> Will the special Janizary
> Whose office it is to bury
> The dead of the commissary
> And heaving him high in air,
> Carries him out of there.
> No one stands round to stare.
> It is nobody else's affair.

Among the pyrotechnics of "Departmental," one should not lose sight of the contribution made by the rapid trimeter: that dancing meter which piles the rhymes atop one another almost beyond the reader's ability to assimilate. No sooner has one pair of rhymes hit its mark than another comes flying on its way. "Departmental" represents a near-perfect combination of thought with art. It does consummately what the craftsman intends it to do—and with economy and precision. In its genre, it is unsurpassed in the verse of this century.

## "Perfect-Paired as Eagle's Wings"

Frost agrees wholeheartedly with Emerson's observation that rhymes should be as perfectly matched as a pair of eagle's wings.[26] The ability to conjure up twin sounds that carry the idea forward without making themselves felt was one of the principal marks by which he differentiated between genius and talent. Anyone who has tried his amateur hand at verse or who has attempted to instruct a class of neophytes in the composition of rhymed poems has some notion of what Frost is driving at. The results can be ludicrous: tortured phrases, hopelessly inverted order, sentences pinched and squeezed, contractions and archaisms, wild graspings-at-straws. One has little difficulty discerning the tortuous mental gymnastics of a writer who has at last by the sweat of his brow located two words that rhyme and who must now torment his lines so that, whether they be logical or illogical, stilted or ungrammatical, they lead toward these hard-found nuggets. After experiencing the incompetency of a weak craftsman, one is tempted to go all the way with Frost's insistence upon the attention to be paid to rhyme-pairs.

Yet this very insistence upon perfect rhymes identifies Frost as being out of tune with modern trends. His criticism, for instance, of Emily Dickinson's near-rhymes is unconvincing to anyone exposed to the horrors created of her poems by well-meaning editors who "improved" them for publication. He felt that once Miss Dickinson had committed herself to convention, she should have remained true to the rules. Otherwise, she would have done well to operate within a different framework. He cannot bring himself to condone her practice of giving rein to her ideas and images and of letting rhyme fend for itself.

Frost does not belabor what he considers to be Emily Dickinson's chief weakness as a poet, perhaps because he does not absolutely believe himself to be right. But he did believe that she had compromised her art. Compromising with the rules was an act he had difficulty accepting. He spoke of it often in regard to rhyming, but generally the examples he cited were not from Miss Dickinson. It is crucial to know the difference between a well-rhymed verse and a poorly rhymed verse, to be able to distinguish a good quatrain from a bad one. A bad quatrain, says Frost, is essentially an epigram of perhaps two lines which the poet is determined to expand, so he concocts another pair of lines to precede it or to splice with it. In a good quatrain, it is difficult to determine "which member of the rhyme-twins the poet thought of first."[27]

One example that he was fond of using to illustrate the evil of compromise in rhyming came, surprisingly, from Emerson's "Ode Sung in the Town Hall, Concord, July 4, 1857":

> For He that worketh high and wise,
>     Nor pauses in his plan
> Will take the sun out of the skies
>     Ere freedom out of man.

To Frost, the first two lines are sheer padding. Their "scanty scaffolding" leads up to the meat of the verse in the last lines. Emerson, he reasoned, had happened on the poem by looking at the sky and noticing how much a part of it the sun was. Then he thought of how much a part of himself freedom was. Emerson set out to compare the two, and that took the form of his epigram in the last two lines: "He had to have two lines to rhyme with them. He picked out 'wise' and 'plan,' and they do not come anywhere near the top of the others. They are weak. They do not form a perfect working part of the rest of the lines. Remember that we go on line by line in poetry, building up from the idea, trying to make a rhyming that will not seem the tiniest bit strained."[28]

By way of contrast, Frost was fond of offering an example from Walter Savage Landor's "On His Seventy-Fifth Birthday":

> I strove with none; for none was worth my strife.
> Nature I loved and, next to Nature, Art;
> I warmed both hands before the fire of life;
> It sinks, and I am ready to depart.

Landor's quatrain, thought Frost, was "well-nigh perfect."[29] Nothing was extraneous, nothing but what served to carry forward the thought, nothing—including the rhymes—but it was functionally defensible. "Suspect those rhymes as hard as you can. Try your darndest."[30] The second line, he felt, might possibly have been improved, but, over-all, the rhyming was good.

## "My Heavy Duty Poem"

"Stopping by Woods on a Snowy Evening" is widely regarded, metrically, as Frost's most perfect poem. He himself always offered it as the prime example of his commitment to convention, describing it as "my heavy duty poem to be examined for the rime pairs."[31] Frost said that he wrote it after an extended night of work on his long poem "New Hampshire." Whether it was inspired by "auto-intoxication" and sheer tiredness, as its author suggested, or by some more ethereal influence, it has come to be the single poem with which most readers identify Frost.

Whose woods these are I think I know.
His house is in the village though;
He will not see me stopping here
To watch his woods fill up with snow.

My little horse must think it queer
To stop without a farmhouse near
Between the woods and frozen lake
The darkest evening of the year.

He gives his harness bells a shake
To ask if there is some mistake.
The only other sound's the sweep
Of easy wind and downy flake.

The woods are lovely, dark and deep,
But I have promises to keep,
And miles to go before I sleep,
And miles to go before I sleep.

It will be instructive to observe his own account of the creative process which ended in this lyric.[32] No better demonstration could be desired for explaining what Frost may have meant when he spoke of a poet committing himself to convention—to form.

One begins with the principle that poetry is organic, that thought takes precedence over form. This principle requires one to fall into accord with Emerson: "The thought and the form are equal in the order of time, but in the order of genesis the thought is prior to the form."[33] One begins then with the concept; this is genesis. Any poem has three parts, Frost pointed out: the point or idea; the details which develop it; then the technique with which it is crafted.

The idea must be well in mind initially, as well as the details that will give it flesh. This problem taken care of, the very first line of the poem—particularly if it is being written in conventional form—constitutes a first step into deeper commitments. What is the meter? What length is the line? Supposing that rhyme is to be used, the last word in the first line is vital. Frost, in his composition, came up with a first line of iambic swing containing four beats: *Whose woods these are I think I know.* So far so good. Now the second line: *His house is in the village though.*

At this point, the poem can go any one of several ways. It can continue in iambic tetrameter couplets. It can verge into tercets. It can build toward a quatrain or toward one of the five- or six-line stanzas. Finally, it can edge over, despite its beginning couplet, into another of the free-form poems like "Storm Fear." The third line of the poem, however, rules out at least the tercet. But the meter is retained. The rhyme *here* is so far uncommitted. With the choice of his fourth line, the poet has pledged himself to the quatrain and to the rhyming pattern *aaba*.

Now one arrives at the most critical step in the creative process. Frost often spoke of the indulgent smiles he received "for the recklessness of the unnecessary commitment I made when I came to the first line in the second stanza."[34] By picking up—casually, one would like to think—the odd-rhyme *here* and establishing it as the major rhyme of the new quatrain, Frost bound himself to a most difficult pattern. It would require all his powers to carry this intricately interlocked form to conclusion. If he succeeded, it could assure his reputation as a craftsman. If he botched the job or weaseled out of it halfway through, he could shatter the poem. The delicacy of maneuver at this particular point resembles that of a diamond cutter who must consciously make his decisions and then follow through with sure, deliberate strokes.

By the time the poet reached the third stanza, he had a good idea of how long the poem would be; for the idea was developing swiftly, and the details dramatized it adequately. Now, how was he to conclude? The chosen pattern has set up an expectation that the third lines of every stanza will lead into another verse. It cannot simply halt without doing violence to the maxim that all things possess a natural beginning and ending. If that third-line rhyme is left dangling, it would destroy the art thus far apparent. The poem has become self-perpetuating, like terza rima. Fittingly, the device used for closing off terza rima suggests a solution for this new form also.

"Every step is a further commitment." In the fourth stanza the poet masterfully abandons the odd-rhyme pattern of his third lines, rhyming that line instead with the first two in the quatrain. The last line, a simple but profound underscoring of the third, concludes the poem in the most natural way possible.

Surely this poem shows Frost at his best: he composes strong sentences that flow along with the meter, not straining it or themselves; he uses rhymes so natural and inevitable that one cannot decipher whether they arrived first or last in order of thought. "Stopping by Woods" should be read as an illustration of Frost's description in "In A Poem":

> The sentencing goes blithely on its way
> And takes the playfully objected rhyme
> As surely as it keeps the stroke and time
> In having its undeviable say.

"Stopping by Woods" does supremely well what Frost says a good poem will do: it rides on its own melting, like a piece of ice on a hot stove.[35] The townsman who stood outdoors on a spring day chopping his own wood was watched by two tramps from the logging camps who "judged me by their appropriate tool." To show how he "handled an ax," Frost liked to point to "Stopping by Woods" as the supreme example of his craftsmanship and let it do his boasting for him.

# Chapter Four

# The Aim Was Song: Frost's Theories

Robert Frost has offered a good many definitions of poetry. Most are fragmentary, and some of the most colorful might be termed impressionistic. They illuminate the subject like sputtering flares, brilliant and short-lived; but they provide no steady light to see by. When these bolts of ecstatic lightning have spent themselves, one is left again in the dark of wondering:

A poem is the emotion of having a thought while the reader waits a little anxiously for the success of dawn.[1]

. . . . . . . . . . .

Every poem is an epitome of the great predicament; a figure of the will braving alien entanglements.[2]

. . . . . . . . . .

A poem is a momentary stay against confusion.[3]

. . . . . . . . . . . . . .

My definition of literature would be just this, words that have become deeds.[4]

These definitions leave little to build on, stimulating as they are. Search as one will, nowhere does one find Frost, despite his flashes of intuitive knowledge, communicating a patterned theory of his art, not even a brief one. His various essays in criticism provide surprisingly little, even though what he has to say in them is aimed at the heart of the matter, spoken with a voice of authority, and delivered with lucidity of phrase.

One is left to patch a theory together from the scraps the past has thrown to us. "Thrown" may be too facile a term; one understands that his formalized pronouncements on poetry were almost literally dragged from him after the most prolonged coaxing by interested editors or persuasive compatriots. Even then, Frost acceded reluctantly for he had no genuine relish for the role of critic. To be a poet seemed plenty in itself; he desired to leave the theorizing for those who relished it, or for those unequipped to compose the songs themselves. He believed, for instance, that Louis Untermeyer had done himself ill by attempting simultaneously to sit upon the twin stools of creation and criticism. He wrote his friend, who had encountered great success in 1919 with his critical study, *The New Era in Poetry:* "I was afraid that book would be too good to be good for you. And it is. It is dangerous in two ways. It calls for another book like it to pile on top of it about all the poets here and in England taken together. . . . before you are free to get back to writing your own poetry again. . . . it will make you your own worst rival."[5]

Frost saw little compatibility between the roles of critic and poet, no satisfactory compromise. Energy expended to achieve excellence in one direction was provided only at the sacrifice of the other. A poet is an artist; a critic, a scholar. A tremendous gulf separates the two: the artist necessarily is intuitive; the scholar, logical. The scholar, having sliced out his self-assigned task, sticks to it doggedly, pursues it to completion. The artist recognizes no assignment, nor does he admit to any obligation to stick to what he has been inspired to take up. On the contrary, an artist invites whatever will stick to him "like burrs" do when he tramps across a wild field.[6] Obviously, this method is not one by which coherent theories of poetry are written.

Nevertheless, what Frost believed about the poetic process is not impossible to come by, even if it does require the piecing together of a jigsaw puzzle.

## Poems and Pears

To begin with, poetry is organic. Upon this principle Frost insisted, maintaining it both in his essays and in his finished verse. In asserting the freedom of poetry from prior discipline, he reaffirmed Emerson's doctrine that it is not meter but a meter-making argument that produces poetry. "The freshness of a poem," Frost insisted, "belongs absolutely to its not having been thought out and then set to verse."[7] To do so would involve the poet in a fatal compromise, one similar to composing music to suit a pre-selected set of lyrics. It would result in art only by happenstance and against great odds.

Walt Whitman, who also was dedicated to Emersonian doctrine—although he and Frost are in many ways the most different of artists—gave American literature the most vivid description of organic verse when he compared poems directly with flowers and fruits: "The rhyme and uniformity of perfect poems show the free growth of metrical laws and bud from them as unerringly and loosely as lilacs or roses on a bush, and take shapes as compact as the shapes of chestnuts and oranges and melons and pears, and shed the perfume impalpable to form."[8] It goes without saying that one does not command a lilac how to bloom or instruct an orange about what shape it will take. One allows organic things their intrinsic freedom and then waits for the pleasure of fruition. With a poem, one "waits a little anxiously for the success of dawn."

Form, then, as a consideration falls secondary to inspiration. Organic structure is easily discerned in Whitman's products, where the forms are indeed new. Whitman's poems, which startled when they first appeared, do not follow established patterns in their composition, nor do the beginnings create rigid molds which might bind their own nether parts. Frost, using for the most part established forms, is not so readily comprehended to be a truly organic poet. Yet he insists that this is the case.

Even though he keeps at his disposal a variety of conventional forms which poems in the long poetic tradition have assumed, Frost cannot apprehend for certain toward which of these patterns—or hybrid of them—the verse at hand may be inclining. The organic writer shares with his reader some of the mystery and suspense of never being exactly certain how things will come out. He may have a good idea he is on his way to a sonnet, for instance; but he cannot be positive about it: "He doesn't even have the say of how long his piece will be. Any worry is as to whether he will outlast or last out even the fourteen lines—have to cramp or stretch to come out even—have enough bread for the butter or butter for the bread. As a matter of fact, he gets through in twelve lines and doesn't quite know what to do with the last two."[9] At the heart of poetry, says Frost, stands its identity as "a wild tune."[10] How an individual poem can retain its pure organic function and unique wildness, its meandering and free tune, and at the same instant be committed to "such a straightness as meter" is to be recognized as the first mystery of poetic art.

The logic of this wildness in poetry cannot be projected or fully perceived in advance. It can be discerned only in retrospect, after the poem has grown to ripeness and assumed the shape its own necessity demanded from the start. Only then can the reader understand the poet's role as co-conspirator with nature. Only then can the poet comprehend what he has wrought. The poetic art, then, takes on shades of necromancy: it is a sleight-of-hand performance in which even the prestidigitator is not quite fully aware of the process through which he works his wonders.

In advance of writing, the "only discipline" Frost admits being held to is an "inner mood," nebulous and indefinable, which leads him into the poem and may cause him to commit a series of false starts before the shape that the poem itself demands is understood and submitted to by the writer. "He must be entranced to the exact premonition" appears to be Frost's way of explaining that poets are not essentially rational but intuitive. If he is unwilling to go so far as to subscribe to the "trance" theory, yet he lingers just outside the door, sorely tempted, and not more than a step or two removed from it. The generative impulse often made itself known to Frost by a sudden exaltation, the "surprise of remembering something I didn't know I knew. I am in a place, in a situation, as if I had materialized from cloud or risen out of the ground. There is a glad recognition of the long lost and the rest follows."[11]

His description of the intuitive poetic process is brushed with mysticism. But there is no mysticism—and no contradiction—in his description of what a poem becomes once it has assumed its chosen shape. One cannot very well delineate the mystery through which a pear at one moment in time is a silken snowflake of blossom and at another dangles globed and yellowflecked from its stem. But when the pear is picked and set on the shelf for ripening, it can be described easily enough and with pinpoint accuracy.

Frost provided a generic description suitable for defining that which would call itself poetry. The essential poem arrives in a homogeneous trinity of three parts, all of them crucial to the fulfillment of a verse. Frost refers to these three elements as the *point,* or *idea;* the *details;* and the *technique.* Technique has already been examined, but one should consider the others.

## "Look at the Fuzz on Plants"

Although poems seen from one important viewpoint are experiments in sound, the object being "to make all poems sound as different as possible from each other,"[12] Frost is explicit in emphasizing the necessity for significant subject matter. Experiments in sound alone soon pall; they lack staying power; and Frost, one eye forever cocked cannily in the direction of his career, strove to "lodge a few pebbles" in permanence. Edgar Allan Poe's "The Bells" illustrates quite satisfactorily the versatility and range of language, yet the poem is not generally included among Poe's memorable handful because ultimately it must be recognized as mere *tour de force* of the onomatopoeic: it possesses beauty without substance and does not tease the mind. "The Bells" remains a novelty, a marvelous toy. The durability of any linguistic finger-exercise, no matter how flamboyant, is limited severely, for "all that can be done with words is soon told."[13]

However, that unique sound of a poem—that "wild tune," as Frost liked to call it—derives from more than language alone. It stems from something beyond meter and rhyme, and it demands more than linguistic expertise. The meaning of a poem provides limitless "possibilities for tune."[14] A poem must contain the ballast of idea— theme—to tie the poem down, to anchor it securely to the world and to hold it back from soaring into orbits of blank space, propelled there by its own linguistic fuel. It is a verse, not a tree, that is the thing next most diffuse to a cloud.

The balance for imagination is sagacity. When Frost in his well-known essay "The Figure a Poem Makes" refers to poetry as beginning in delight and ending in wisdom, he has in mind this balance of sensibility and substance, of emotion and thought, of airiness and weight. A poem must be not merely a trick, but a performance; and to Frost the difference is considerable. "Enthusiasm passed through an idea" is what poetry must become if it aspires to the heights.[15] The poet must never falter in his knowledge that his audience demands of him both virtuosity and communication.

Lucidity does count. Somehow, somewhere, a point of meaningful contact with the reader has to be registered. This particular obligation

Frost met with supreme skill. That he communicates, however, is only partially responsible for his unparalleled success with the general reader. He cared for texture, that supreme idol of many modern poets, but never was it to be achieved at the expense of thought. Using a homely image that might have found an appropriate place in his verse, he compared the contemporary worship of texture to weaving a piece of fabric which, while delightful and decorative in itself and suitable perhaps to serve as "a decoration for the wall of a studio,"[16] would never be made into a useful article. He preferred a good solid bolt of goods, one not lacking texture, surely, or decorative qualities, but fabric which might easily serve a variety of purposes. The most exquisitely poised balance of beauty and utility, this was his aim—a song with sense.

The details that Frost assigned an integral place in verse were to result from masterful observation. He joined with the Imagists in their insistence upon particularized diction, language which would flesh out the bones of thought solidly. He was with Emerson in his rejection of "poetic" diction in favor of language that reflects the life around us with precision. Emerson was a strong supporter of intuitive speech, regardless of its conformance with arbitrary rules, the speech of life before it is fossilized in books:

The language of the street is always strong. What can describe the folly and emptiness of scolding like the word *jawing?* I feel too the force of the double negative, though clean contrary to our grammar rules. And I confess to some pleasure from the stinging rhetoric of a rattling oath in the mouth of truckmen and teamsters. How laconic and brisk it is by the side of a page of the *North American Review*. Cut these words and they would bleed; they are vascular and alive; they walk and run.[17]

Wherever possible, Frost carried this advice into his own verse, never apologizing for showing preference for the real, the genuine, and the colloquial over the more turgid literary phrase. As he matured as a poet, this trait became stronger and more typical of his performance. The speakers in his poems were increasingly allowed to use their voices, never for the delivery of froth, but of "a shower of bullets"[18] that hit their marks with rare and immediately felt accuracy.

Acute observation was the means: painstaking, alert, continuous observation of one's immediate environment. During his later years

Frost became generous in offering advice to young aspirants. The hints he extended were the same as those given earlier by Henry James. Essentially, one should strive always to be a person on whom nothing is lost. "Look at the fuzz on plants," he urged, recalling how as a young man he had bent down to examine the Calypso orchid and found it to be primarily seedpod with a tiny tuft of flowers puffing from the pod-end.[19]

One need feel no compulsion to be inventive, to discover a new continent. The old would do as well, so long as one possessed skill in the art of renewal. Taking "the things people have known all their lives," one could renew them simply by calling attention to them in one's own unique and identifiable style: "Be observant. In the work on the farm, notice the people, the way they cut up meat, harness horses, and the way they use words. Put them down. Don't worry about understanding people too much. If you work with them, observe and talk with them, you will come to know enough for your poetry. Always use what you know about. . . . Observe everything—that is the point I am stressing."[20] From observation will emerge the details that everyone sees but that only a poet *notices.* By calling attention, one encourages the others to notice. Through its details a poem gains the sense of life and reality it must have.

Critics have been unanimous in praising Frost's use of infinitely observed detail in the rendition of true portraits. It is emphasized that *true* does not necessarily imply scientific exactness. Among the first merits of Frost's poetry to which a general reader will be likely to respond is this ability to delineate in strong, definite, precise strokes the immediate environment. Few possess the gift, whether innate or acquired, to become, in Emerson's phrase, "a transparent eyeball." But nearly any page of *The Poetry of Robert Frost* illustrates that Frost's skill in observation accounts for a large measure of his wide appeal:

> Often you must have seen them
> Loaded with ice a sunny winter morning
> After a rain. They click upon themselves
> As the breeze rises, and turn many-colored
> As the stir cracks and crazes their enamel.
> Soon the sun's warmth makes them shed crystal shells
> Shattering and avalanching on the snow-crust—[21]
> . . . . . . . . . . . . . . . . . . .

And life is too much like a pathless wood
Where your face burns and tickles with the cobwebs
Broken across it, and one eye is weeping
From a twig's having lashed across it open.[22]
. . . . . . . . . . . . . . .
The warping boards pull out their own old nails
With none to tread and put them in their place.[23]
. . . . . . . . . . . . . . .
Yet oh! the tempting flatness of a book,
To send it sailing out the attic window
Till it caught wind, and, opening out its covers,
Tried to improve on sailing like a tile
By flying like a bird (silent in flight,
But all the burden of its body song),
Only to tumble like a stricken bird,
And lie in stones and bushes unretrieved.[24]
. . . . . . . . . . . . . . .
He dumped himself like a bag of bones,
He sighed himself a couple of groans,
And head to tail then firmly curled
Like swearing off on the traffic world.[25]
. . . . . . . . . . . . . . .
The mountain held the town as in a shadow.
I saw so much before I slept there once:
I noticed that I missed stars in the west,
Where its black body cut into the sky.[26]

## "The Tones of Everyday Talk"

In Robert Frost's poems, close ocular investigation is joined by a
superior ear for language. Ear, not eye, for Frost aims at the spoken
word, not the printed page. Life is his dictionary, and it provides him
with the elemental American mode of expression. From the beginning
of his career, but particularly after the appearance of *North of Boston,* he
was acclaimed for his uncanny knack of catching the authentic native
accents. Credit goes in part to his development of the loose iambic. The
more strictly patterned cadence might be considered more artistic, but
it would be sadly handicapped in direct proportion to its removal from
the actual conversational mode, which abhors the metronome.

On the other hand, one cannot merely unload the tape recorder onto an innocent page and call it verse; and here is the dilemma. Frost's verse does convey a most convincing illusion of real conversation. His speakers deliver a sense of spontaneous dialogue that tallies with the reader's observation of speech under normal and relaxed conditions. But this fluency *is* an illusion, as other writers have taken pains to emphasize. It stands far removed from any kind of precise reproduction of what actually was or might have been said.

Frost, universally regarded as synonymous with New England, is even praised for bringing into literature the New England tongue. But his verse in fact is not regional at all. Amy Lowell knew her New England dialect and felt its absence when Frost brought out his first books. His people, so true to the locality in most respects, do not speak with any degree of local authenticity—and this lack irked the Boston poetess. In his characters and situations she found little to cavil at, but where was the peculiar Yankee turn of speech? The down-east region was well known for its strong dialect, not a difficult one to catch, as it had, for example, been caught by her own cousin, James Russell Lowell: "We're curus critters: Now ain't jes' the minute/That ever fits us easy while we're in it."[27] and by Alice Brown:

I tried to do all I could for them that was in need. But I never lived my life with 'em, even when I was tendin' upon 'em and gittin' kind of achey trottin' up an' down stairs.[28]

But this is not the speech of Frost's poems at all. Missing are both the peculiar pronunciation unique to New England and the specialized vocabulary of that area. "Speech like that is of the essence of New England," said Amy Lowell, "and yet Mr. Frost has ignored it absolutely. He feels the people, but he has no ear for their peculiar tongue."[29]

As a possible explanation, Miss Lowell proposed that Frost was striving to provide his work with the greatest possible universality and permanence. He was aware, she reasoned, that the use of exact dialect undeniably narrowed a writer's immediate appeal. Dialect also, by rendering a work subject to fashions in literature, was likely to shorten perhaps by decades one's eventual literary life. She recognized that the

Yankee dialect required very noticeable deviations from normal spelling, yet she cited Robert Burns as an example of a writer whose work not only survived with dialect but apparently derived a good share of its continuing charm from the very fact of its being in dialect. Frost's decision not to employ dialect in his monologues and dramatic narratives seemed a serious error; it flawed the authenticity of his verses. But few other critics appeared to care—indeed, even to notice. Amy Lowell's criticism, well founded as it may be, did nothing whatsoever to hamper the steady growth of the pervasive myth that insists that Frost writes poems not only of the New England scene but in the New England speech. Frost himself did nothing to dispel this myth, but then why should he trouble himself to contradict a notion which was pleasing both to himself and to those who believed it?

What readers hear and respond to in the poems are the recognizable rhythms of standard American colloquial speech. His own speech patterns were firmly established long before he returned to New England, and they were shaped on the West Coast. He would likely view the Yankee dialect of the Northeast as an oddity. Whether or not he realized that precise use of localized speech would restrict his audience, a great measure of his success is due entirely to the fact that readers all over the nation intuitively recognized that the poet and his common folk were speaking the language of the land. That this everyday speech placed in the mouths of his rural speakers could also, in defiance of tradition, be poetic was no surprise to Frost, for he was convinced that "The common speech is always giving off . . . the special vocabulary of poetry. The same thing happens with the tones of everyday talk."[30] It is now axiomatic that the nation's joyful reception of his poetry owed a good deal to his readers' elation at discovering in verse their own idiom, syntax, and colloquial expressions.

The myth of dialect has been systematically demolished in John F. Lynen's close study of Frost's poetic diction.[31] In his thorough analysis Lynen locates only "five or six localisms" in the whole of Frost's output. He cites the use of "ile" for "oil" in the last stanza of "Brown's Descent" and the rhyming of "Ira" with "inquiry" in "Of the Stones of the Place." One must hunt diligently to find even these examples. It may be that one is so attuned to meeting in print only the more formal written language that one really fails to hear his own spoken words, with their more casual air, even when they are presented to him. One tends instead to regard them as a picturesque dialect peculiar to some distant locality.

The speech Frost concocts is *trompe l'oeil*. It tricks, deceiving its hearer exactly as the painstakingly rehearsed action on a stage deceives an audience with an artful illusion of natural gesture. Who, in real life, ever saw a person cross a room, turn on his heels, or sit in a chair precisely the way an actor must in order to be convincing? The artificial, behind the footlights, becomes the genuine. So it is with the honest duplicity of Frost's "talk." It is founded upon his loose iambic swing and proceeds in an apparently wandering train of thought, a zigzag pattern which at the same time takes a remarkably straight path toward its goal. A generous use of idioms and contractions characterizes this speech. Interspersed with its loosely connected phrases, the mark of a relaxed conversationalist, are enough "you know's" and "anyway's" and "sort of's" to provide the flavor of the real thing. The result is a well-crafted counterfeit of spontaneous, impromptu American chatter:

> "He'll know what he would do if he were we,
> And all at once. He'll plan for us and plan
> To help us, but he'll take it out in planning.
> Well, you can set the table with the loaf.
> Let's see you find your loaf. I'll light the fire."[32]
> . . . . . . . . . . . . . . . .
> Call it a day, I wish they might have said
> To please the boy by giving him the half hour
> That a boy counts so much when saved from work.
> His sister stood beside them in her apron
> To tell them "Supper." At the word, the saw,
> As it to prove saws knew what supper meant,
> Leaped out at the boy's hand, or seemed to leap—
> He must have given the hand. However it was,
> Neither refused the meeting.[33]
> . . . . . . . . . . . . . . . .
> "You know Orion always comes up sideways.
> Throwing a leg up over our fence of mountains,
> And rising on his hands, he looks in on me
> Busy outdoors by lantern-light with something
> I should have done by daylight. . . ."[34]
> . . . . . . . . . . . . . . . .

The only fault my husband found with me—
I went to sleep before I went to bed,
Especially in winter when the bed
Might just as well be ice and the clothes snow.
The night the bones came up the cellar-stairs
Toffile had gone to bed alone and left me,
But left an open door to cool the room off
So as to sort of turn me out of it.[35]
. . . . . . . . . . . . . . . . . .
My father's brother, he went mad quite young,
Some thought he had been bitten by a dog,
Because his violence took on the form
Of carrying his pillow in his teeth;
But it's more likely he was crossed in love,
Or so the story goes. It was some girl.
Anyway all he talked about was love.[36]

It is Lynen's thesis that Frost's language, when coupled with his infinitely observed and deeply understood regional characters, becomes an integral part of the dramatic situation in a poem. The resultant fusion of speaker and language produces the authentic "local" flavor for which the poems are praised. This may well be so, for Frost himself declared that a point existed at which all the discrete elements of a projected work came together—met in mid-air, as it were—and joined to make the poem. In particular the theme must meet and fuse harmoniously with the details—one of which would surely be speech.

## How Poems Arise

The ineffable drive of one poetic element toward the other as a successful poem takes shape is not a sudden thing. A long time may be required for the creative process to ferment. When an idea is grasped, the poet must draw a workable parallel before he can express himself in language. Frost liked to cite the parallel of Walt Whitman's "A Noiseless Patient Spider" to illustrate his point. Whitman observed the spider casting his filament again and again, failing each time until at last the line caught on a solid base and anchored there. Then the spider sped across his bridge and went about his business. Likewise, the mind of man throws out its own lines, its ideas, until at last the intellect fastens, says Frost, on the idea of death. Then, it scurries into the darkness, away forever.[37]

Frost formalized his notions of the creative process no more than he did his poetic theory, but he did leave instructive hints as to how his own poems took shape. Any poem is the result of "enthusiasm passed through an idea," and this process will not be hurried.[38] Unborn poems gestated for long periods in his mind, teasing the imagination. His painstaking observations might seem to lead nowhere apparently, until at last a day came when idea and detail entwined naturally and became deed. He records "the surprise of remembering something I didn't know I knew,"[39] the sudden materialization—as if from cloud—of the complete poem. The mind recognizes gladly "the long lost." Work then proceeds swiftly as, the mental dam now broken, one step leads easily to another. Everything comes piling out, ready for use. "The impressions most useful to my purpose seem always those I was unaware of," Frost remembered, "and so made no note of at the time when taken, and the conclusion is come to that like giants we are always hurling experience ahead of us to pave the future with against the day when we may want to strike a line of purpose across it for somewhere."[40]

Poems then are created out of the storehouse of observations meticulously gathered—apparently without concern for immediate utility—in the mind. False leads abound, as successive lines thrown out by the mental process fail. But seemingly all things drive toward an ultimate ripeness, one unknown perhaps even to the poet. Failures are plowed back into the loam, "building soil" for future growth. "Many a quatrain," he pointed out, "is salvaged from a sonnet that went agley." Nothing is wholly lost; everything finally is used, if only to serve as compost for richer verses to come. A couplet, a line, a detail from one abortive start may yet bear fruit at another time.

Only when the time is ripe do all circumstances combine under favorable auguries for the creative artist. Then idea and detail at last experience their happy collision, triggering the chain reaction. "As I lie awake or walk myself every week or so a little poem will make in my head as sudden as an exclamation."[41] But the poems come from something, not from nothing—from somewhere, not from nowhere. Only at this point, with the concept fully shaped, can the craftsman take over and polish the artifact to a higher sheen by consciously selecting the very best word, one that will perform perfectly the work of ten; and by squeezing, compressing, and trimming all excess, he attains an ultimate economy. The resulting poem, if it is good and true and not malformed, recalls to Frost the napkin tucked into the napkin ring of bygone years. "The small end is stuck through. You pull it through—and it gets smaller and compressed. All the way through, it suddenly bursts out, opens up."[42] This is the alchemy of poetry.

## Direct Poems

As a poem emerges from its "ring" it may—or it may not—reveal itself wholly to its reader. Some poems unfold at once, with scarcely a crease left, ready for immediate use. For instance, a good number of Frost's lyrics are based upon the least complex of notions: a comparison, perhaps, or a contrast or simple parallel. "What Fifty Said" is representative of this type:

> When I was young my teachers were the old.
> I gave up fire for form till I was cold.
> I suffered like a metal being cast.
> I went to school to age to learn the past.
>
> Now I am old my teachers are the young.
> What can't be molded must be cracked and sprung.
> I strain at lessons fit to start a suture.
> I go to school to youth to learn the future.

Lying as it does directly upon the surface of the poem, the point is easily grasped: the interesting reversals, tinged with the irony of the inevitable, that occur as one ages. Education, Frost is saying, must continue in an unbroken line if an individual is to avoid rigidity. No school child would have much difficulty providing a clear, comprehensive paraphrase.

The simplicity of "What Fifty Said" characterizes also most of the minor poems that are constructed as definitions. For instance, "Devotion" defines its virtue by means of a breathtakingly appropriate, yet uncomplicated figure. The result is immediate illumination, utter clarity:

> The heart can think of no devotion
> Greater than being shore to the ocean—
> Holding the curve of one position,
> Counting an endless repetition.

Directness is employed also in lyrics where the purpose is to record a simple emotion, when perhaps he wishes to join poetic tradition by affirming that nature through trivial actions creates huge effects upon the human heart. Bryant's healing power of nature permeates "Dust of Snow." But it is not Bryant's property exclusively, for Wordsworth expressed the same thought earlier through his field of golden daffodils, and Hardy later did so through his darkling thrush. One might ask whether any poet has neglected to take notice of the theme.

The charm of "Dust of Snow" then lies not in the depth of its message or in any unique quality of thought, but in its utter simplicity, its perfection of image, and in its superb and economical craft:

> The way a crow
> Shook down on me
> The dust of snow
> From a hemlock tree
>
> Has given my heart
> A change of mood
> And saved some part
> Of a day I had rued.

His direct approach is particularly evident in poems stressing the didactic. When Frost wishes to instruct, he characteristically lays bare the message he chooses to convey. Particularly in his satirical poems on topical themes this trait predominates. One sees it clearly in his verses on the Bomb. Following the atomic blasts over Nagasaki and Hiroshima, and during the ensuing dispute over use of thermonuclear weapons, Frost was struck by the irony involved. On the one hand, use of these weapons was defended pragmatically as the most direct and utilitarian means of victory. On the other, banishment of the bomb was called for on humanitarian grounds. Frost manages to intensify the ironic center of the dispute by comparing it in "U.S. 1946 King's X" with the simple expedient employed in children's games to achieve immunity:

> Having invented a new Holocaust,
> And been the first with it to win a war,
> How they make haste to cry with fingers crossed,
> King's X—no fairs to use it any more!

At times the poet appends his lesson for today in much the same manner as the nineteenth-century "moral" was utilized to round out the verses of the Cambridge poets. He uses the tacked-on coda, for instance, in "The Tuft of Flowers" when he closes his couplets with a statement of the ultimate conclusion reached through the progression of thought: "'Men work together,' I told him from the heart,/'Whether they work together or apart.'" One could scarcely ask for a more succinct summary of the essential content of the poem than what the poet himself supplies in these two lines.

The same directness of statement occurs throughout the spectrum of Frost's achievement. It is observable in poem after poem, sometimes as a tag-line, as in "Tuft of Flowers"; sometimes it is worked into the heart of the verse itself. These examples will ring familiar:

And of course there must be something wrong
In wanting to silence any song.
                              —"A Minor Bird"

A theory if you hold it hard enough
And long enough gets rated as a creed:
                              —"Etherealizing"

Nothing can make injustice just but mercy.
                              —"A Masque of Mercy"

"Good fences make good neighbors."
                              —"Mending Wall"

There are roughly zones whose laws must be obeyed.
                              —"There are Roughly Zones"

Won't this whole instinct matter bear revision?
Won't almost any theory bear revision?
                              —"The White-Tailed Hornet"

Only where love and need are one,
And the work is play for mortal stakes,
Is the deed ever really done
For Heaven and the future's sakes.
                              —"Two Tramps in Mud-Time"

Heaven gives its glimpses only to those
Not in position to look too close.
                    —"A Passing Glimpse"

            but nothing tells me
That I need learn to let go with the heart.
                    —"Wild Grapes"

It must be I want life to go on living.
                    —"The Census-Taker"

Nothing gold can stay.
                    —"Nothing Gold Can Stay"

We love the things we love for what they are.
                    —"Hyla Brook"

Frost appears to have recognized the temptation of pushing didacticism too far and thereby becoming a poet of rhyming fables. Although he could never relinquish his prerogative—his duty—to generalize or add marginal notes, he did sometimes in revision cut the lessons that appeared to hammer at his point excessively. As an instance, "At Woodward's Gardens" originally closed with two lines of direct message: "It's knowing what to do with things that counts./Resourcefulness is more than understanding." Aware that the final line reiterated the lesson already stated, and perhaps was at the same time weakened by its vocabulary, he eliminated it when the poem appeared in *A Further Range*. But he was reluctant to part with his line entirely—building soil, no doubt—so he slipped it into his table of contents as a subtitle for the poem.[43]

## "Tell the Truth but Tell It Slant"

It may be a truism that the more explicit a poem is, the more easily it can achieve popularity. At least with a mass audience this characteristic appears to hold true, for traditionally the masses have exhibited a preference for the simple over the complex. The broadly underscored adage goes down well, is assimilated at once, and is easily recalled for quotable occasions: *Only God can make a tree; It takes a heap o' living to make a home.* But popularity won so effortlessly can just as suddenly and easily be lost. Frost has his moments of being in danger of becoming a merely "popular" poet, a versifier. Those who in the 1930s and 1940s derisively labeled him "the Edgar Guest of the Intellectuals" made capital of this aspect of his work.

If any of his poems are overly direct, they stand in a minority, and they never sink quite to the level of the "line-a-day" journalist. Here and there the reader may believe that he detects just the slightest echo of Sinclair Lewis's Chum Frink, but only in poems deliberately executed with the light touch as distinguishable postscripts to the more serious works. But the intent is not to deride Frost's achievement in the direct manner. Some of his most excellent work parades ideas wholly on the surface—or so close to it as to be seen like a lamp through gauze. Frost never allowed a piece to go to print, of course, until it was satisfactorily representative of his meticulous craftsmanship. At the same time, it is doubtful whether many of his direct poems—particularly those on topical subjects—are destined for long life. Time will winnow out the handful that are to be saved. Most critics can only guess at which these might be.

However, one need not be a crystal-gazer to predict that Frost's ambition of lodging a few poems in history will be realized. One may hazard also that the majority of the survivors will come from works that achieve their major effects through indirection. If one considers only the practical eventualities, an implicit poem, being subject from the beginning to interpretation, adapts more readily to changing circumstances. A work that lends itself easily to meaningful reinterpretation stands a better chance of surviving from era to era.

Shakespeare's plays are a case in point. They have managed to mean all things to all men, being interpreted variously as each generation views them through its own unique spectacles. One has only to experience Sir Lawrence Olivier's film version of *Hamlet,* for instance, to be impressed by the facility with which sixteenth-century Shakespeare absorbs twentieth-century Freud to its own profit.

A fair share of Frost's poetry also will take Freud in stride, notwithstanding its author's professed scorn for "Viennese" interpretations of his work. But then, he never expressed patience with analysis, psychological or poetic. As a matter of fact, if Frost, speaking without a poet's-cap as public figure, is listened to with an overly susceptible ear, he may leave the distinct impression of being opposed to any type or degree of interpretive reading at all. He has said so often enough and in plain-spoken terms. Indeed, interviews and lectures present him as forever fulminating against the analytical dissection of verses. Or else he is warning against the dangers of pressing a poem beyond its ability to yield meaning. But the continual expression of this attitude, at times seemingly at white heat, has to be tempered. Publicly, Frost said a good many things calculated to preserve his widespread image.

Frost obviously cherished the mezzotint of himself, in antique frame, which his countrymen held close to their hearts something like the Bibles that soldiers are said to have carried in breast pockets to avert a shot. He fought to preserve this picture, just as William Faulkner helped perpetuate the story that he was nothing but a backwoods, hound-dog man who just happened to pump out *The Sound and the Fury* while stumbling back from delirium tremens. It seems true that Frost's resistance to excessive intellectual probing and symbol-finding was sincere, but many of his protestations have to be considered for what they were, mere word play for effect: campaign oratory.

Were this not so, he simply would not have been a poet at all, for he would be working toward the demolition of one of the chief *raisons d'être* for poetry. Even when they break with the past, poets continue to work within conventions, not only of syntax and form, which are relatively superficial, but also within conventions of figure. Metaphor has been, is, and will be a poet's lifeblood. No amount of "modernizing" is likely to alter that. Metaphor separates poets from poetasters; without it, a poet dwindles to a mere jingle man. The unique personality with the grand touch of metaphor is not to be confused with the versifier of prose notions.

Fortunately, Frost not only had metaphor coursing in his veins—a good high blood-count, too—but he admitted it. Statements made in his infrequent critical works flatly contradict his more impetuous declarations from the speaker's podium. When he agreed to drop his rural mask and act like the grown-up, classically grounded, intellectually mature adult he was, he disclosed that much more than a swarm of airy visions populated the space beneath his familiar white thatch. When the poet in him did the speaking, he was ready to admit with pride that he labored always within "the constant symbol" and to declare aloud that "education by poetry is education by metaphor."[44]

These admissions are no more than should be expected from a devotee of Emerson, who saw Nature and all her parts as one gigantic interlocking complex of symbols, parables, and exempla. It is highly doubtful that serious readers of Frost were ever fooled even for an instant by his implying otherwise. One reading of "Fire and Ice," a poem which employs symbols in an indispensable role, which in fact names its symbols outright, should be sufficient enlightenment even for the most naive. Critics have from the start appreciated his skill in handling metaphor and symbol. Perhaps it is a part of his basis for protest that in their zeal the critics overdid it, as they have generally overdone so much in the twentieth century and as they have specifically overdone Frost's own "Stopping by Woods on a Snowy Evening."

To say that "Stopping by Woods" has been one of the most discussed poems of the twentieth century is an understatement. It has been analyzed, explicated, dissected—sometimes brilliantly—but altogether to the point of tedium. One falls under the illusion that no other poem is available for critical study, with the exception of Eliot's *The Waste Land.* Proud as Frost was of this lyric, and only partly because it got into the anthologies more frequently than any other, he felt that readers made themselves too busy over "my heavy duty poem" and squeezed it for meanings not present: "That one I've been more bothered with than anybody has ever been with any poem in just pressing it for more than it should be pressed for."[45]

Up to a point he was ready to agree that poems become the property of those who read them and therefore are open to innumerable interpretations. As he slyly put it, "The poet is entitled to everything the reader can find in his poem."[46] Yet readers sometimes exceed themselves. Frost ordinarily gained amusement from the meanings people located in his work, meanings he claimed to have been totally unaware of. Sometimes he was moved to shake his head wryly. But he became downright touchy about the "busymindedness" that inspired the ceaseless flow of questions, many of them asinine indeed, concerning the minutiae of "Stopping by Woods."

He was irritated by people who asked to know the name of the man who did the stopping. It appalled him to have someone write inquiring whether those woods would really fill up with snow. Unbelievable questions came his way: Who would be going home that way so late at night? What did the woods mean? What did the snow stand for? Could a horse really ask questions? Frost's reply to this last inquiry, made with the aid of J. Frank Dobie—yes, they could, and decidedly better questions than some professors could ask!—inspires support for his skeptical approach to poetic explication.[47]

Like other major poets, Robert Frost writes on multiple levels of meaning. Throughout his poems he employs symbolism and metaphor to achieve his ends. He communicates indirectly as well as directly. T. S. Eliot is widely regarded as a symbolist and Frost is not. Eliot in a poem will leap at once to the secondary meanings of his symbols, while Frost weaves his emblems into a surface fabric of solidly intelligible texture. This surface by itself satisfies so completely that the danger exists that secondary meanings will be ignored. Eliot's symbols lie in the open, where the reader's attention is forced to them. Frost's symbols are hidden like children's Easter eggs—barely out of reach and easily found.

Nor did Frost, when speaking of poetry in a serious tone, dispute this point. His gift was for creating an artifice so vivid, moving, and significant on the initial level that any probing for further rewards can seem like meddlesome prying, an intrusion upon an otherwise wholly satisfying performance. Yet he spoke to the English School at Bread Loaf concerning the "honest duplicity"[48] of poetry, a term reminiscent of Emily Dickinson's "tell the truth but tell it slant." Poetry is the true lie.

Elsewhere he stood firm in declaring that out of all the manners in which he had defined poetry, the chief definition "is that it is metaphor, saying one thing and meaning another, saying one thing in terms of another, the pleasure of ulteriority."[49] To those who question why he did not say what he meant outright and literally, his answer was the only honest one a poet can offer, and it was sufficient: "We never do that, do we, being all of us too much poets. We like to talk in parables and hints and in indirections—whether from diffidence or some other instinct."[50]

So all poetry is hinting, is metaphor, is duplicity. As such, it may give the reader trouble. Those handicapped by insufficient education to develop their taste and judgment "don't know when they are being fooled by a metaphor, an analogy, a parable."[51] But this handicap will not affect solely their judgment of poetry. It will affect also their judgment of all arts and books, as well as simpler forms of communication such as newspaper editorials or political orations. For the sophisticate, a poem can be peeled away layer by layer like a plump artichoke until its delicate heart can be savored. Poetry is adult entertainment.

## "After Apple-Picking"

As an illustration of the "honest duplicity" of Frost's better verses, the early lyric "After Apple-Picking," although often analyzed, serves ideally. Some readers admire this poem because the deceptive simplicity of its surface picture has charmed them with a rich vision of idyllic New England harvest. Others treasure the poem as exemplifying the truth of John Ciardi's reminder that "a poem is never about what it seems to be about":[52]

> My long two-pointed ladder's sticking through a tree
> Toward heaven still,
> And there's a barrel that I didn't fill
> Beside it, and there may be two or three
> Apples I didn't pick upon some bough.
> But I am done with apple-picking now.
> Essence of winter sleep is on the night,
> The scent of apples: I am drowsing off.
> I cannot rub the strangeness from my sight
> I got from looking through a pane of glass
> I skimmed this morning from the drinking trough
> And held against the world of hoary grass.
> It melted, and I let it fall and break.
> But I was well
> Upon my way to sleep before it fell,
> And I could tell
> What form my dreaming was about to take.
> Magnified apples appear and disappear,
> Stem end and blossom end,
> And every fleck of russet showing clear.
> My instep arch not only keeps the ache,
> It keeps the pressure of a ladder-round.

I feel the ladder sway as the boughs bend.
And I keep hearing from the cellar bin
The rumbling sound
Of load on load of apples coming in.
For I have had too much
Of apple-picking: I am overtired
Of the great harvest I myself desired.
There were ten thousand thousand fruit to touch,
Cherish in hand, lift down, and not let fall.
For all
That struck the earth,
No matter if not bruised or spiked with stubble,
Went surely to the cider-apple heap
As of no worth.
One can see what will trouble
This sleep of mine, whatever sleep it is.
Were he not gone,
The woodchuck could say whether it's like his
Long sleep, as I describe its coming on,
Or just some human sleep.

Among the available interpretations of Frost's lyric, perhaps the most lucid and readily accessible is that based upon the Emersonian pattern of natural analogies: "things admit of being used as symbols because nature is a symbol, in the whole, and in every part."[53] Emerson's doctrine of analogy between human life and the seasons, for instance, in which spring, summer, fall, and winter parallel the various ages of man, is seconded by Thoreau, who observed the same analogy operating within the span of the day: "The phenomena of the year take place every day in a pond on a small scale. Every morning, generally speaking, the shallow water is being warmed more rapidly than the deep, though it may not be made so warm after all, and every evening it is being cooled more rapidly until the morning. The day is an epitome of the year. The night is the winter, the morning and evening are the spring and fall, and the noon is the summer."[54] Building upon the suggestions of Emerson and Thoreau, and noting the centrality that Frost has afforded both to the yearly cycle and to the daily span, the reader begins to absorb the implications radiating from "After Apple-Picking."

On the surface of the poem, however, all seems serenely concrete and straightforward. An apple grower, eager for his awaited harvest of ripe red russets, has worked for days against the imminent arrival of autumn frost. Freezing temperatures, signs of which are already apparent, will close out his opportunities to profit fully from his year's labor. In tending his trees from springtime bud through summer growth, the man's toil has been buoyed by a tremendous stimulus of anticipation. But now the exertion of the harvest itself has wearied him. Tedium has set in. He knows he will not be allowed to pick every apple on his trees, nor does he expect to. Much more realistic now than in the spring and summer, he possibly no longer even desires to account for every piece of fruit.

The harvest has taught the apple-grower something of value. He has attempted to do more than one man can hope to do alone in a season. His excitement—as well as his weariness—has caused many apples to fall to earth. Bruised, ruined, spiked on stubble, these become relatively worthless. The energies of man and nature lavished upon bringing them to perfection seem to have been poured out for naught. Yet such accidents are to be expected in the normal course of any human scheme. It is natural also that some fruit will necessarily be left to freeze as winter closes in; for this is real, not ideal, harvest.

Sleepiness of late autumn pervades the air. All around the harvester nature is preparing herself for rest: trees are defoliating as the summer sap recedes; woodchucks are hibernating, snug in readied burrows. The harvester himself lies in bed after what he realizes may be the very last day of his harvest. He is tired to the bone, leaden-limbed; but ironically he is too fatigued to pass easily into his exhausted and well-earned slumber. His eyes swim. His feet ache from standing on the ladder rung for hours at a time. All ambition spent, he is ready to call a halt and take his rest, knowing that—like anyone totally committed to a task—he will continue the harvest of apples even in his sleep.

So accurately and so economically does Frost capture the essence of apple harvest that one cannot be faulted for finding adequate satisfaction within his portrayal of the apple-picking itself, needing no more. The sights and sounds are all there. Every sensation is recorded vigorously. No one who has used a ladder or labored long hours driven by desire, or nodded in the heady drowsiness of Indian summer, is likely to forget soon the achievement of this verse. As rural idyll, it gratifies.

Even so, the simple application of natural analogies to the poem discloses an entirely new dimension, and it does so without exertion or distortion. The explicit meaning of the poem communicates with the clarity of crystal. Just as clearly does the metaphor, camouflaged only slightly by the impressive veneer of sensory detail, make itself felt. Just as every line, detail, and word contributes to transmitting the essence of the harvest experience, so does every aspect of the poem fall into place as well within the analogies and press for their development.

One notes first that Frost selects as his setting both the night of the daily span and the winter of the yearly cycle. Either would guide the mind toward a prospect of death, but the conjunction of night and winter renders that prospect unmistakable. Numerous references to drowsiness and sleep, to strangeness of sight, and to the harvest itself all reinforce the parallel between the terminations of day, season, and existence. The span of life is embraced within the curve of season, spring to winter. But what completes the circle? Ordinarily spring again, returning after winter to bring rebirth. Hints emanate from at least two references and suggest that the resurrection of spring is probable. The first comes with an unobtrusive gesture in the poem's second line, its seemingly gratuitous reference to the ladder's pointing "toward heaven still." Without straining the issue, the word *heaven* elicits subconscious responses involving death and immortality. The second hint occurs at the finish, as the verse concludes with a whimsical contemplation of the woodchuck's sleep, the hibernation, the little imitation of death which also will terminate in springtime "resurrection." And obviously even "just some human sleep" implies a reawakening.

Snuggling within the curve of the natural cycles is another arc, that shaped by the harvest process fulfilling itself. The harvest is awaited expectantly, with nerves atingle for rosy signals of ripeness to appear on the fruit. With the "russet showing clear," the picker goes to work, heady with grandiose visions of a bumper crop gathered to the last plump apple. The elixir of enthusiasm is steadily diluted. First come endless hours of labor. Then a weariness engulfs what energy is yet unspent. Desire wanes. Then a realization grows that the original goal will not be reached without compromise forced by circumstance. Surprisingly, it no longer seems so very critical to finish. Finally comes the letting-go, first with the hands, then with the mind, but never with the heart. The apple-picker, a sadder but wiser man, relinquishes his task altogether. Now is the time to rest from toil, to accept the verdict on his performance, to listen to himself harshly judging himself.

This harvest action, complete in itself, slips so neatly into the convenient circle created by the natural symbolism, and the whole tallies so comfortably with the surface events of the poem, that the reader arrives at the final period in a euphoria of "rightness." Surface and symbol coincide neatly.

How fortunate that Frost resisted any impulse he may have felt to press his poem into the didactic mold. A phrase or two would have shaped the verse into a substantiation of the orthodox religious view— and would have done untold violence to the lyrical purity so far sustained. But he fortuitously elected instead to suggest, to hint. Whatever sleep it is, only a woodchuck, he says fancifully, could tell for sure. The poem thus ends in deliberate ambiguity. But if a reader chooses to see "After Apple-Picking" as an allegory of man's life ascending from the eager grasping of youth to the letting-go of age, Frost will not object. Nor will he frown upon his poem viewed as a moral tale of the world having its inevitable way with human ambition. Let there be no mistake; all poetry is hinting—is metaphor. Poetry is the legitimate means of saying one thing and meaning another, an "honest duplicity."

In few poems do a complex of symbols work together with such ease and precision. They interlock honestly, apparently without effort, yet with such pure calculation. Art conceals art. Not a single false note is sounded. Every word making for the metaphorical interpretation works as well toward the concrete rendering of the harvest-scene veneer which clothes that metaphor. The "careful casualness"[55] for which Paul Engle praised Frost is nowhere more fully realized or more apparent than in "After Apple-Picking."

Were a definitive example of Frost's achievement required, this poem could easily suffice. It is illustrative of his major poetic traits. His close observation of the world and man, these are present, depicted in terms of an original relation with nature. The true colloquial flavor of American speech invigorates each line, beginning with the opening observation: *My long two-pointed ladder's sticking through a tree.* At the same time that the verse strains against the bonds of orthodox form, finding its old way to be new, the poet's solid commitment to convention is undisguised. Idea, detail, and technique link hands in solidarity, each cooperating with the other to achieve wholeness. "After Apple-Picking" obeys its author's dictum requiring that a poem epitomize the great predicament: portray the will braving alien entanglements. Finally, with its double and perhaps triple layers of meaning revealed suddenly through metaphorical extension, the poem assumes the shape of the napkin drawn tightly through the ring. When its constraint has been achieved, it emerges, unfolding brilliantly to disclose its full import.

# Chapter Five

# Roughly Zones: Frost's Themes

Hand in hand with the common opinion of Robert Frost as a regional poet, rather strictly limited to portraying the rural Northeast, comes a corollary opinion that holds that he is restricted also in his handling of major themes. Nothing could be more misleading. It is true that Frost, in confining himself by choice largely to things "rustic," fed this very misinterpretation. At times he does present the illusion of perching serenely on his own little New England hill while the rest of the world races by. But what appears to be an avoidance of basic themes is not timidity at all but a calculated reluctance to deal with purely topical subject matter. Many of the overwhelming subjects of the twentieth century appear to have scarcely grazed his awareness: the two world wars are glaring examples. Likewise, the specific problems deriving from urbanization and mechanization, so rich an area for other artists, seem to pass unnoticed. The skyscrapers and skid-row alleys of Sandburg, for instance, have no place in the neat circle Frost scratched for himself on the earth's face. Frost's people suffer, but not from the "modern" diseases. While personal problems and dislocations abound in Frost's poems, a reader would not expect his characters to reflect much of the horror of that particular type of loss of identity, for instance, which megalopolis imposes upon the anonymous citizen in Kenneth Fearing's "Dirge."

Yet when it comes to those universal experiences that a poet evades only at the price of being thought trivial, there is little shirking on Frost's part. He is as deeply involved as any poet whose style glitters with the fashionable linguistic trappings of contemporary urban society. Already the wisdom of his approach is becoming clear. By some sacrifice of immediacy, he has outpointed many of the moderns. Each passing year dates the work of poets whose work depends upon topical labels. Meanwhile, Frost's poems manage to retain their freshness because they are less reliant upon day and year, less adorned by names, idiom, and actions of the passing moment. Frost referred to himself as a "synechdochist." He had no doubt but that in exploring one representative corner of humanity, he was probing a sample of the larger crowd. If, in writing honestly of New England, he faced life squarely on its own terms, then why should he extend his range?

That he did face up to life, not averting his glance from its bitter interludes any more than from its tranquil moments, is revealed when the full range of his work is scrutinized. With equanimity he investigates the basic themes of man's life: the individual's relationships to himself, to his fellow man, to his world, and to his God. These are the unavoidables. If readers, compulsively seeking reassurance, skip by the more stark pages of his books, that is their omission and not Frost's. When President John F. Kennedy dedicated the Frost Library at Amherst in 1963, he stressed this very thought: "If Robert Frost was much honored during his lifetime, it was because a good many preferred to ignore his darker truths."[1]

## The Trial by Existence

As Frost ponders the lot of individual man, he stresses the human being as an entity. One among many, man yet remains single and alone with his fate. Life holds the possibility of terror and the potential of beauty. To know which it is to be, man first must educate himself. He must learn his place among the final truths of existence. Only by knowing these verities for what they are can he work toward acceptance of them and of his own lot.

By observation man gradually becomes aware of his own position in the inexorable cycles of being. Life arches outward from youth toward age somewhat in the way a seedling first shoulders its way through the crust of soil in order that it may end as an unpicked fruit that drops in autumn, its stem nipped by cold. Frost's pages are soaked in mutability. Spring and autumn scenes crowd his poems. New life burgeons through last year's waste. Old life goes under to build soil for the new growth. The great pulse of the seasons throbs its message. In "Blueberries," he calls attention to the mystery of rebirth as berry bushes sprout from slag:

> There may not have been the ghost of a sign
> Of them anywhere under the shade of the pine,
> But get the pine out of the way, you may burn
> The pasture all over until not a fern
> Or grass-blade is left, not to mention a stick,
> And presto, they're up all around you as thick,
> And hard to explain as a conjuror's trick.

In contrast to his landscapes of resurgent life, he provides scenes such as in "The Wood Pile" with its cord of maple abandoned to the processes of nature, the carefully cut and stacked wood serving only the cosmic welfare as it warms the swamp "with the slow smokeless burning of decay." But the wood is not altogether worthless, surely, because it goes to build soil for the new. Man, impressed with the urgency of this natural cycle, recognizes his own reliance upon it:

> Before the leaves can mount again
> To fill the trees with another shade,
> They must go down past things coming up.
> They must go down into the dark decayed.
> They must be pierced by flowers and put
> Beneath the feet of dancing flowers.
> However it is in some other world
> I know that this is the way in ours.[2]

Contributory to the basic lesson of mutability are repetitive portrayals of harvest and mowing, and particularly poems centered upon abandoned dwellings. A home may be untenanted but cared for, as in "The Black Cottage." It may be opened to the ravages of weather, as the home of the poetess in "A Fountain, a Bottle, a Donkey's Ears and Some Books." Both are headed down the final path. "The Census-Taker" finds a house "in one year fallen to decay." Only the cellar walls of "Ghost House" are standing; from its ruins sprout wild raspberries. The uninhabited dwelling in "Directive" has decayed into: ". . . only a belilaced cellar hole,/Now slowly closing like a dent in dough." Like the abandoned maple stack, these human woodpiles are fast disintegrating into compost for another cycle. And the process cannot be avoided.

The lesson for today is simple and explicit: all things change. Man's time is terrifyingly limited. Seemingly with caprice, he is "doomed to broken-off careers." The natural cycle preaches this lesson, intensified by the intrusion of accident, which leaves man as exposed as a bird's nest unroofed in a new-mowed field. The same tune dins in his ears. "Nothing gold can stay." It is man's doom to bloom.

The facts of change, hard as they might be, nevertheless do not justify despondency. This is not the way out:

> May my application so close
> To so endless a repetition
> Not make me tired and morose
> And resentful of man's condition.[3]

What cannot be altered must be understood and accepted. Life is far from being unlivable. "As long as life goes on so unterribly," there is no need, declares Frost, for writing the Russian novel. But man must "bow and accept the end," even if graceful reception of the inevitable end seems no less than treason to his human hopes and dreams. "Acceptance" tells the reader this:

> When the spent sun throws up its rays on cloud
> And goes down burning into the gulf below,
> No voice in nature is heard to cry aloud
> At what has happened. Birds, at least, must know
> It is the change to darkness in the sky.
> Murmuring something quiet in her breast,
> One bird begins to close a faded eye;
> Or overtaken too far from his nest,
> Hurrying low above the grove, some waif
> Swoops just in time to his remembered tree.
> At most he thinks or twitters softly, "Safe!
> Now let the night be dark for all of me.
> Let the night be too dark for me to see
> Into the future. Let what will be, be."

## Finalities Besides the Grave

Frost's poems are studded with individuals who accept the inevitable or who resist it. Included are those spied when just in the act of learning. The little girl in "Wild Grapes" responds to her older brother's tutelage but is not yet able to act upon his advice "to let go" of the branch she clutches. For her life is difficult. It will continue to be until she acquires the ability to release her human hold on transitory things. In contrast, the gathered witnesses in "'Out, Out—'" have already mastered the difficult art of allowing what will be to be. A young boy has had his hand ripped off by a buzz saw, a senseless accident infuriating in its conditions. The witnesses do what they can: they call the doctor, attempt to stanch the flow of blood. But nothing helps. One moment the lad is alive, the next dead: "And they, since they/Were not the one dead, turned to their affairs." Cold and heartless as this ending seems to many, Frost apparently approves of it. He appends it as the coda of the poem to express the only possible course of action guaranteed to preserve equilibrium. The boy has loosed his hold on life. Now those gathered around must loose their hold on him. If accused of cruelty, the survivors might answer with the old woman in "A Servant to Servants": "By good rights I ought not to have so much/Put on me, but there seems no other way."

What happens when man cannot accept the facts of his condition is graphically portrayed through the young wife of "Home Burial," unable to reconcile the death of her child. Day after day she drifts compulsively to the tall stairway window looking out upon the nearby family plot. Every sight of the raw mound where her child lies buried reopens her wound. She clutches her grief. Already her resistance to consoling arms has driven a wedge between herself and her husband. He feels his loss no less painfully than she; but, knowing that life is for the living, he has released the past to itself. The wife finds this incomprehensible:

> "You could sit there with the stains on your shoes
> Of the fresh earth from your own baby's grave
> And talk about your everyday concerns. . . .
> I can repeat the very words you were saying.
> 'Three foggy mornings and one rainy day
> Will rot the best birch fence a man can build.'
> Think of it, talk like that at such a time!
> What had how long it takes a birch to rot
> To do with what was in the darkened parlor.
> You *couldn't* care!"

One grants that the young husband is considerably less than tactful, but he has spoken from deep compulsions, freely associating as one will do. Under stress, conversation must be made to break the silence. The wife cannot forget. Nor can she forgive. She can only hate and shrink icily away from any human touch. Her husband bears the brunt of the contempt she feels for her race:

> "Friends make pretense of following to the grave,
> But before one is in it, their minds are turned
> And making the best of their way back to life
> And living people, and things they understand.
> But the world's evil. I won't have grief so
> If I can change it. Oh, I won't, I won't!"

Because she cannot "change it," the reader anticipates deeper abysses opening for her on the path ahead. Estrangement from her husband, the poet implies, may be only the first step to loss of reason.

The young woman of "Home Burial" seems likely to join a number of Frost's people who have plunged into madness through failure to accept their lot. When life shatters, man must piece together the shards. There is no alternative. Over those unable to adapt, the night of the mind closes down with finality. Loss of equilibrium, the failure of whatever stabilizing gyroscope maintains man on a steady keel, this is the storm fear to which the poet so often refers when probing the darker corners of individual lives.

There is a wind working "against us in the dark." Like some voracious beast, the fear orders man out of his secure niche into the night, there to devour him. All his strength is required to resist the commands of the monster:

> And my heart owns a doubt
> Whether 'tis in us to arise with day
> And save ourselves unaided.[4]

When man is summoned into the night with an offer of release from life's storm, capitulation often seems the simplest route.

Without dwelling on it to the point of morbidity, Frost described

himself as "one acquainted with the night." He knew, he said, what it
was to "outwalk the furthest city light," past the security of familiar
lighted windows into a question mark. In "Desert Places" the theme is
treated again, this time as loneliness that "will be more lonely ere it will
be less." Here, loss of reason is figured in a blank expanse of snow which
smothers familiar landmarks "with no expression, nothing to express":

> They cannot scare me with their empty spaces
> Between stars—on stars where no human race is.
> I have it in me so much nearer home
> To scare myself with my own desert places.

With this human void so close at hand, so accessible, what need is there
for anyone to contemplate the constellations for a glimpse between the
streetlight stars into empty black vacuum? Man lives always, Frost
implies, just a short step removed from the crevasse; he is sustained by
props of terrifying frailty.

While mental aberration or even absolute madness lurks near enough
to anyone to serve as a reminder of the thin red line that makes all the
difference, Frost lived in a shadow darker than most men experience.
For many years his sister, Jeanie, exhibited unbalanced propensities. By
degrees she became so alienated from the world that it was necessary to
institutionalize her. Jeanie was unable to accept "the coarseness and
brutality" of existence; in particular she found the facts of birth, love,
and death revolting. Jeanie Frost's ideal world could never be reconciled
with the actual world of daily life, nor could she "let what will be, be."
The advent of World War I, with its torrent of atrocity stories and its
genuine slaughter, unsettled her fragile mind permanently. However,
as Frost wrote Louis Untermeyer, the symptoms had been apparent for
many years:

She has always been antiphysical and a sensibilist. I must say she was pretty
well broken by the coarseness and brutality of the world before the war was
thought of. . . . She has had very little use for me. I am coarse for having had
children and coarse for having wanted to succeed a little. She made a birth in
the family the occasion for writing us once of the indelicacy of having
children. Indelicacy was the word. Long ago I disqualified myself for helping
her through a rough world by my obvious liking for the world's rough-
ness. . . . One half the world seemed unendurably bad and the other half
unendurably indifferent.[5]

To Jeanie, sympathy, to be genuine, meant that a mourner should die of sorrow for another's passing. Frost's sadness in being unable to dissuade his sister from this view of things is strikingly like the plight of the husband in "Home Burial." Without implying any autobiographical ties between his life and that poem, it is apparent that in sketching his painful portrait of inconsolability, he knew whereof he wrote.

So soundly is the optimistic note struck throughout Robert Frost's poetry that many fail to respond adequately to his compassion for individuals who have toppled into the pit. With a particular poignancy, he traces the decline of the young woman in "The Hill Wife." Having nothing to fill the emptiness of her isolation, she snaps under the gradual tension of a stark environment. She was one who "ought not to have to care so much," but did. She was one who ought not to have been alone, but was. Fear of the dark was the first symptom. This deepened. Then came imaginary plots against her life. A tramp who wandered by, begging a meal, was "watching from the woods as like as not," planning attack. The tree outside her window was trying to undo the latch; her sleep was torn by such dreams. At last, but suddenly also, "the ties gave." She found release from the world she could not endure.

Even more unsettling is the tale of the uncle in "A Servant to Servants." He went mad supposedly from intolerable disappointment in love. Given to violent rages, he was confined like a beast in a hickory cage in the attic. In this perch he might scream all night through until exhaustion quieted him. The bars of his prison were worn smooth from his efforts to pull them apart. The poet offers a gratuitous shock when the madman's niece discloses that she herself has "been away once" at the state asylum, but this news is mitigated by her apparent reconciliation with the world, expressed in stoic terms: "I s'pose I've got to go the road I'm going:/Other folks have to, and why shouldn't I?" This woman's acceptance of the common lot of mankind is the key Frost offers for rendering life tolerable, as tolerable mankind must find it in order to survive and drive onward.

Frost cannot find much sympathy for the man who merely rails against his lot. The Miniver Cheevy syndrome has no claim upon his heart. Always the great inescapable fact is that man comprises an imperfect being who operates within a larger but equally imperfect universe. Freighted with impossible dreams, man labors toward impossible goals. No salvation can be had without the twin keys to release. First comes recognition of man's common plight; next, acceptance.

## Together and Apart

The precise relationship of man to his fellows lies at the heart of the second of Frost's central themes. As a strong advocate of individualism, Frost saw man as learning from nature the zones of his own limitations. Within these naturally imposed boundaries, man struggles to achieve whatever he might with whatever talents he has been granted. Conversely, Frost saw man as achieving little so long as he considers only himself, isolated from those around him. At the best, this preoccupation leads to egocentrism; at its worst, to lonely madness. Always a moderate—Frost was fond of emphasizing that he considered himself neither radical nor conservative—he searched for an ideal reconciliation between the opposing claims of the individual and the group. He never found it.

Throughout his poetry, his statement of man's relationship to man remains ambiguous. One poetic credo is balanced against its opposite—a pattern established in his earliest published books. For instance, "The Tuft of Flowers" in *A Boy's Will* rests upon the question of apartness–togetherness. Two field hands work the same field. One mows the grass; later another comes to turn it for better drying:

> And I must be, as he had been,—alone,
> "As all must be," I said within my heart,
> "Whether they work together or apart."

But the grass-turner comes upon a tuft of flowers left standing by the scythe—almost—probably—certainly by design. Instantly the mood changes, the proposition is reversed:

> "Men work together, I told him from the heart,
> Whether they work together or apart."

Were "The Tuft of Flowers" his sole rendering of the theme, he would be tied unmistakably to the romantic tradition of the great brotherhood of man, wherein one mortal was bound to the other by ties of spirituality.

However, Frost's very next volume, *North of Boston,* begins with the converse of this comfortable stance. In "Mending Wall" two neighbors labor together so closely that their hands can touch, and they engage in extended conversation. Yet between them stands a wall of solid rock which holds one apart from the other; the men are engaged in raising this wall even more solidly and securely. But the wall of field-stone is a relatively insubstantial symbol of the real barriers dividing men. That particular wall can come down. In fact, it does, every fall and winter. Were it not for spring mending-time, it would topple altogether.

Between these two neighbors is another wall, impervious, built slowly of set ways and habits, mortared firmly of tradition, upbringing, and environment. One neighbor recites over and over again his creed: "Good fences make good neighbors." The other counters: "Something there is that doesn't love a wall, that wants it down." To the passing eye these two men give the appearance of working closely, but their cooperation is deceptive. In actuality, they stand so far apart from each other that even the simplest communicative act proves futile. The closed mind slams harder than granite against an unwelcome idea.

Do men work together or apart? Obviously they do both, says Frost, and poems such as "Mending Wall" document his case.

## Storm Fear

Whether apart or together, men exist as individuals. They coalesce as individuals, not as groups. If drawn together, it is love and need that motivate. The need is that of sharing fears and frailties held in common. The love is that of individual human companionship. The human hunger for relief from the scary darkness of the universe impels Frost's people to huddle near whatever lights are available. Be they lanterns, bonfires, hearths, or stars, these lights are as candles to moths.

Loneliness and the fear of loneliness are entrenched in the human heart. They are lodged there by man's knowledge of his isolation on a whirling planet poised precariously in space. They are anchored by man's awareness that he is no more than grass for the mower. Always there is the tremulous reaching out of the hand for a warm, reassuring clasp. There is the search for warmth and illumination from a spark of light, all to drive back into the dark woods the knowledge that man stands alone. One thinks of the girl in "The Fear of Man" who sets forth for home at midnight with a thudding heart. When solitude and the dark pour down upon her, she dashes breathless through the desert spaces between "little street lights she could trust."

The theme is strong throughout the dramatic narratives, particularly in *North of Boston,* where it impinges upon the majority of poems. As the shadows fall, Old Silas in "The Death of the Hired Man" creeps back like a wounded dog to the only home he has ever known. He wants to die by a familiar hearth, to be solaced by those he trusts will welcome him. As he often does, Frost employs two characters to conduct the dialogue. Mary argues to take Silas in; Warren, to put him out. Mary wins, as she must. Or rather, Silas wins, dying in at least the illusion of a last embrace.

"A Hundred Collars" dramatizes a familiar human conflict. The need for companionship struggles against innate fear of the unfamiliar. A timid professor, stranded overnight in a one-hotel town, is given the opportunity to share the last half-bed with a stranger. The professor's apprehension is stimulated by knowledge that another guest has refused the bed by virtue of fear "of being robbed or murdered," but his apprehension is overcome by his greater need for rest. Confronted by his roommate, whom he hopes desperately to get on with, the professor's fear mounts. The man is huge. He wears a size eighteen collar, to the professor's own fourteen.

Lafayette, hulking collector for the *Weekly News,* is first amused by the little man's fright. Then he is angered to learn that the fear is motivated by thorough mistrust. After all, Lafayette has in his own wallet ninety dollars compared to the professor's five. Now who has the greater right to suspicion? In an ironic tone Lafayette advises his new roommate:

> "You'd better tuck your money under you
> And sleep on it the way I always do
> When I'm with people I don't trust at night."

Later he unpacks his whiskey bottle and storms out, leaving the professor quaking on his pillow and scathing him with the information that, when he returns from his debauch, he will make himself known by purposive knocking at the door: "'There's nothing I'm afraid of like scared people/I don't want you should shoot me in the head.'" Man must have companionship, but he is afraid. When suspicion blights his fellowship, he is left even more unsheltered than his natural state demands.

That man *is* alone, Frost never forgets. "An Old Man's Winter Night," with its unforgettable image of the old man scaring the outer night as he clomps here and there from one room to another of his empty house, solitary lamp in hand, is enough to make this fact graphic. If aloneness is the final reality, then man's self must suffice. Like the drumlin woodchuck, he must be instinctively thorough about his own crevice and burrow, building for both security and escape.

As a last resort, a type of inferior friendship can be purchased like any other commodity. The fallen movie star of "Provide Provide" does precisely this, and the poet praises her for ensuring herself half a loaf in place of none. Sometimes, he seems to be advising, this assuagement cannot be avoided. Anything is better than being wholly isolated. Complete isolation from society is the greatest catastrophe that can befall. "On the Heart's Beginning to Cloud the Mind" is concerned with the plight of those existing in the desert. Looking out of his lower berth at night, the poet spots a single light on the landscape:

> A flickering, human pathetic light,
> That was maintained against the night,
> It seemed to me, by the people there,
> With a God-forsaken brute despair.
> It would flutter and fall in half an hour
> Like the last petal off a flower.

This desolate thought is countered by the poet's realization that the "pathetic" flickering of the light is an illusion wrought by the rapid movement of the train through the landscape. The light, he believes at last, burns in a home where husband and wife provide for each other.

### Set the Wall between Us

In most of his poems the possibility exists for people to work together. Individuals can offer a friendly hand like the cook in "A Servant to Servants" who tells the itinerant campers, "I'd *rather* you'd not go unless you must." The same is true of the farmer in "A Time to Talk" who recognizes from the gesture his neighbor makes in slowing his horse to a walk that companionship is being asked for:

> When a friend calls to me from the road
> And slows his horse to a meaning walk,
> I don't stand still and look around
> On all the hills I haven't hoed,
> And shout from where I am, "What is it?"
> No, not as there is a time to talk.
> I thrust my hoe in the mellow ground,
> Blade-end up and five feet tall,
> And plod: I go up to the stone wall
> For a friendly visit.

One *must* respond to such invitations, to such needs. There are walls enough between individuals in a world already imposing solitary existence without one's erecting unnecessary barriers.

The walls that wall men in or wall them out are three, says Frost in "Triple Bronze." They constitute their hides, their homes, and their nations. This threefold defense against "too much" seems essential. Yet men sometimes go too far: they too quickly erect walls where none should stand, shut themselves away from things and men, close off the hand that gropes for help. Anything will serve for a reason or for bricks. The death of a child, which should bind husband to wife closer in their common grief, may pry them apart instead. As "Home Burial" unfolds, the husband pleads with the deranged mother:

> Tell me about it if it's something human.
> Let me into your grief. I'm not so much
> Unlike other folks as your standing there
> Apart would make me out. Give me my chance.

Alienation may spring from the fear of "A Hundred Collars," or it may rise from the slightest breach of respect—from the very way a thing is said without prior thought, as in "The Code."

Respect for the other person and awareness of his precise needs are indispensable. "The Housekeeper" records the tale of John and Estelle, living together fifteen years in common law, apparently with satisfaction and deep respect. Estelle suddenly elopes with a man who has promised marriage. "That's a long time to live together and then pull apart," comments Estelle's old mother. But Estelle needed one thing more, a ceremony which would tie her as wife in the eyes of the world. John lacked the discernment to see this need or respond to it.

Men's deliberate acts can mark them and leave them abandoned without hope. "The Fear" recounts the story of a woman haunted by the faith she broke when she deserted her husband to run away with another man. Her life is one of apprehension, of hiding away in a secluded spot, ever certain that her husband is ferreting her out, spying upon her, and preparing to take vengeance. Retribution hangs like the sword of Damocles, obliterating peace. The witch of Coös has boarded up her attic door to restrain the clacking "chalk-pile" bones of the man her husband murdered and buried in the cellar. Her life and her son's pivot around the eternal threat of a ghostly skeleton from the past.

Yet a thread of the possibility of communication runs through the poems like the promise of spring. Fellowship is never more than a handclasp away, although ironically it sometimes hovers precisely there, out of reach. At times the link between men is represented by mechanical devices, such as telegraph or telephone. In "An Encounter" the forest walker searching out the orchid Calypso confronts a lineman "dragging yellow strands of wire with something in it from men to men." "The Line-Gang" portrays laughing, shouting workers stringing the dead trees "together with a living thread" which will carry words from man to man "as hushed as when they were a thought."

In "Snow" the reader eavesdrops on the Fred Coles, routed out of their warm bed on a blizzard midnight to provide shelter for their three-mile neighbor, Brother Meserve, preacher of a small fundamentalist sect. Meserve checks his horses in the barn and prepares to embark upon a final venture through the storm. Against heavy odds, he is determined to push home that night. The Coles debate his merits, much as Mary and Warren debated the merits of their hired man. The Coles, who do not like Meserve or what he represents, mistrust even his motives in undertaking what seems a foolhardy trip. It would be so much more sensible for him to spend the night with them and leave by daylight after the storm abates. Why is he compelled to face the snow?

> "He's getting up a miracle this minute.
> Privately—to himself, right now, he's thinking
> He'll make a case of it if he succeeds,
> But keep still if he fails."

If Meserve fails, he will be dead under the snow. This consideration gives them pause. And more than that, despite their disapproval of his actions, Meserve has claims upon the Coles; they had called him "Brother" Meserve and wondered why. The title goes beyond their unconscious use of his sect's appellation: man is brother to man in spite of all.

Once Meserve leaves, blustering and cocksure, the Coles are unable with any serenity to return to the warmth of their blankets. The poem centers around the telephone, now the only hope for reassurance. Will the telephone ring, telling them the fool is safe at home? They cannot slough off their fear for Meserve's wife and for the future of his family should he perish. At three in the morning the Coles are on the telephone talking with Mrs. Meserve; but she has no news. Only later, when the wife calls to let them know that her husband has reached the house, do they relax. Then, in a supremely human touch, their deep concern becomes righteous indignation. What was the point of this upstart Meserve's subjecting all of them to such an ordeal?—

> "The whole to-do seems to have been for nothing.
> What spoiled our night was to him just his fun.
> What did he come in for?—To talk and visit?
> Thought he'd just call to tell us it was snowing.
> If he thinks he is going to make our house
> A halfway coffee house 'twixt town and nowhere—"

But of course they would do it all over again if he came knocking. They can't help themselves, nor would Frost have it any other way. Anger at Meserve's lack of consideration, once past, quickly fades. The Coles have no reason to hold it against him; nothing is gained that way. Intolerance of others' foibles holds men too far apart for humanity's sake: "'But let's forgive him./We've had a share in one night of his life.'" The worry, the inconvenience, all are part of life, if life is to be lived. Sharing of lives, so that one overlaps into the other, is called for.

Frost's theme is pinpointed with clarity in "The Figure in the Doorway," a record of a railroad trip across scrub-oak mountains. Beside the tracks in a tiny cabin dwells a gaunt figure, self-sufficient with his oaks for heating and light, his hen and pig, his well and garden. He seems a hermit, stranded by more than miles from men, yet his life is "evidently something he could bear." The grim sense of separation which the train's passengers feel is caused by much more than just the pane of glass in the dining-car window which comes between them and him. But a single gesture evaporates it. They see the man "uncurl a hand in greeting" as the train roars past. Sometimes that is all it takes to tell whether men work together or apart.

## Our Hold on the Planet

If a reader, even the most superficial, takes anything at all from Frost's poems, it is likely to be a memorable impression created by the overwhelming presence of nature. His people prosper amid profusion. When they contain themselves in a room, nature presses against the window panes until she is strongly felt. Mountains rear high above man's head; valleys curve to his inquiring eye; roads, open or leaf-strewn, invite his curious foot. Everywhere crowd the trees, singly or in dense dark woods. Brooks race downhill with silver-singing waters. Beside them, or against outcropping rocks in fields where the mower has recently passed, bloom tufts of flowers.

As autumn's chill approaches, dry leaves darken the flinty soil. Dropping temperatures warn the woodchuck to prepare for windy blasts. And then comes the snow, flakes piling deep over the roads, snow falling fast, drifting to the window sills. In just-spring the hills of snow cave in heavily. Silver lizards of run-off water boil into creeks and rivers. Every hoof print is a pond. The warming sun stimulates buds of blueberry and sends men out to split good blocks of maple.

It is time for putting in the seed. The cycle of growth is on its way again, whirling with the planet, the seasons, and the years. Far overhead a vast sky roofs the entire cyclorama in solid bands or in fragmentary blue. Light gives way to dark. A parade of stars sweeps by, too far for man's grasp but close enough for aspiration. This memorable world of Robert Frost is pervasive, constant; it touches men's lives at all points and never is too much with them.

As Frost's vision expands beyond its focus upon man and society, he reveals his concept of the human relationship to this planet upon which the human race is destined to live out its days. Again he acts as moderator between extremes of attitude. He is, for example, far too much the realist to swear fealty to the concept of natural man, although a superficial contact with his work may suggest a perceptible drift in that direction. It is possible to extract from his poems only the Edenic strain of man blissfully removed from urban squalor and solaced by an original relation to woods and fields. But those who see only this concept are probably reading within the confines of their own hopeful wishes.

Nature, for Frost, is scarcely what it was for Bryant and other worshippers of the woods of the nineteenth century. The landscape is no panacea to soothe the ills and cares of society; the natural features do not invariably solace with warm companionship or bring a flush of hope to the pallored cheeks of despair. Nature does not exist to work continual miracles of revelation. Nor will it impart transcendental truths to any poor, bare, forked creature who straggles near a brook or tuft of flowers. For nature is hard as she is soft. She can destroy and thwart, disappoint, frustrate, and batter. She may prove as flinty as the rocky soil of New England, and as difficult to till profitably. On the other hand, the poet is unwilling to declare outright that man is marooned on a desert isle called "earth." His experience with the world would not permit him to go that far—not as far, for instance, as Robinson Jeffers.

Others might cry that man perches on a cinder drifting in the void, dying even as it cools—but not Robert Frost. Others might see nature possessed of unmitigable violence matched only by the brutality of society, but Frost is far too much like Emerson to drift in that direction. Again, neither a radical nor a conservative, he steers a middle path. Nature is at once harsh and mild. Man's relation to nature, as to his fellows, is both together and apart.

## There Are Roughly Zones

In keeping with his legacy from Emerson, Frost visualizes man always cradled within nature, totally immersed in environment. Nature is first of all the open book with lessons on every page awaiting the sensible reader. The need for self-reliance and individualism becomes apparent even to the least perceptive. The lesson of mutability is taught by repetition of days, seasons, years.

Beyond this, man learns his limitations, another lesson for survival. What man can do and cannot do; where he is allowed to stray and where he is prohibited; the length, breadth, height, and depth of his domain:

these recognitions must be absorbed. At war against nature's posted territories is man's unquenchable desire to reach beyond his grasp. He longs to break through the barriers set against him. If a thing is impossible, then this is what he lusts after. If a further step is mined with danger, then it is the one he must take. With the example of a peach tree carried perhaps too far north to survive the intense cold of winter, Frost illustrates man's refusal to accept decreed limits. The tree may live, but most probably will freeze, and all to satisfy the farmer's passion:

> Why is his nature forever so hard to teach
> That though there is no fixed line between wrong and right,
> There are roughly zones whose laws must be obeyed.

Limits imposed by nature are variously obeyed. "The Mountain" describes a hill-country township so dominated by the "black body" of the mountain Hor emanating from its center that:

> "Hor is the township, and the township's Hor—
> *And* a few houses sprinkled round the foot,
> Like boulders broken off the upper cliff"

An elderly citizen recognizes the limits which Hor places upon expansion by pointing out that sixty voters cast ballots in the last election, and "We can't in nature grow to many more" because "that thing takes all the room!" The land is vertical and stony; the few hill intervals are already under cultivation. There simply is no room for expanding the agriculture needed to sustain the population. Like it or not, man must accept. His alternative is to defeat himself in the attempt to do otherwise.

Man learns also, and quickly enough, that he cannot range beyond what his own physical nature permits. The woods tramper in "The Road Not Taken," coming upon a fork in the path, recognizes to his sorrow that he cannot travel both roads "and be one traveler." Not often is it given to man to have things all his own way. He learns not only that choices must be made but that his decisions prove irrevocable. Neither can he expect to pluck all the treasure from a lode. Time, space, and capability see to that; they set the zones within which nature allows man to harvest. The eye is doomed always to encompass more than the arms can glean.

"After Apple-Picking" doubtless contains the best presentation of this theme. The harvester, long before his plan is carried out, finds himself blocked from success by winter's approach and physical weariness: "I am overtired/Of the great harvest I myself desired." The same limitless ambition that impels one man to plant his peach tree too far north causes another to formulate a plan of superhuman capacity. Here, too, nature imposes her zones by dragging across man's path roadblocks labeled *halt*. Why should it be cause for cynicism that his "missiles always make too short an arc"? Out of this failure, man learns his human limits, painful lessons sometimes, like a child's finger burnt on the stove. But he learns. If he accepts and profits, then he has good reason for rejoicing:

> May something go always unharvested!
> May much stay out of our stated plan,
> Apples or something forgotten and left,
> So smelling their sweetness would be no theft.[6]

## Temples in the Woods

With his ringing declaration that "the groves were God's first temples," William Cullen Bryant launched into his "Forest Hymn" and made the most overt statement of his pantheism. The overreaching forest was a true cathedral, the woods the object of veneration as well as the proper spot for it. In nature's chapel God himself was immediately present:

> Thou art in the soft winds,
> That run along the summit of these trees
> In music; thou art in the cooler breath,
> That from the inmost darkness of the place,
> Comes, scarcely felt; the barky trunks, the ground,
> The fresh moist ground, are all instinct with thee.
> Here is continual worship:

And God was inherent also in every aspect of the landscape, in trees, soil, rock, and bush. For Bryant, these physical features were no more than God's palpable raiment:

> that delicate forest flower,
> With scented breath and look so like a smile,
> Seems, as it issues from the shapeless mould,
> An emanation of the indwelling Life,
> A visible token of the upholding Love,
> That are the soul of this great universe.

Because of Frost's own stress upon the tutorial function of nature, it may seem inevitable that he should join Bryant with an easy step forward into full altruism, portraying nature as Bryant did, "like one that loves thee nor will let thee pass ungreeted."

But Frost comes to an abrupt halt well before passing over the line. He specifically dissociates himself from the pantheistic tradition. Citing the sin of Ahaz, which was worship of nature, Frost writes of Matthew Hale who tends his orchard of Gold Hesperides with such zeal that he slides over into deification of the apples he has raised. The man dances in his orchard on a Sunday. No one sees him, except God; and He mercifully turns others' eyes away to save Squire Matthew from disgrace.

"New Hampshire" contains Frost's most explicit break with the pantheists. Out for a walk in the forest, he comes upon charcoal and blackened stones, remnants of a fire. In imagination the ashes seem an altar which purports "to say the groves were God's first temples." Because the statement shifts the central light from man, the poet must frown:

> on these impoverished
> Altars the woods are full of nowadays,
> Again as in the days when Ahaz sinned
> By worship under green trees in the open.
> Scarcely a mile but that I come on one,
> A black-cheeked stone and stick of rain-washed charcoal.
> Even to say the groves were God's first temples
> Comes too near to Ahaz' sin for safety.
> Nothing not built with hands of course is sacred.

Certainly then, nature is not to be worshipped as a benevolent deity. But neither is nature to be tarred as a black-browed adversary, hands loaded with thunderbolts to hurl toward man's obliteration. Rather, both elements are present. Nature becomes friend and foe together:

> There is much in nature against us. But we forget:
> Take nature altogether since time began,
> Including human nature, in peace and war,
> And it must be a little more in favor of man.

In tune with this evaluation, cited from the poem "Our Hold on the Planet," Frost displays nature as being predominantly man's benefactor. Nature provides, in Emerson's terms, "all sorts of things and weather" to fashion the year and sphere amenable to man's pursuits.

This same world that spills the cornucopia stands alert to remind one of "the line where man leaves off and nature starts" by nipping apples at the stem before there are hours enough left to harvest them. When man asks for rain, the world answers with a vengeance, sending "a flood and bid us be damned and drown." This is the nature of "Snow," raising its voice to a thin pitch, asserting its heavy power, bombarding man with plummeting thermometers and towering drifts:

> "This house is frozen brittle, all except
> This room you sit in. If you think the wind
> Sounds further off, it's not because it's dying;
> You're further under in the snow—that's all—
> And feel it less. Hear the soft bombs of dust
> It burst against us at the chimney mouth,
> And at the eaves."

It is against this adversary that Brother Meserve pits his will. It is not because the Coles want him to that he opposes the storm, even less that his wife would wish it, and surely not because of any message from God. He goes because he must:

> "Well, there's—the storm. That says I must go on.
> That wants me as a war might if it came.
> Ask any man."

In "Snow" man's relation to nature is no less intimate than it is in "Tree at My Window." In that poem the sympathetic blending of human head and tree head, of inner and outer weather, draws man and nature so close in understanding as to fit them together like twin hemispheres. So Brother Meserve and the blizzard lock together, but in combat, not love.

## Man the Preserver

If nature showers gifts and also confounds those gifts, so are the actions of man toward nature double-edged. On the one hand, man assumes the stewardship of his environment. On the other, he pillages the natural scene. A runaway Morgan colt, stampeding a wall with whited eyes and stand-up tail, summons the best in an alert observer:

> "Whoever it is that leaves him out so late,
> When other creatures have gone to stall and bin,
> Ought to be told to come and take him in."[7]

A young couple stumbling upon a nest of fledglings unroofed by the cutter-bar are stimulated into constructing from cuttings a new roof, and thereby: "restore them to their right/Of something interposed between their sight/And too much world at once."[8]

The men who keep vigil over the world include the owner of the pasture where young balsam firs spring up like a blessing, making the pasture "a place where houses are all churches and have spires." That man rejects the thirty pieces of silver to be gained by betraying his firs into the hands of the Christmas-tree seller: "But thirty dollars seemed so small beside/The extent of pasture I should strip. . . ./And leave the slope behind the house all bare."[9] The preservers include also the orchard owner who, leaving his trees to the winter, knows he will be haunted by the danger of their being prematurely warmed by a February sun masquerading as April. If the trees are induced to bud out of season, they place themselves in jeopardy of freezing in the first subzero gale. "Good-by and keep cold" is this man's parting word as he commits his trees to the snow and to providence.

This theme becomes most emphatic in verses devoted to preservation of clear running water, emblematic of the life-gift of the natural world. In these poems Frost's reverence for nature most closely approximates the religious. A double motif of winter and spring dominates, with scene after scene of death closing in upon the year and of snow piling over trees, road, hill, and roof. Ultimately springtime thaws release a "wet stampede" which resurrects grass and flowers, causes birds to "redouble song and twitter," and most significantly gives fresh tune and speed to the racing brooks.

Like Eliot, Frost equates water with fertility and vigor. Winter and drouth are death-dealers. In place of Eliot's bleak wasteland stretches of dry rock and sand, his "dry brain in a dry season," Frost pictures Hyla Brook in low-water season: "Its bed is left a faded paper sheet/Of dead leaves stuck together by the heat—" or he speaks of a brook's desecration by being channeled into underground conduits away from human eyes and hands.

The most fully developed appreciation of the stream as an emblem occurs in "West-Running Brook" in which a young couple recognize the running water as completing the triumverate of their marriage. In a scene of near-nuptial celebration, the two speak of being "married to the brook." As it gushes out of unknown into unknown, the white water is simultaneously with them, behind them, and beyond them. It becomes the stream of life itself:

> It is from that in water we were from
> Long, long before we were from any creature.
> Here we, in our impatience of the steps,
> Get back to the beginning of beginnings,
> The stream of everything that runs away.
> Some say existence like a Pirouot
> And Pirouette, forever in one place,
> Stands still and dances, but it runs away,
> It seriously, sadly, runs away
> To fill the abyss' void with emptiness.
> It flows beside us in this water brook,
> But it flows over us. It flows between us
> To separate us for a panic moment.
> It flows between us, over us, and *with* us.
> And it is time, strength, tone, light, life, and love—

Toward the corollaries of the brook, Frost expresses the same delight and reverence. The spring pools, deposited by "snow that melted only yesterday," stand clear and still. They reflect the total blue of the sky until their last drop is sucked up to sustain the enclosing trees, "to bring dark foliage on."

A spring, source of water and life, is placed high atop the bulge of stone dominating the local scene of "The Mountain." Too high to be ferreted out, it has eluded all climbers seeking it. It is known to the natives, nevertheless, in a mystical, even magic, way. From its source "right on the top, tip-top," it feeds a brook, "cold in summer, warm in winter," that flows evenly through drought and freeze. Could the spring be reached, "there ought to be a view around the world" from the spot where it gushes out of rock. The rain too is prayed for, welcomed. A downpour provides life at its fullest, sometimes almost too full to bear. Although flowers in a dry region "Contrive to bloom/On melted mountain water led by flume" how much better are the drenching rains that pour unsparing on petals and heads together:

> 'Tis not enough on roots and in the mouth,
> But give me water heavy on the head
> In all the passion of a broken drouth. . . .
> As strong is rain without as wine within,
> As magical as sunlight on the skin.

From whatever source, by whatever means, water is necessary to man. "We love the things we love for what they are," Frost says of the brooks. What they are becomes apparent through his dedicated concern for their preservation. His poems celebrate the fruition of growth along the margin of pond and stream. He seems always engaged in restoring the clarity of water by sweeping away contaminating debris of stem, twig, and leaf.

Of more than passing significance is his choice of epigraph for *A Boy's Will*. "The Pasture" encompasses not only his passion for tending the fount of life but also includes his invitation to the reader to participate:

> I'm going to clean the pasture spring;
> I'll only stop to rake the leaves away
> (And wait to watch the water clear, I may):
> I sha'n't be gone long.—You come too.

That quatrain might serve as motto for the entire Frost canon. His retention of its leading position in *Collected Poems* and in *Complete Poems* could affirm its import. Dependence upon running water is reasserted in "Going for Water." When the local well is dry, inhabitants seek their sustenance from the woods-hidden brook with tinkling fall and "drops that floated on the pool like pearls." At all costs, these brooks must be kept clear and flowing. So much depends upon them, and not only for material subsistence: "It is from this in nature we are from."

## Man the Destroyer

For the most part, man as "tenant farmer" of his environment performs his function with love and ability. But there are occasions when his depredations come close to wiping out every brave deed. He is capable of callously disposing of a brook's "immortal force" by running roughshod over it with his houses, curbs, and streets, throwing the brook

> Deep in a sewer dungeon under stone
> In fetid darkness still to live and run—
> And all for nothing it had ever done
> Except forget to go in fear perhaps.[10]

Man's sins against water fade to child's play beside his brooding urge to play with fire. Sometimes on a local scale, for his own amusement, or even more to scare away his desert places and create a lighted clearing in the dark, a man builds a bonfire on the hills. Then "something or someone" blows a gust that spreads the torch well beyond the natural hearth he thought would contain it:

> The place it reached to blackened instantly.
> The black was almost all there was by daylight,
> That and the merest curl of cigarette smoke—
> And a flame slender as the hepaticas,
> Blood-root, and violets so soon to be now.
> But the black spread like black death on the ground,
> And I think the sky darkened with a cloud
> Like winter and evening coming on together.[11]

Man's irresponsible playing with bonfires, destructive as it may be, seems scarcely worth mentioning in the same breath with man's perversity in toying with gunfire. War is not a subject Frost treats often, but he felt its presence deeply. When he does devote his talents to it, he usually speaks of its effect upon the race and particularly upon individuals. But its baleful sin against nature is not overlooked. "Range-

Finding" describes the havoc worked on the battleground by shells long before "a single human breast" is pierced. Underplaying the destruction, limiting himself to "trivial" details such as the rending of a "diamond-strung" cobweb and the snapping of a flower's stem, Frost manages to convey the ominous upheaval of the entire ecology. War's poison spreads over hill and pasture like a creeping fog. The starkest horrors to be unleashed by man's picking the lock on Pandora's box eluded Frost or lay beyond him on a road not taken. By choice or disposition, he no more than hinted at the cosmic scope of the ruination upon which man seemed bent. To deal adequately with the Frankenstein aspects of the contemporary scene, someone of Robinson Jeffers's stamp was needed. Someone else—not Frost—would have to hold before men's eyes the specter of a universe hurling itself into flaming extinction, not requiring any help from the human race to accelerate the process, but perversely being given a hand nevertheless toward the end.

Only in his later years, past the chronological age of ordinary retirement, when the vision of nuclear holocaust was inescapable, did Frost take up the challenge on a global scale. Then, almost as a valedictory, he published his handful of poems on the post-Hiroshima world. "Sarcastic Science" and her "complacent ministry of fear" were addressed. He used his satiric pen, the one that required only a simple twist to be turned on its knife-edge for verses like "U.S. 1946 King's X," "Bursting Rapture," "The Planners," and "Why Wait For Science."

But it was too late now to play a new part, and Frost was too old to become Cassandra. He could only try. The night sky over the plot of earth he had chosen to tend was still the sky where "showers of charted meteors let fly," not intercontinental ballistic missiles. Frost's eyes were set only for watching to see whether that small sailing cloud—not an Apollo rocket—would hit or miss the moon.

## God Speaks at the End

When Frost considers individual frustrations and joys, or when he writes of his "lover's quarrel with the world," he does not hesitate to probe deeply and offer explicit statements of his findings. But as he approaches the boundary between things of this world and the next, that thin line "beyond which God is," his approach is more timorous. Many who have noticed the poet's hesitance at dealing with the larger mysteries cite his habit of averting his eyes or of withdrawing before he has reached out far or in deep.

It must be assumed that Frost is not a cosmic poet in the same sense as Whitman was. He does not aggressively embrace the whole of creation, including its Creator, lips pressed against the bosom of existence. Nor does he, like Emily Dickinson, dwell upon the next life until it overpowers man's life on earth and transforms the imponderable into the tangible here and now. At the same time, he does not ignore final queries, even though his direct gaze is upon the terrestrial shadows of eternity, not upon eternity itself.

The body of Frost's nature poetry contains decipherable dimensions beyond physical nature. He can show his willingness to question life's meaning outright:

> The universe may or may not be very immense.
> As a matter of fact there are times when I am apt
> To feel it close in tight against my sense
> Like a caul in which I was born and still am wrapped. [12]

Still this direct approach is not typical of the poet. He is much more apt to approach his topic obliquely rather than head-on, through symbolism rather than concept, by hinting rather than by saying, and with a question rather than a statement.

## Out for Stars

Among the traditional symbols employed by Frost to depict his thoughts on the eternal, his reliance upon stars stands out. Stars figure prominently in his poetry, either as centers of interest or as background. *The Poetry* is quite literally a star-ridden book. These are the lights that brighten the black desert spaces of the sky like street lamps, the stars whose unchanging courses impress the sense of never-ending serenity upon a man who looks up by chance at the constellations. They are "old skymarks in the blue" whose friendly constancy can be relied upon as a palliative against the "shocks and changes" of earth.

In choosing something like a star to place their faith in, mortals gain an antidote for earth's excesses. Some go mad for stars. Not content to view them with the naked eye, they must approach a more perfect vision:

> I knew a man who failing as a farmer
> Burned down his farmhouse for the fire insurance,
> And spent the proceeds on a telescope
> To satisfy a life-long curiosity
> About our place among the infinities.[13]

And when the arsonist has collected his six hundred dollars insurance money and squandered it on a star-splitting telescope, he spends his evenings searching up its brass barrel at the sky. What more does he discover?

> We've looked and looked, but after all where are we?
> Do we know any better where we are
> And how it stands between the night tonight
> And a man with a smoky lantern chimney?
> How different from the way it ever stood?[14]

Frost's reply is, of course, that man doesn't know any better where he is. He can't. Bound by the globe, with his feet planted in soil, he cannot approach the stars closely enough. The telescope brings him more proximity than the birch tree brings the boy who likes to climb toward heaven on its branches and then swoop back down again; but the telescope is not a final answer. Even a zoomar lens would not land man near enough to see what he hungers after.

## Dust of Snow

If human beings can do no more than stand under the light of the stars and reverence them almost to the point of prayer, the stars do sometimes visit the earth. They come in "showers of charted meteors," flashing through the black to bury themselves in a field, a road, a tree. But in the process of abandoning their own natural zone, they lose their luster. On earth they exist as stony ash. They speed downward "dark and lifeless from an interrupted arc," unfit to inspire. If found at all, they are good for loading into a boat for building walls. Even then, however, the star retains some faint hint of its former glory:

> Such as it is, it promises the prize
> Of the one world complete in any size
> That I am like to compass, fool or wise.[15]

The stars that disarm the darkness of the unknown sky are unable to make passage. They cannot carry their message unburnt to men. But another element can and does—the stars of snow which are forever drifting down like psalms into Frost's world. Falling from the same source as stars, they blanket the earth and obliterate darkness with their white tide:

> In the thick of a teeming snowfall
> I saw my shadow on snow.
> I turned and looked back up at the sky,
> Where we still look to ask the why
> Of everything below.[16]

On Frost's continent all seasons lead out from winter. Autumn is merely its herald; spring is full of winter memories; and midsummer is practically nonexistent. The poems could not exist without winter and its flood of white snow, that paradoxical life-in-death without which spring can never awaken. "The Trial by Existence" clarifies the religious connotations of this snow:

> The light of heaven falls whole and white
>     And is not shattered into dyes,
> The light forever is morning light;
>     The hills are verdured pasture-wise;
> The angel hosts with freshness go,
>     And seek with laughter what to brave;—
> And binding all is the hushed snow
>     Of the far-distant breaking wave.

## Spring Pools

Snow then partakes of "the light of heaven" as fully as the stars. And that same light appears in a third form. The water that runs in brooks or stands in gem-like pools reflects fragments of blue from the sky. It quenches the thirst, but is far more precious. Like the snow, it derives from the great Reply to man's inquiry; but, like the snow, it gives no final answer itself but provides only the next best thing: continual reassurance. Even if buried in the darkness of the forest, spring pools manage to reflect somehow "the total sky almost without defect."

West-Running Brook carries a slight backward wave running counter to the slope of its hill, "the tribute of the current to the course." Man aspires to the source of life, but he cannot attain it any more than he can reach his star. He can become "too anxious for rivers," just as he can become too ravenous for stars or snow. But even one too eager can sometimes arrive tantalizingly close to success, as the poet explains in "For Once, Then, Something." In the habit of kneeling at wells to peer down and discern whatever is to be found, he has always been, as he puts it, "wrong to the light." The water yields not its secret, but the mirrored image of himself:

> *Once,* when trying with chin against a well-curb
> I discerned, as I thought, beyond the picture,
> Through the picture, a something white, uncertain,
> Something more of the depths—and then I lost it.
> Water came to rebuke the too clear water.
> One drop fell from a fern, and lo, a ripple
> Shook whatever it was lay there at bottom,
> Blurred it, blotted it out. What was that whiteness?
> Truth? A pebble of quartz? For once, then, something.

Something, a glimpse through the veil, provides. It is enough to sustain hope.

## The Enormous Outer Black

In star, snow, and water man locates scraps of heaven's light. He clings tenaciously to them, as reluctant to let them pass as the old woman in "The Night Light" resists extinguishing her lamp—and for the same reason:

> She always had to burn a light
> Beside her attic bed at night.
> It gave bad dreams and broken sleep,
> But helped the Lord her soul to keep.

> Good gloom on her was thrown away.
> It is on me by night or day,
> Who have, as I suppose, ahead
> The darkest of it still to dread.

Enveloped in darkness which threatens to close in tightly, engulfing him, man must have some candle, however small and meager, to burn against the black. Lights provide security to push back the terror. They furnish knowledge to dissipate fear—to give the faint hope of eternity which subdues apprehension.

That an "enormous Outer Black" exists to make light essential is evident throughout the range of his poetry. At many times and in many places he has observed the night make threatening gestures. He has watched dark waters of the sea batter the cliffs of man's continent "as if a night of dark intent was coming." He has seen a woman driven mad with fear by the night brushing tree-fingers across her windowpane. He has followed an apple-picker overcome by twilight and discerned an appalling "design of darkness" even in a pure white scene, where an albino spider, moth, and flower combine "like the ingredients of a witches' broth."

The predominant image of darkness recurs like a major theme against which all else is variation. Dark woods, mixing fear and desire, typify the great concern of man for knowledge of the unknown that awaits him. Dark woods, full of mystery and promise, draw man like a filing to the magnet. They do their best to suck him in. He can only plant his feet in resistance, wanting all the while to enter but in mortal terror of setting a single toe past the forest's rim.

For fifty years this pattern repeats itself in poems which at times are so similar that they read like variants. The very first verse of Frost's first book recounts this wish to enter the woods, "into my own":

> One of my wishes is that those dark trees,
> So old and firm they scarcely show the breeze,
> Were not, as 'twere, the merest mask of gloom,
> But stretched away unto the edge of doom.
>
> I should not be withheld but that some day
> Into their vastness I should steal away,
> Fearless of ever finding open land,
> Or highway where the slow wheel pours the sand.

"A Dream Pang," also in *A Boy's Will,* tells of the wanderer in a dream who came to the forest edge, looked and pondered, "but did not enter, though the wish was strong."

"Stopping by Woods on a Snowy Evening" in *New Hampshire,* the most expert of all versions of the enticements of the dark woods, again looks upon a traveler mesmerized by the black trees yet unwilling to enter. This time, with his "promises to keep," the traveler has a ready rationalization for withstanding the bait. In *A Further Range,* "Desert Places" reproduces a scene almost identical to "Stopping by Woods":

> Snow falling and night falling fast, oh, fast
> In a field I looked into going past,
> And the ground almost covered in snow,
> But a few weeds and stubble showing last.
>
> The woods around it have it—it is theirs.
> All animals are smothered in their lairs.
> I am too absent-spirited to count;
> The loneliness includes me unawares.

This time the traveler feels no need to enter the black woods. Accustomed to contemplation of the "empty spaces between stars," he has already passed far beyond the mere echo of outer blackness which the woods represent. He does not need them to scare him. "Come In" adds emphasis to the inviting quality of the forest's "pillared dark." Dusk has fallen. Thrush music beckons from the branches, even though it is too dark in the woods for birds:

> Almost like a call to come in
> To the dark and lament.
>
> But no, I was out for stars:
> I would not come in.

It happens too often for coincidence that Frost's forest images carry light as an antidote—the blue sky, snow, water, or the stars. And in his last treatment of this theme, in the title poem of his final volume, *In The Clearing,* the human beings living in the woods possess two means of protection against hazard: lamp and clearing. The lamp is lit against the dark, but it is the clearing that provides the greater security:

> They've been here long enough
> To push the woods back from around the house
> And part them in the middle with a path. . . .
> All they maintain the path for is the comfort
> Of visiting with the equally bewildered.
> Nearer in plight their neighbors are than distance.

In his poems Frost never enters these dark woods, although his life was spent approaching them and peering in as far as human eyes can see. This is not far or deep enough to return with any secrets found.

Critics are quite correct in noticing that while Robert Frost steps up shoulder to shoulder with the final questions, he invariably withdraws, veers off on a tangent, or changes the subject. There is a reason, and a good one, for doing so. He has no answer to the greatest query. Death remains the undiscovered country from whose bourne no traveler returns.[17]

In his honesty, Frost the seer penetrated only as far as he was able. He was too honest either to deny the existence of the dark woods or to ignore its appeal. He was too honest also to affirm a solution to a puzzle he felt no human can solve and still be flesh and blood. In 1963 his opportunity came, and he did enter the woods, bound away "for the outer dark," promising whimsically to return if dissatisfied with what the forest had to offer.

# Chapter Six

# Testing Greatness: Frost's Critical Reception

During his eighty-eight years, Robert Frost became the most read and honored American poet of the twentieth century. It is no exaggeration to suggest that in the final years of life he was known to millions and regarded not only as something of a national celebrity—a role he cherished—but as a great natural resource, an American institution; surely he was the best-loved American poet since the day of Henry Wadsworth Longfellow. Few writers have maintained a steadier claim upon the attention of reviewers, students, critics, scholars, and biographers. Since 1913 the appreciation and evaluation of his poetry has consistently gone forward, always gaining momentum, and to judge from the numbers of articles and books which appear annually, America's interest in Robert Frost and his verse will continue to increase for some time to come. The possibility of mastering Frost criticism is rapidly slipping beyond the ability of any but the specialist; however, the general student of Frost will benefit from knowing at least the outlines of that criticism and its history.

## Discovering Frost, 1913–1920

"Whatever you do," wrote Robert Frost to his daughter Lesley when she was invited to speak on modern poetry in 1934, "do Pound justice as the great original."[1] It was Ezra Pound, after all, who discovered Frost in London in 1913 and brought him belatedly to the attention of America, and it is fitting that a survey of Frost criticism should begin with Pound and his review of this "Vurry Amur'kin" fellow's *A Boy's Will*, sent to Harriet Monroe for the pages of *Poetry*. Both Pound and Amy Lowell, who also came upon Frost in London during his brief expatriatism, took it upon themselves to convey the happy news of their discovery to their countrymen. With such help Frost quickly caught on at home and congratulatory notices soon cropped up on all sides as his first two books appeared in American printings. In *The Dial* William Morton Payne's response was typical; he expressed his admiration for the "simple phrasing and patient sincerity" of Frost's poems and compared his achievement to that of A. E. Housman's popular book *A Shropshire Lad*.[2] Another reviewer, Sylvester Baxter, depicted Frost upon his return to America as being ready to go back to farming the "beloved soil" of his New Hampshire and helped to set in motion the myth of Robert Frost as a paragon without blemish: "a winsome personality, unassuming but not shy . . . well built; a finely modeled head, mobile features and sensitive, dark brown hair of youthful abundance . . . expressive blue eyes, tinged with a lightness as of summer mist at dawn."[3] Nothing here to suggest imperfection, surely. This romantic image would swell in proportion during the bulk of Frost's career; eventually it would so possess the minds of Frost's admirers that it would inhibit possibilities for viewing the writer whole.

The earliest notices of Frost's work, published by British critics during his 1913 debut, had been mixed in their evaluations. But the American criticism published during the first years of Frost's prominence was dominated by the sense of glad discovery which had been established by Pound, Lowell, Baxter, and others in the vanguard. The words *new, American,* and *New England*—either alone or as combined by Sylvester Baxter in his title "New England's New Poet"—became something of overnight clichés, easy handles for reviewers to attach to their notices. Actually, Frost's American reception mirrored the times, for by 1915, during the unprecedented upsurge of enthusiasm for the New Poetry, most emergent poets could count upon being greeted warmly (although holding one's lead against the latest genius to be discovered might take some doing). If America in those years of the first World War was perceived by her somewhat insular citizens as a noble and altruistic land motivated by idealism, then Robert Frost rather quickly came to embody all good qualities for a people who would have it no other way. The tenor of his American reception after 1915 can be summed up by the titles given prominent appreciations during the years following his debut: "The Neighborliness of Robert Frost," "The Sincerity of Robert Frost," "Robert Frost: Good Greek out of New England."

The first serious evaluation of Frost to appear in book format was that offered by Amy Lowell. Her *Tendencies in Modern American Poetry* (1917) recognized the modern movement as an accomplished fact and identified six poets as being worthy of individual attention: E. A. Robinson, Edgar Lee Masters, Carl Sandburg, H. D. (Hilda Doolittle), John Gould Fletcher, and Frost. Among these six, the relative preeminence of Robert Frost was signified by his being discussed in a separate chapter. The others, except for Robinson, were considered in groups. The Lowell evaluation of Frost's verse is now thought by many to be wrongheaded, and surely it is marred by biographical errors (many of these occurred because Frost withheld the data she had requested). But Amy Lowell's chapter on Frost and his work is notable in accepting him as an established figure—more than that, as a major American poet whose verse is deserving of the most serious consideration.

In writing of Frost's tragic sense (which she felt to be overly obsessive) and the quality of disillusionment that touched so much of his work, Miss Lowell introduced topics that would not be dealt with easily by other commentators for decades to come. Hers was the first important criticism to imply that the emerging Frost myth—the happy, cheer-bearing farmer—might be one-sided. To her the poet seemed to betray a weakness of breadth by limiting his subject matter to the tiny canvas of New England. She was not entirely correct, of course, as Frost's later achievements would establish, and yet her apprehensions were justified in the context of the three books that Frost had so far published. Readers of a later day may disagree with her judgment that Frost in 1917 had touched the limits of his growth, but they will be hard pressed to deny the incisive understanding which led Miss Lowell to declare that *North of Boston* is "a very sad book . . . [which] in spite of its author's sympathetic touch . . . reveals a disease that is eating into the vitals of our New England life, at least in its rural communities."[4] Lowell's remains the first effort at a balanced evaluation of Frost's strengths and flaws. In all it remains a generous tribute from a fellow poet.

In 1919 Louis Untermeyer, then and always a booster of Frost, gave his friend the lead chapter in his *New Era in American Poetry*, which was the first volume to be designed as a comprehensive survey of the modern verse movement. Untermeyer centered his praise upon Frost's unique powers of concentration and language, and he singled out the dramatic poems from *North of Boston* as the most powerful and authentic of their kind to have come out of America. In Frost more than in any other poet of the day Untermeyer found a modern expression of the "poetic feeling for ordinary life" which was Walt Whitman's bequest to his countrymen.[5] Untermeyer's essay is essentially a paean to a new-found idol. Even so, and while he lavishes his praise upon individual Frost poems, Untermeyer remains sufficiently discerning to hint (with phrases such as "seeming simplicity" and "apparently inconsequential") that something deeper, more complex and paradoxical is restive beneath the calm surfaces of these poems which then were attracting admirers on every side.

The years between 1913 and 1920 were devoted to introducing Robert Frost to the reading public and to establishing him as a major voice in American poetry. In three volumes rapidly published, *North of Boston* (1915), *A Boy's Will* (1915), and *Mountain Interval* (1916), Frost's work was placed before readers and simultaneously boomed by friendly reviewers in a campaign which Frost himself often directed from the wings. Upon his return to America from London, Frost had expressed his own private fears that he might lack staying power.[6] He recognized that his first books had been composed of verses backlogged from earlier, less receptive times, or else written under the pleasant stimulus of having one book out successfully and his British publisher eager for another. His apprehension that the poems he would produce following his auspicious debut might prove to be anticlimactic was shared by others, and that fear was not wholly allayed by the appearance of *Mountain Interval* or, indeed, even in later times, for the poet never again produced a volume as consistently fine as *North of Boston*. *Mountain Interval* did prove, however—and what is more, to Frost himself—that the poet was no flash-in-the-pan. He had not lost his magic, and upon occasion he could surpass the best of his earlier efforts. This knowledge, coupled with lavish praise on the critical front, served to bolster the poet's belief in himself and to renew the inner confidence that had sustained him while undertaking his English venture in 1912.

## Flush Times, 1920–1930

The 1920s proved to be boom years for Robert Frost. His service as Poet-in-Residence/Fellow in Creative Arts at the University of Michigan from 1921 to 1923 and his subsequent professorship at Amherst were but two of the prominent academic posts that enhanced his prestige and widened his visibility. Reading tours took him to far parts of the nation, enlarging his already considerable audience through the display of his winning personality in public recitations and lectures. He possessed great charm and he learned how best to use it; as Lawrance Thompson has put it, "his platform name dramatized his ideal image of how he wanted to be viewed."[7] Following Frost's Pulitzer Prize for *New Hampshire* in 1923, no doubt existed that any serious study of American poetry must consider his achievement.

Critics now built upon the foundation that had been established prior to 1920. While little that was truly new was introduced into the study of Frost, the myth of the poet as a genial farmer-philosopher grew more pervasive. A minor strain of criticism recalled Amy Lowell's judgment, which had been followed by Waldo Frank's depiction of Frost's universe as "starved" and "sick,"[8] and by Bruce Weirick's suggestion that Frost's poetry (along with Edwin Arlington Robinson's) was dominated by "a note of futility rather than any great national or spiritual hope." Weirick saw Frost as retiring "into a seclusion of homely rural nature" where life has "lost its opulence." This to him seemed clearly the message conveyed by Frost's poetry overall, even though it was clear that Frost's lyrics at times commanded an idyllic sense of beauty: "Suddenly into the tumult of the scene there slips a calm. The sky breaks open and a flood of peace for a moment possesses the narrative."[9] To these voices Clement Wood added his depiction of Frost as the laureate of the "dimming" world of New England, a "sad-eyed" man who wrote of sad people, sad lives.[10]

But these reservations were overwhelmed by more sanguine views. The majority of critics, preferring to emphasize the happy Frost personality, harkened back to Sylvester Baxter's description of him as one of the most endearing men in the world. Percy Boynton, who had no way of knowing in 1924 the extent to which the poet had labored to establish himself in the literary world, saw Frost as a man determined to live "relaxed and unhurried," one who almost always preferred to work with his hands than to write. As evidence, he pointed to the tardy beginning of Frost's career, which to him indicated that Frost had been preoccupied with other concerns during his first forty years. He cited also the fact that seven years had passed between *Mountain Interval* and Frost's next volume, an infrequency of publication which had led many to believe him "not really a poet, but only a man who writes poetry."[11] It was a fine distinction, perhaps, but one which suggested that Frost's rustic persona was perhaps succeeding only too well.

For Carl Van Doren the word *Yankee* became the key to Frost's character and writing alike. He advised his readers that one might properly disregard the fact of the poet's California birth and childhood, because "New England was in his blood," seeded there by generations of forebears. That dormant blood strain eventually drew the man back to his native habitat, a true Yankee, son of the soil, willing to work with what tools he possessed upon those homely materials lying close at hand. All the best Yankee traits were his: he was properly individualistic, and his attitude was utilitarian, as befitted a "rustic" of the Yankee stamp. Neither cynic nor philanthropist, Frost trod the middle ground of the highly aware neighbor, his speech and his poetry alike conforming to the voice of reason which was the voice of New England.[12] Without question, Van Doren spoke for many.

Elizabeth Shepley Sergeant, who later would write a fine biography of Frost, imagined him as the *genius loci* of New England, a genial and somewhat puckish creature who, if one were lucky, might surprise a watcher by poking his head up from behind any New Hampshire blueberry bush or mountain boulder. His face was the mirror of his virtues. He might best be rendered in stone by the ancient sculptor Skopas "who added shadows of human passion to calm Greek faces." Sergeant was struck by Frost's "musing eyes" and thought his brow resembled Dante's. Observing him on his fiftieth birthday celebration, she perceived him "shining with a clear Renaissance beauty of the Christian sort." She believed that he ought to have wrapped himself in a white Dominican robe because "he carried almost visibly the consecration and weight of his ascetic priesthood."[13]

With the Frost reputation as a gentle, kind, and wise soul becoming ever more firmly lodged in the national consciousness, greater attention began to be paid to his biography and to discussion of his range in verse technique. Readers who had come to love the poet's verses were eager to learn more about Frost the man and to be guided toward a definition of his work. Most beneficial of all to Frost's overriding wish for permanence was the pronounced movement toward a fresh perception, one which saw him as less parochial than had been supposed. Critics now began to speak of his New England connections as being less constraining; happily, he was not as limited as had been feared, but could speak of life from a more universal vantage point. Geography proved to be no barrier. New England might dominate the surfaces of Frost's poems, but his appealing verses were appreciated equally in the South and throughout the great West. The image of Robert Frost as a national poet, as opposed to a regional figure, began to emerge more clearly. Acceptance on that wider landscape was crucial to Frost's expanding fame. In critical reviews by 1929 his identity as "Poet" was considerably less likely than in 1920 to be accompanied by the modifier "of New England."

No small part in the dissemination of Frost's poetry and the concurrent fostering of his reputation was played by the anthologies which carried the message of the new verse far beyond the restricted clientele for individual volumes of poetry. The influence of two extremely popular and widely circulated anthologies should be credited, Harriet Monroe's *The New Poetry* and Louis Untermeyer's *Modern American Poetry*. From her influential editorial post in Chicago, Miss Monroe was in a better position than anyone in America to comprehend the full extent of the ferment in verse across the continent. Some of the new poets—Carl Sandburg and Vachel Lindsay were the chief examples— had been her personal discoveries, and dozens of the others had appeared at one time or another in the pages of *Poetry*. In the first edition of her comprehensive anthology, edited in collaboration with Alice Corbin Henderson, Robert Frost was represented by seven poems.[14] Even today that edition provides a reader with a quite respectable sampling of the early modern movement in America, and very few later anthologies have managed to equal the breadth and depth of the major revision of 1923, in which Frost's group of poems was increased to sixteen, including the five verses that constitute "The Hill Wife."

Untermeyer in the modest five-page preface to his slender first edition of *Modern American Poetry*[15] paid a balanced tribute to the current pacesetters. He restricted his praise of Frost—by now a close and good friend—to a pair of sentences: "Notice, for instance, in the direct but fully-flavored blank verse of Robert Frost, how the words are so chosen and arranged that the speaker is almost heard on the printed page. Observe how, beneath these native sounds, we hear the accents of his people walking the New England farms and hillsides."[16] In 1919 four poems served to represent Frost's output to date: "Mending Wall," "The Tuft of Flowers," "Birches," and "The Road Not Taken." All of these remain standard anthology pieces to the present day. *Modern American Poetry* underwent rapid and continuous revision. By 1921 it had burgeoned from 165 pages to nearly 400. Its new preface occupied thirty-one pages, two of them devoted solely to Robert Frost, whose representation doubled to eight poems although he had not published another book of verse in the interim. Whereas in 1919 Untermeyer had scrupulously avoided comparisons, three years later he made them with confidence, and always they were made to Frost's advantage, particularly over Edgar Lee Masters, whose potential for rivalry Frost especially feared. In the revision of 1925, a volume whose weighty 600 pages testified to the impressive establishment of the New Poetry, Frost improved his position still further; in six years his representation in *Modern American Poetry* had nearly quadrupled. Yet that growth was not at all out of line with the soaring increase in his national reputation.

The certification of Frost's poetic stature by both the Monroe-Henderson and the Untermeyer anthologies reached tens of thousands of readers both in and out of classrooms. The books became the poetic bibles of uncounted study groups which sprang up in cities coast to coast. The 1920s were flush times for American verse, and for Robert Frost they verged upon the unbelievable. By the time the decade ended in the Wall Street Crash of 1929, he had become the most appreciated poet in the nation, and his career was about to culminate in his *Collected Poems,* for which he would be awarded a second Pulitzer Prize.

## Years of Trial, 1930–1940

The principal literary effect of the financial debacle of 1929 was the resurgence of politics as a legitimate hallmark in judging writers and their works. The 1920s had fostered a spirit of unbridled individualism and experimentation in which Frost had prospered, but it was inevitable now that, given new and radically different times, Frost would suffer in company with others who had written without heed of political considerations. After 1930, more than one literary career came to grief either temporarily or permanently under the pressures placed upon the lyric strain by the Marxist critics, for whom activism and a strong social thesis were not only valid criteria but often became the sole determinants of worth in literature.

The conscious effort to topple Robert Frost from his pedestal began in timely fashion with reviews of *Collected Poems*. Granville Hicks, a major Marxist spokesman, attacked Frost first in the pages of *New Republic*[17]; and later, in his revisionist literary study *The Great Tradition* (1933), he did his utmost to establish the total irrelevance of Frost's poems to those for whom communism seemed the only logical solution for a battered capitalist society apparently on the brink of economic and political collapse. "One can scarcely think of any writer commonly recognized as great," wrote Hicks, "who did not immerse himself in the life of the times, who did not concern himself with the problems of his age," and among these "greats" he emphatically did not include Robert Frost.[18]

In having elected to emphasize rather than to soften his identification with New Hampshire and, further, to concentrate upon special aspects which ignored such phenomena as modern factory towns and state politics, Robert Frost was more vulnerable than many others to criticism from the political left. His work was now perceived by the politically oriented only within the narrow limits permitted by their ideologies, and he was criticized severely, called not only unrepresentative of American life but fully as "moribund" as the vanished way of life that his poems were accused of espousing. Where, inquired Hicks and others, could one find anywhere in Frost's poems the least inkling of the automobiles, radios, mechanics, or shopgirls who pervaded contemporary New England? In support of Hicks, Frederic I. Carpenter delivered an even more stinging rebuke in *New England Quarterly*, comparing Frost with Whitman, Stephen Vincent Benet, and E. A. Robinson, and finding him seriously deficient in imaginative scope.[19]

Critical derogation of Frost accelerated noticeably following his Pulitzer Prize for *A Further Range* (1936), in which for the first time Frost published verse that made overt his conservative political stance. Typically the charges against Frost appeared in magazines such as *New Republic, Nation, New Masses,* and *Partisan Review,* whose literary pages were dominated by critics with a perceptible leftist tilt. Such commentators were prone to suggest that Frost's political sense equalled that of Calvin Coolidge ("The business of America is Business"); Frost's poetry was lumped with the doggerel verses of Edgar A. Guest, the popular newspaper rhymer. But even Frost's staunchest admirers took small pleasure from the poet's venture into the current political scene with its clash of ideologies. In *New England Quarterly* Dudley Fitts judged poems such as "Build Soil" faded in diction, imprecise in expression, and uneasy in tone, and he felt obliged to apply the words *ineffectual* and *sterile* to his evaluation of Frost's most recent efforts.[20]

It might be anticipated that unrestrained jabbing at Robert Frost would call forth an equally vigorous defense from his supporters. The most notable essay in that rebuttal arrived in the form of an infuriated piece written by Bernard DeVoto for *Saturday Review of Literature*.[21] To be defended vehemently was balm for Frost's battered ego, to be sure, but the most far-reaching effect of the critical fray between 1930 and 1940 was to establish the principle that variant schools of thought concerning Robert Frost might legitimately coexist. This was a salutary development. To proceed further upon the older basis of unquestioning admiration which had characterized the Frost reception through 1929, teetering forever on the brink of sentimentality, was unhealthy for Frost's reputation long-term. Somewhere along the line a turnabout was inevitable. A balance had to be struck, and to lay open the poet's weaknesses as the Marxists had done suggested that Frost's adherents must come up with truly persuasive arguments if they were to renew their claim for his greatness. By 1940 it was abundantly clear that while the opening years of Frost's career had been devoted to achieving his acceptance and the 1920s to widespread appreciation and a continuing effort toward defining his contribution, then the Depression decade had opened a new phase of serious evaluation. At issue now was the relative permanence of Frost's role in literary history.

The first important volume designed specifically to counter the negative critics and support the contention that Robert Frost not only had achieved major stature but also was a writer whose reputation would endure was conceived in the mid-1930s. *Recognition of Robert Frost,* edited by Richard Thornton, appeared upon the twenty-fifth anniversary of the publication of *A Boy's Will.*[22] This retrospective collection of reviews and essays offered a sampler of opinion published in America, England, and on the Continent over the preceding quarter century. Works by a formidable array of critics, beginning with the early estimates by Amy Lowell, Ezra Pound, and William Dean

Howells, were gathered. Most important commentators of the 1920s were well represented, among them Sidney Cox, Louis Untermeyer, T. K. Whipple, Alfred Kreymborg, Llewellyn Jones, and Ludwig Lewisohn. The volume concluded by reprinting the four prefaces that had been written for the 1936 British edition of Frost's *Selected Poems* by W. H. Auden, C. Day Lewis, Paul Engle, and Edwin Muir.

*Recognition* was in no sense an effort to present a "balanced" verdict on Robert Frost. Conspicuously absent from the collection were any of the recent and hostile remarks printed by Frost detractors Horace Gregory, Richard Blackmur, Newton Arvin, and Granville Hicks. Such a lapse might be anticipated in a celebratory volume which was issued by Henry Holt and Company, Frost's publisher since 1915, one to which Frost himself referred candidly (but in private) as "their book advertising me." Against Frost's hunger for praise must be placed his own speculation that in a volume as supposedly comprehensive as *Recognition*, perhaps Henry Holt "should have gone the rest of the way and included a fair proportion of the out-and-out hostile in my criticism."[23] Something of the complexity of the man emerges when it is learned that Frost himself played a major role in bringing *Recognition* into being, not only approving the works to be included but himself drawing up both the plan for the book and its preliminary table of contents. He also suggested the book's title.[24] All this aside, however, *Recognition* succeeds admirably in its purpose. Despite its having long since been superseded in substance by later studies and collections, it remains a valuable introduction to the poet and his work.

## Times of Triumph, 1940–1960

Having survived the turmoil of the 1930s with his readership undiminished, Robert Frost saw his public reputation widen and grow ever more secure, while his honors, including a fourth Pulitzer Prize for *A Witness Tree* (1942) accumulated further. Critical evaluation proceeded on the more healthful double-tier structure established during the 1930s. In 1942 Lawrance Thompson, who had already agreed to become Frost's biographer, published his *Fire and Ice*, the first scholarly attempt to place Frost and his poetry solidly within the long tradition of English-language verse, both in theory and form. Finding metaphor in its many guises to be the key to Frost's creative principle, Thompson examined rigorously its use in Frost's dramatic narratives, lyrics, and satires, and made an admirable attempt to define the poet's philosophy of art and life.[25]

In comparison to the flood of encomium which now greeted Frost's every public appearance on the platform or in print, the negative strain was muted; but it gained in credence from being tied less directly to ideologies of the moment. Serious dissent to prevailing views of Frost continued to find expression, notably by Malcolm Cowley. In his two-part essay, "The Case Against Mr. Frost,"[26] Cowley questioned whether Frost could properly be called a complete or even a suitable representative of the New England tradition, particularly when the history of liberal thought inherent in that tradition was considered. He maintained, for instance, that little could be found in Frost's poems to remind one of Emerson's attempt to reform society through reforming the individual. For Cowley, Frost appeared to be trapped in an unfortunate "hands off" attitude toward change, while his eyes remained fixed upon the irrecoverable past. Strongly liberal himself and proceeding on the thesis that recommendations for social action (which Frost avoided) are incumbent upon a poet who aspires to greatness, Cowley suggested that one secret of Frost's large and devoted following might lie in the conservatism of his audience, retreating for reassurance behind the poet as behind a kindly bulwark of the status quo.

For much the same reasons as Cowley, Frost's fellow poet Louise Bogan had little good to report of him while summarizing the modern movement in her *Achievement in American Poetry 1900–1950*.[27] Harold H. Watts and Yvor Winters in major articles carried the argument further.[28] Both critics concluded that Frost, however interestingly he may have explored the universal experiences of human beings, had failed to deal pertinently with the man-society relationship. Later, Roy Harvey Pearce in *Kenyon Review* elaborated upon the proposition that Frost's chief flaw resided in his renunciation of the modern in favor of an older, simpler, and more cheerful way of life.[29] The damaging charge that Frost at heart was a poet of nostalgia would necessarily receive serious consideration as the passage of time made obvious the poet's reluctance—or his inability—to delve directly and deeply into issues concerning his own time and place.

Offsetting these reservations, which always represented a minority view, a multitude of major essays appeared during the latter years of Frost's career, thoughtful and scholarly works by writers whose judgments could be based upon all but Frost's final efforts. The common purposes of these later critics were: (1) to enlarge the reader's understanding of individual poems; (2) to distinguish among the important thematic strands running throughout Frost's total work; (3) to analyze Frost's use of literary devices and symbols; (4) to clarify Frost's relationship to other writers in the Anglo-American tradition; and (5) to evaluate Frost's craftsmanship in verse. A good many, though far from all, of these writers are represented in James Cox's *Robert Frost: A Collection of Critical Essays,*[30] which aims to present the cream of critical thinking regarding Frost up to 1960. In making his selections, Cox has taken pains to represent all dominant strains of criticism, balancing detractors such as Malcolm Cowley and Yvor Winters with admirers such as Randall Jarrell and Lawrance Thompson. Given the responsible nature of the critics who are represented and the importance of the lines of thought they pursue, the Cox collection remains of permanent worth to Frost students.

As Robert Frost's life neared its close, friends of long standing began to publish evaluations based upon their personal acquaintance with the poet. Chief among these was Reginald L. Cook, in whose *Dimensions of Robert Frost* the poet's work is linked at every point with his personality. Far from apologizing for his subjectivity, Cook allows it to stand as a central virtue of his discussion. Thus, Cook's Frost is a man shaped by the Victorian age in which he was raised, and the "high, purposeful optimism" of that time dominates the ethics of the personality whom Cook knew and visited with over a span of thirty years. The farmer-poet image which multitudes of Frost's readers bore so fondly in their minds is found here writ large, an amiable fellow whose sterling qualities include friendliness, cheer, cordiality, warmth, courage, and independence, and whose passion for truth is matched by his sense of humor: all good things and all to be found abundantly throughout the verses of *Complete Poems* as well.

"There is no pose, no pretentiousness, no mask" in Cook's Frost.[31] The poet's outward appearance tallies absolutely with his inner traits: strong of arm, full of chest, rugged of build, and honest of eye—the relaxed and highly physical presence of a master workman so infinitely secure in his craft that he can afford to be generous. Given this image of Frost, the man and the New Englander—for Cook the two are one— the reader must be prepared, in a discussion of organicism, for instance, to be informed of the organic within the man as well as the organic within the poems. And when Cook reports that Frost's dominant theme is affirmation, one cannot truly plead surprise when he hears that the glad spirit of the verse derives directly from Frost's temperament: "There is no backdown in the man; there is no half-heartedness in the poetry."[32] What Cook has to say of the poems themselves will probably, in time, fade away, but his portrait of Frost the man, though controversial, is a permanent contribution to a popular and continuing point of view.

In much the same vein as Cook's *Dimensions* are the memoirs of Frost's friend Sidney Cox. In 1929 Cox had offered a brief and tentative portrait, *Robert Frost: Original "Ordinary Man,"* a rather idealized portrait which served to strengthen the current myth of Frost as a paragon in both the personal and artistic spheres; a Frost, Donald Greiner suggests, who stood "just this side of sainthood."[33] Cox's worshipful attitude is repeated in his later expansion of that memoir, *A Swinger of Birches,*[34] in which numerous anecdotes are added as well as direct quotations taken down during his association with Frost.

A pair of book-length appraisals which first appeared in 1960 sum up two major strands of Frost criticism. The first is George W. Nitchie's *Human Values in the Poetry of Robert Frost,* which concentrates upon Frost's central theme, the man-nature relationship. Nitchie argues that Frost, probably deliberately, avoids deep probing of this complex topic, and restricts himself instead to the simpler, easier task of describing human reactions to natural phenomena. The prospect that the world around us may be discovered to possess some final and illuminative "meaning" is avoided by Frost in favor of treating nature as an incomprehensible force, and this stance, for Nitchie, reveals a serious weakness. When placed alongside an Emerson, a Wordsworth, or even a Robinson Jeffers, in all of whose work nature's ultimate purpose (whether for good or for evil) is clearly delineated, Frost's stature dwindles.[35]

John F. Lynen's *The Pastoral Art of Robert Frost* offers a rather different interpretation of Frost's use of nature. Lynen sees Frost, not as a rustic, certainly, nor as the practicing farmer who inhabits the surface of the poetry, but rather as a sophisticated artist who consciously adopts the pastoral mode and uses rural New England symbolically, making of it a metaphor through which the problems confronting man may be approached, albeit obliquely. In perceiving a virtue where others had seen a flaw, Lynen explains that Frost, despite appearances, really is less concerned with surfaces than with attitudes, points of view. This always-concealed motive explains for him why a reader so often is impelled to believe that there is "something else" in a Frost poem, more than meets the eye, whether the verse be "Mending Wall," "Stopping by Woods," or another. Lynen's conviction that Frost invariably strikes toward that "something" that lies beyond the apparent boundaries of the poem is, he maintains, the reason why a work such as "After Apple-Picking" will succeed in creating its planned effects whether or not the reader possesses any familiarity with New England orchards. Frost, concludes Lynen, is not an escapist at all, but a genuinely modern artist fully immersed in his own time.[36]

## Criticism since 1960

The death of Robert Frost in 1963 inaugurated a new era in Frost criticism, particularly in the realm of biographical revelations. The first items of value to appear in print were Frost's letters, led by *The Letters of Robert Frost to Louis Untermeyer,*[37] containing 220 letters written by the poet to the anthologist during a friendship which began in 1915 and never flagged. For the first time the public was given a cumulative self-portrait of Robert Frost, one which often was quite startlingly different from the mythical author readers had imagined. In his poems Frost had never given full rein to his pervasive sense of humor, but his letters at once revealed him to be an inveterate punster. His correspondence with Untermeyer is peppered with inventions, as when he playfully spells his name "Robbered Frossed" or writes "To some I am known as the Guessed of this University because I came as a riddle and was so soon solved."[38]

Of greater importance is the unexpected—and often shocking—sardonic edge which sharpens much of Frost's humor, and his open delight in relating any embarrassment or mischief which may have befallen what he called his "contemptuaries." Indeed, the sinister aspect of the Frost personality so often exceeds its links with the innocently humorous that many a reader nurtured on the image of Frost as generous neighbor comes away from the letters with shaken faith. Because Untermeyer from the first had become the poet's confidant, he was privy to plans and opinions that otherwise were kept strictly under wraps. The Robert Frost of these letters is an extremely human figure, often a sad one, subject to every shade of insecurity, ambition, and petty jealousy, a sometimes mean-hearted man who connived to diminish and even to destroy those whom he perceived to be potential rivals to his crown of poetry. The letters made startling reading when they first appeared in print, but as the shock of seeing Frost in a new light diminished, they have served as a valuable corrective to the excessively idealized image preserved in too many of his readers' minds.

A more comprehensive collection appeared in *Selected Letters of Robert Frost,* edited by Frost's biographer Lawrance Thompson.[39] These 556 items of correspondence served to confirm the darker portrait inherent in the Untermeyer letters, but their scope, of course, was considerably broader in the numbers and types of correspondents and in the topics of concern. For the reader who is interested in testing the breadth of Frost's correspondence the Thompson collection remains the standard edition. A more limited volume is Margaret Bartlett Anderson's *Robert Frost and John Bartlett,*[40] which reproduces some sixty letters written between 1912 and 1949, most of them personal in nature, to a man who had been Frost's student at Pinkerton Academy from 1907 to 1910 and who remained a lifelong admirer and booster of Frost's poetry. Another 182 letters, including 133 by Frost himself, are gathered in *Family Letters of Robert and Elinor Frost,* edited by Arnold Grade.[41] Here a reader encounters yet another dimension, a considerably more intimate Frost, without axe to grind or career to promote, a husband and father as much as a poet, a man genuinely concerned for his children and wife. *Family Letters* is of value for the light it casts upon Frost's relationships with those nearest and dearest to him and also for implications concerning the nature of those relationships as they may affect the poetry.

By all odds the most valuable document to appear since Frost's death has been Lawrance Thompson's massive life, published in three volumes.[42] The new work superseded earlier and necessarily incomplete attempts at biography by Gorham Munson, Elizabeth Shepley Sergeant, and Jean Gould, and corrected their numerous errors of fact and interpretation (often the result of Frost's own ambiguity or direct obfuscation). As his first biographer, Frost had handpicked a young professor at Ohio State University, Robert S. Newdick, with whom he had established an easy rapport in 1934. But Newdick died quite unexpectedly of appendicitis in 1939, and within three weeks Frost selected his successor, of the faculty of Princeton University, agreeing to work closely with him provided that no biography was published during his lifetime.

Thompson was awarded the immense advantage of associating intimately with Frost for a period of twenty-four years, was given first-hand accounts of events in Frost's life, and heard the poet's own interpretations of those events. In addition, by observing Frost's attitudes as they emerged from word and action, Thompson became aware of the man's numerous prejudices, unexpressed in the poems and scarcely revealed by the bare facts of biography. The most important lesson that emerged from this association, says Thompson, was a caveat made explicit by Frost himself: the poet was not invariably to be trusted to reveal the complete truth about himself.

It became clear to Thompson that he would have to do much digging for himself. His task was not only to collect information but to weigh and measure Frost's variant versions of events, comparing them with established fact and with versions offered elsewhere to other acquaintances. Much of what resulted from Thompson's spadework appears in the highly readable footnotes to the biography, so that the complexity of the man Frost is conveyed to the reader effectively and with profit. Thompson's first volume of Frost's biography appeared in 1966. The second, published in 1970, was awarded the Pulitzer Prize for biography; it makes explicit the less savory portrait of Frost which had been implicit in the published volumes of letters. When Thompson became aware of his own terminal illness in 1972, he took on the services of a graduate student, R. H. Winnick, as an aide. These two, working together for the better part of the next year, managed to assemble a draft for the final volume of the biography. Following Thompson's death in April 1973, Winnick completed the work, published in 1977.

After Frost died, it became known that Robert Newdick's preliminary efforts toward a biography were extant, his papers having been preserved for three decades by his widow. Arrangements were made to bring these materials before the public, and in 1976 *Newdick's Season of Frost* appeared, edited by William A. Sutton.[43] Thirteen "mini-chapters" represented Newdick's aborted attempt at a script for the biography. Appended to these narratives, which carried the Frost story through publication of *A Boy's Will*, were numerous examples of Newdick's research findings as well as a substantial narrative record of the Frost-Newdick association contributed by Sutton. Of greatest interest to the general reader, perhaps, are the letters of reminiscence regarding Frost, which Newdick was able to obtain from many who had known him in the early days, and Newdick's own detailed observations for which he anticipated a use when it should come time for him to describe the poet and his demeanor in mid-career.

Among the minutiae that Newdick felt worth recording—details insignificant separately but valuable in the aggregate—were notations that Frost smoked cigarettes but never a pipe or cigar, that drinking tended to loosen Frost's tongue rapidly, that he preferred nightshirts to pajamas, clung to hightop shoes, was fond of blue ties and wore cheap cotton socks but sported an expensive Stetson hat. Having observed Frost preparing for his public lectures, Newdick knew even what the poet allowed himself to eat during the stressful period preliminary to speaking: a pair of raw eggs, the juice of a lemon, perhaps a cup of tea with lots of sugar and a few crackers, then a dish of his favorite ice cream.[44] A fascinating account in its own right, *Newdick's Season of Frost* adds to our knowledge of Frost a host of details, facts, and anecdotes which apparently were not made available to Lawrance Thompson. Because of its interrupted status, the document should probably be considered a memoir rather than a biography.

The first memoir to appear after Frost's death was *Robert Frost Speaks*[45] by Daniel Smythe, who had known Frost since 1939 and had corresponded and held private conversations with him besides attending a good number of the poet's public readings and lectures. The volume centers upon Smythe's notes dictated to himself immediately following each personal encounter. Its great virtue is the presentation of events, thoughts, and opinions unavailable elsewhere. Unfortunately, the book cannot be considered wholly reliable as a source, as Lawrance Thompson has noted, because of the author's reliance upon his own memory and his willingness to present as direct quotations materials that apparently represent Smythe's own paraphrases of Frost's speech.[46] Again, Frost's habit of leaving different accounts with his various friends haunts Smythe's record and affects its validity. Yet the volume does furnish an extended look at the private Robert Frost and never shies away from the man's shortcomings, a view all but closed to public scrutiny at the time of its publication.

A more extensive memoir, one approaching biography in scope, is Louis Mertins's *Robert Frost: Life and Talks-Walking.*[47] Like Smythe, Mertins relies upon diary notes he recorded during the thirty years since 1932 when he and Frost first met. The greatest merit of Mertins's valuable book lies in his presentation of the many experiences that he and Frost shared and in the private remarks that he noted during and subsequent to their private moments together. While Mertins does hint at Frost's character flaws, he tends to minimize them, obviously preferring the more prevalent idolatory tone, and his extensive use of quotation marks in recording Frost's speech remains open, finally, to the same question as Smythe's.

Lesley Frost's *New Hampshire's Child*[48] is a personal account of the life of the Robert Frost family during the years 1905–1909. This unique contribution to the biographical record has been preserved because of the special at-home education that the Frost children received while living on the Derry farm prior to their father's emergence into fame. The information carried in the childhood journals that Lesley Frost kept during that residence is supplemented by an introduction in which she expands upon the methods and subject matter employed by her parents.

A fellow poet and resident of Amherst, Massachusetts, Robert Francis in 1972 published his reminiscences in *Frost: A Time to Talk,*[49] which offers Francis's detailed records of conversations held with Frost during the 1930s and again for a time during the 1950s. Francis is diligent in cautioning his reader that the records of conversations always rely upon his own memory and often are paraphrases. While he is open to preserving whatever Frost may have said, Francis emerges as an admirably critical listener, one who will pause to suggest how remarkable it is that Frost should inform him that he had never lifted a finger to further his own career; in his role as creative writer he wonders openly whether Frost is to be trusted entirely when he lavishes upon Francis's poems praise which seems more effusive than even their author is convinced they deserve.

*A Time to Talk* was soon followed by a similar volume by Reginald L. Cook based upon his many conversations with Robert Frost and supplemented with transcriptions of tape recordings in which Frost both reads his poems and comments upon them. Cook was clearly aware of questions concerning the validity of previously published conversations and undertook to assure the authenticity of his own volume by stressing that *Robert Frost: A Living Voice*[50] credited no word, phrase, or sentence with quotation marks unless he had heard it from the poet's lips. The reader will find Cook's volume to be a gold mine of off-the-cuff remarks upon a variety of Frost poems, as well as an intriguing commentary upon Puritanism, Marx, Darwin, Freud, Einstein, Emerson, Thoreau, religion and science generally, and upon the hazards of *explication de texte.*

With Robert Frost's life-work completed, general studies of his poetry have become more frequent. The focus of Reuben A. Brower's *The Poetry of Robert Frost*[51] is indicated by its subtitle "Constellations of Intention." Brower declines to write of Frost the man, preferring instead to concentrate upon the poems. In so doing he provides valuable analyses of a variety of titles, particularly in terms of form. His presentations of "After Apple-Picking," "Stopping by Woods on a Snowy Evening," "Design," and "The Death of the Hired Man" are notable examples of his success. Frost's major themes, with emphasis upon nature, are approached in the context of the two poets, Wordsworth and Emerson, whom Brower identifies as Frost's principal forebears, and his comparisons of Frost's verse with theirs is a stimulating contribution to our understanding of Frost's links with the Romantic tradition.

Frank Lentricchia in *Robert Frost: Modern Poetics and the Landscapes of Self*[52] is adamant in declaring Frost to be " a major poet" over objections to the contrary by George Nitchie, Cleanth Brooks, Malcolm Cowley, Yvor Winters, and others. Lentricchia identifies Frost as a man ever aware of the "struggle between the fiction-making imagination and the antifictive of the given environment, social and natural."[53] That the human being is forever stranded upon an inhospitable globe, separated from his environment no matter how ardently he desires unity with it and regardless of his efforts to achieve that happy resolution, is identified as being the central fact of existence in Frost's scheme of life. In this context, Lentricchia examines basic symbols—the book, the house, the woods—and sets out to rescue Frost from overly narrow classification as the Poet of New England, spokesman for a dead era. He asserts that the "American" quality of Frost's work has been too greatly (and often mistakenly) emphasized; he prefers to position the poet upon the broader landscape of the "timeless world" inhabited by all great poets. Lentricchia sees little difficulty in linking Robert Frost advantageously with other spokesmen for the modern age.

Richard Poirier mounts a formidable defense of Frost as "a poet of genius" in *Robert Frost: The Work of Knowing*.[54] Frost's stature, says Poirier, must be determined by considering his work within the limits he himself established. These would include his deliberate self-exclusion from the elitist literary modernism of Joyce and Eliot and from participation in concerns of the political left. While Poirier grants that Frost's chief deficiency was his inability to see as deeply into social systems as he saw into nature, this failure is not perceived as being of sufficient importance to deny Frost the labels "major" and "great." Poirier's provocative reading of the poems includes an unanticipated contempt for certain old favorites customarily exalted by readers and critics alike. "Directive" he finds to be both contrived and stagy, a poem which involves "no daring at all." In "The Death of the Hired Man" Poirier discerns a Frost much too ready to sell out to his popular audience. "Design," on the other hand, is read as a major work, and if Poirier's extrapolation of the poem's language is pushed to the snapping point, Frost's debt to William James's *Pragmatism* is brilliantly demonstrated.

A considerably more specialized study is John C. Kemp's *Robert Frost and New England*,[55] with its focus upon the long-standing tradition of viewing Frost as a New England farmer-poet. Kemp reminds us that Frost, far from being New England born or bred, was in actuality an outsider, an observer, and that he consciously allowed his poetry to slip into the regional mode. After 1915, finding that the New England aspects of his poems appealed to readers and drew praise from reviewers, Frost himself fostered the farmer myth, going so far as to settle in New Hampshire in his effort to promote it. In doing so, he joined a galaxy of writers—Ellen Glasgow, Willa Cather, E. A. Robinson, Carl Sandburg, Edgar Lee Masters, and soon to be, Sherwood Anderson and Sinclair Lewis—who had taken pains to identify themselves with discrete American localities. In truth, as Kemp points out, neither Frost's temperament nor his experience coincided with the insular and laconic persona of the Yankee. Yet he managed more often than not subtly to provide his poems with an acceptable "feel" for the region (this despite the fact that a mere handful of Yankee localisms appear in all his works). It is Kemp's judgment that a time came when Frost found himself overly committed to the rustic persona he had donned, that the possibility—or the wisdom—of breaking out from this mold troubled him considerably, and that his renewed commitment to it caused his later work to suffer, becoming at times melodramatic, at other times "sententiously smug and pompous."[56] Within the New England context, Kemp presents a valuable analysis of individual poems.

Among miscellaneous works of Frost criticism, noteworthy additions have been made by the three volumes of *Centennial Essays*[57] published under the editorship of Jac L. Tharpe and offering discussion by dozens of Frost scholars upon a far-ranging variety of issues. Linda W. Wagner's *Robert Frost: The Critical Reception*[58] collects the important periodical and newspaper reviews of all of Frost's books of verse. Her collection makes it feasible for a student to examine first-hand the contemporary reactions to Frost which gathered while his career expanded.

A pair of fine compilations have taken us in the direction of a complete and authoritative bibliography of works by and about Robert Frost. The first to appear was Peter Van Egmond's *The Critical Reception of Robert Frost*,[59] an annotated bibliography. It was followed by *Robert Frost: A Bibliography, 1913–1974*,[60] compiled by Frank Lentricchia and Melissa Christensen Lentricchia. A different and highly useful approach to the question of bibliography is taken by Donald J. Greiner in *Robert Frost: The Poet and His Critics*.[61] In six major essays—"Frost the Man," "The Early Criticism," etc.—Greiner identifies and also evaluates the most important books and essays written about Frost. While the opinions expressed are, of course, Greiner's, most readers will find him to be eminently fair and perceptive in his appraisals.

Collections of essays on Frost continue to appear, the most recent being *Studies in the Poetry,* edited by Kathryn Gibbs Harris[62] and consisting of fifteen essays arranged according to *Form, Attitude, Problems,* and *Background.* Without doubt there will be more collections coming along, as well as continued work toward a standard bibliography. It is not unlikely that further editions of letters will appear, culminating in as complete a collection as can be gathered. And those who knew Frost either for brief or extended periods, or who were associated with him in special circumstances, will continue to record their remembrances in print as Peter Davison, Alfred Kazin, and Donald Hall have done in recent years.[63] The study of Robert Frost is an ongoing process.

# Notes and References

*Chapter One*

1. Lawrance Thompson, *Robert Frost: The Early Years*, 1874–1915 (New York, 1966), p. 164.
2. Ibid., p. 261. That Robert Frost was mistaken in his judgment is indicated by the fact that upon his death William P. Frost left the Derry farm to his grandson, along with a trust fund which brought him $800 a year and made it possible for him to take his family to England in 1912.
3. Ibid., p. 380.
4. Elizabeth Shepley Sergeant, *Robert Frost: The Trial by Existence* (New York, 1960), p. 88–89.
5. Thompson, p. 403.
6. Linda W. Wagner, ed., *Robert Frost: The Critical Reception* (New York, 1977), pp. 1–2.
7. Sergeant, p. 129.
8. Lawrance Thompson, ed., *Selected Letters of Robert Frost* (New York, 1964), p. 131.
9. Sergeant, p. 152.
10. William Stanley Braithwaite, ed., *Anthology of Magazine Verse for 1915* (New York: 1915), pp. 199, 231–32.
11. Sergeant, p. 165.
12. Ibid., p. 271.
13. Ibid., p. 311.
14. Reginald L. Cook, *The Dimensions of Robert Frost* (New York, 1958), p. 11.
15. Daniel Smythe, *Robert Frost Speaks* (New York, 1964), p. 149.
16. Ibid., pp. 101–102.
17. Louis Untermeyer, ed., *The Letters of Robert Frost to Louis Untermeyer* (New York, 1963), pp. 361–62.
18. Sergeant, p. 239.
19. Untermeyer, p. 372.
20. "Robert Frost Dies at 88; Kennedy Leads in Tribute," *New York Times Western Edition* (Jan. 30, 1963), p. 5.
21. Stanley Kauffman, "Traveling Light," *New York Review of Books* 2 (June 25, 1964): 11.

22. *New York Times,* p. 5.

23. Frost's Russian trip is comprehensively treated in *Robert Frost in Russia* by F. D. Reeve, who accompanied the poet as guide and interpreter.

24. *New York Times,* p. 5.


*Chapter Two*

1. Henry David Thoreau, *Walden,* ed. Norrhan Holmes Pearson (New York: Holt, Rinehart & Winston, 1957), p. 80.

2. Ibid., p. 167.

3. Ibid., p. 255.

4. Ralph Waldo Emerson, *Selected Prose and Poetry,* ed. Reginald L. Cook (New York: Rinehart, 1956), p. 5.

5. Ibid., p. 25.

6. J. Donald Adams, "Speaking of Books," *New York Times Book Review* (April 12, 1959), p. 2.

7. Hayden Carruth, "The New England Tradition," *Regional Perspectives,* ed. John Gordon Burke (Chicago: American Library Association, 1973), pp. 18–35.

8. Alvan S. Ryan, "Frost and Emerson: Voice and Vision," *Massachusetts Review* I (October, 1959): 7–8, 10.

9. Nina Baym, "An Approach to Robert Frost's Nature Poetry," *American Quarterly* 17 (Winter, 1965): 714–16.

10. Malcolm Cowley, "Robert Frost: A Dissenting Opinion," *A Many-Windowed House* (Carbondale, Ill., 1970), p. 208.

11. Frank Lentricchia, *Robert Frost: Modern Poetics and the Landscapes of Self* (Durham, N. C., 1975), p. 179.

12. Roy Harvey Pearce, "Frost," *The Continuity of American Poetry* (Princeton, 1961), pp. 272–73.

13. John C. Kemp, *Robert Frost and New England* (Princeton, 1979), p. 33.

14. Ryan, p. 11; S. P. C. Duvall, "Robert Frost's 'Directive' out of *Walden,*" *American Literature* 31 (January, 1960): 488.

15. Willard Thorp, ed., *Herman Melville* (New York: American Book Company, 1938), p. 390.

16. Untermeyer, *Letters,* p. 22.

17. Ibid., pp. 88–89.

18. Ibid., p. 59.

19. James M. Cox, ed., *Robert Frost: A Collection of Critical Essays* (New York, 1962), p. 13.

20. Ibid.

21. Untermeyer, *Letters*, p. 129.
22. Harriet Monroe, *A Poet's Life* (New York: Macmillan, 1938), p. 286.
23. Ferdinand Earle, ed., *The Lyric Year* (New York: Mitchell Kennerley, 1912), p. viii.
24. Ibid.
25. Louis Untermeyer, ed., *Modern American Poetry* (New York, 1921), p. xxxi.
26. Amy Lowell, *Tendencies in Modern American Poetry* (New York, 1917), pp. 97–103.
27. Ibid., p. 107.
28. Sidney Cox, *A Swinger of Birches* (New York, 1957), p. 2.
29. Robert Frost, "Introduction to *King Jasper*," *Selected Prose of Robert Frost*, ed. Hyde Cox and Edward Connery Lathem (New York, 1966), pp. 59–60.
30. Emerson, p. 60.
31. Untermeyer, *Letters*, p. 29.
32. Smythe, p. 126.
33. Untermeyer, *Letters*, p. 30.
34. Ibid., p. 29.
35. Ibid., p. 219.
36. Sergeant, pp. 248–49.
37. Untermeyer, *Letters*, p. 10.
38. Ibid., p. 29.
39. Ibid., p. 96.
40. Ibid., p. 299.
41. Ibid., p. 106.
42. Ibid., p. 62.
43. Ibid., pp. 106–7.
44. Ibid., p. 148.
45. Ibid., pp. 91–2.
46. Ibid., p. 113.
47. Ibid., p. 134.
48. Lawrance Thompson, *Robert Frost: The Years of Triumph, 1915–1938* (New York, 1970), p. 696.
49. Alfred Kazin, *New York Jew* (New York, 1978), pp. 230–32.
50. Braithwaite, *Anthology . . . 1915*, p. xvii.
51. Ibid.
52. William Stanley Braithwaite, ed., *Anthology of Magazine Verse for 1917* (New York, 1917), p. 376.
53. Untermeyer, *Letters*, p. 50.
54. Untermeyer, *Modern American Poetry*, p. xlvi.

55. Ibid.
56. T. S. Eliot, *The Complete Poems and Plays* (New York: Harcourt, Brace & World, 1962), pp. 118–27.
57. Untermeyer, *Letters,* p. 262.
58. Ibid., p. 257.
59. Norman Foerster, ed., *American Poetry and Prose,* 3d ed. (Boston: Houghton Mifflin, 1947), p. 1518.
60. Untermeyer, *Letters,* p. 336.
61. Walt Whitman, *Leaves of Grass,* ed. Sculley Bradley (New York: Rinehart, 1955), p. 472.
62. Untermeyer, *Modern American Poetry,* p. xxxv.
63. Lionel Trilling, "A Speech on Robert Frost: A Cultural Episode," *Partisan Review* 26 (Summer, 1959): 448.
64. Ibid., p. 451.
65. J. Donald Adams, "Speaking of Books," p. 2.
66. Trilling, p. 446.
67. Untermeyer, *Letters,* p. 264.

*Chapter Three*

1. Cook, *Dimensions,* p. 78.
2. Robert Frost, "The Constant Symbol," *Atlantic Monthly* 178 (October, 1946): 51.
3. Ibid.
4. Ibid., p. 52.
5. Robert Frost, *Selected Poems* (London, 1936), p. 27.
6. Dudley Fitts, untitled review, *New England Quarterly* 9 (September, 1936): 519. Also, Leonard Unger and William Van O'Connor, *Poems for Study* (New York: Rinehart, 1953), p. 593.
7. Yvor Winters, *The Function of Criticism* (Denver: Swallow, 1957), pp. 160, 185.
8. Fitts, p. 519.
9. Edward Garnett, "Robert Frost's 'North of Boston,'" *Friday Nights* (London, 1922), pp. 239–40.
10. Lowell, *Tendencies,* p. 128.
11. Harris Francis Fletcher, *The Complete Poetical Works of John Milton* (Boston: Houghton Mifflin, 1941), pp. 159, 160, 193.
12. Ibid.
13. Lowell, *Tendencies,* p. 130.
14. Frost, "The Constant Symbol," p. 51.
15. Ibid.

16. Ibid., p. 52.
17. E. E. Cummings, *Poems 1923–1954* (New York: Harcourt, Brace, 1954), p. 286.
18. Robert Frost, *Complete Poems of Robert Frost* (New York, 1949), p. 155.
19. Untermeyer, *Letters,* p. 203.
20. Frost, "The Constant Symbol," p. 52.
21. Untermeyer, *Letters,* p. 264.
22. Ibid., p. 261.
23. Ibid., p. 138.
24. These and other puns occur with considerable abundance throughout the poet's letters to Louis Untermeyer.
25. Untermeyer, *Letters,* p. 166.
26. Emerson, p. 409.
27. Untermeyer, *Letters,* p. 322.
28. Smythe, p. 80.
29. Ibid.
30. Cook, *Dimensions,* p. 58.
31. Reginald L. Cook, "Robert Frost's Asides on His Poetry," *American Literature* 19 (January, 1948): 358.
32. Cook, *Dimensions,* pp. 78–80.
33. Emerson, p. 320.
34. Frost, "The Constant Symbol," p. 51.
35. Frost, *Complete Poems,* p. viii.

*Chapter Four*

1. Frost, "The Constant Symbol," p. 50.
2. Ibid.
3. Frost, *Complete Poems,* p. vi.
4. Untermeyer, *Letters,* p. 10.
5. Ibid., p. 85.
6. Frost, *Complete Poems,* p. viii.
7. Frost, "The Constant Symbol," p. 50.
8. Walt Whitman, *Leaves of Grass and Selected Prose,* ed. John Kouwenhoven (New York: Modern Library, 1950), p. 458.
9. Frost, "The Constant Symbol," p. 50.
10. Frost, *Complete Poems,* p. v.
11. Ibid., p. vi.
12. Ibid., p. v.
13. Ibid.
14. Ibid.

15. Robert Frost, "Education by Poetry," *Selected Prose of Robert Frost,* ed. by Hyde Cox and Edward Connery Lathem (New York, 1966), p. 36.

16. Frost, "The Constant Symbol," p. 50.

17. Emerson, p. 475.

18. Ibid.

19. Smythe, p. 81.

20. Ibid.

21. Robert Frost, *The Poetry of Robert Frost,* ed. by Edward Connery Lathem (New York, 1969), p. 121.

22. Ibid., p. 122.

23. Ibid., p. 56.

24. Ibid., p. 216.

25. Ibid., p. 419.

26. Ibid., p. 40.

27. Lowell, *Tendencies,* p. 125.

28. Ibid.

29. Ibid., p. 126.

30. Untermeyer, *Letters,* p. 92.

31. Mr. Lynen's book is dedicated to a thorough study of Frost's pastoralism, including his use of diction. John F. Lynen, *The Pastoral Art of Robert Frost* (New Haven, 1960).

32. Frost, *The Poetry. . . ,* p. 115.

33. Ibid., p. 136.

34. Ibid., p. 176.

35. Ibid., p. 203.

36. Ibid., p. 65.

37. Smythe, p. 90.

38. Frost, "Education by Poetry," p. 36.

39. Frost, *Complete Poems,* p. vi.

40. Ibid., p. vii.

41. Untermeyer, *Letters,* p. 341.

42. Smythe, p. 120.

43. Untermeyer, *Letters,* p. 274.

44. Frost, "Education by Poetry," p. 6.

45. Reginald L. Cook, "Frost on Frost: The Making of Poems," *American Literature* 28 (March, 1956): 64.

46. Cook, *Dimensions,* p. 97.

47. Smythe, p. 57.

48. Cook, *Dimensions,* p. 63.

49. Frost, "The Constant Symbol," p. 50.

50. Frost, "Education by Poetry," p. 37.
51. Ibid., p. 35.
52. John Ciardi, "Robert Frost: The Way to the Poem," *Saturday Review* 40 (April 12, 1958): 13.
53. Emerson, p. 322.
54. Thoreau, p. 251.
55. Frost, *Selected Poems*, p. 27.

*Chapter Five*

1. Kauffman, p. 11. See Chapter One, note 21.
2. Frost, *The Poetry* . . ., p. 26.
3. Ibid., p. 286.
4. Ibid., p. 10.
5. Untermeyer, *Letters*, pp. 102–3.
6. Frost, *The Poetry* . . ., p. 305.
7. Ibid., p. 223.
8. Ibid., p. 109.
9. Ibid., p. 106.
10. Ibid., p. 231.
11. Ibid., p. 131.
12. Ibid., pp. 389–90.
13. Ibid., p. 168.
14. Ibid., p. 179.
15. Ibid., p. 174.
16. Ibid., p. 303.
17. A more extensive treatment of the implications raised by Frost's continuing predicament with the dark woods may be found in my essay on that subject. Philip L. Gerber, "Bound Away—and Back Again," *Robert Frost: Studies of the Poetry*, ed. by Kathryn Gibbs Harris (Boston, 1979), pp. 65–75.

*Chapter Six*

1. Arnold Grade, ed., *Family Letters of Robert and Elinor Frost* (Albany, 1972), p. 161.
2. William Morton Payne, untitled review, *The Dial* 55, (Sept. 16, 1913): 212.
3. Sylvester Baxter, "New England's New Poet," *American Review of Reviews* (April, 1915), p. 434.
4. Lowell, *Tendencies*, p. 105.

5. Louis Untermeyer, *The New Era in American Poetry* (New York, 1919), p. 16.

6. Untermeyer, *Letters,* p. 29.

7. Thompson, *Robert Frost: The Years of Triumph,* p. xviii.

8. Waldo Frank, *Our America* (New York, 1919), pp. 158–62.

9. Bruce Weirick, *From Whitman to Sandburg in American Poetry* (New York, 1924), pp. 177–78, 182.

10. Clement Wood, *Poets of America* (New York, 1925), p. 150.

11. Percy H. Boynton, *Some Contemporary Americans* (Chicago, 1924), p. 35.

12. Carl Van Doren, *Many Minds* (New York, 1924), pp. 53–58.

13. Elizabeth Shepley Sergeant, "Robert Frost: Good Greek out of New England," *Fire Under the Andes* (New York, 1927), p. 289.

14. Harriet Monroe and Alice Corbin Henderson, eds., *The New Poetry* (New York, 1919, 1923). The poems used to represent Robert Frost are: "Mending Wall," "After Apple-Picking," "My November Guest," "Mowing," "Storm Fear," "Going for Water," and "The Code—Heroics."

15. Louis Untermeyer, ed., *Modern American Poetry* (New York, 1919).

16. Ibid., p. ix.

17. Granville Hicks, "The World of Robert Frost," *The New Republic* 65 (December 3, 1930): 77–78.

18. Granville Hicks, *The Great Tradition* (New York: Macmillan, 1933), p. 301.

19. Frederic I. Carpenter, "The Collected Poems of Robert Frost," *New England Quarterly* 5 (Jan., 1932): 159–60.

20. Dudley Fitts, untitled review, *New England Quarterly* 9 (Sept., 1936): 519–20.

21. Bernard DeVoto, "The Critics and Robert Frost," *The Saturday Review of Literature* 17 (Jan. 1, 1938): 3–4, 14–15.

22. Richard Thornton, ed., *Recognition of Robert Frost* (New York, 1937).

23. Thompson, ed., *Selected Letters,* p. 460.

24. William A. Sutton, ed., *Newdick's Season of Frost* (Albany, 1976), pp. 131–38, 418–20.

25. Lawrance Thompson, *Fire and Ice: The Art and Thought of Robert Frost* (New York, 1942).

26. Malcolm Cowley, "Frost: A Dissenting Opinion," and "The Case Against Mr. Frost: II," *New Republic* 111 (Sept. 11, 18, 1944): 312–13; 345–47.

27. Louise Bogan, *Achievement in American Poetry 1900–1950* (Chicago, 1951), pp. 47–51.

28. Harold H. Watts, "Robert Frost and the Interrupted Dialogue," *American Literature* 27 (March, 1955): 69–87. Also Yvor Winters, "Robert Frost: or, The Spiritual Drifter as Poet," *Sewanee Review* 56 (Autumn, 1948): 564–96.

29. Roy Harvey Pearce, "Frost's Momentary Stay," *Kenyon Review* 23 (Spring, 1961): 258–73.

30. James M. Cox, ed., *Robert Frost: A Collection of Critical Essays* (Englewood Cliffs, N. J., 1962).

31. Cook, *Dimensions,* p. 11.

32. Ibid., p. 146.

33. Donald J. Greiner, *Robert Frost: The Poet and His Critics* (Chicago, 1974), p. 46.

34. Sidney Cox, *A Swinger of Birches: A Portrait of Robert Frost* (New York, 1957).

35. George W. Nitchie, *Human Values in the Poetry of Robert Frost: A Study of Poetic Convictions* (Durham, N. C., 1960).

36. Lynen, *The Pastoral Art of Robert Frost.*

37. Untermeyer, ed., *Letters* (New York, 1963).

38. Ibid., pp. 126, 139.

39. Thompson, ed., *Selected Letters.*

40. Margaret Bartlett Anderson, *Robert Frost and John Bartlett: The Record of a Friendship* (New York, 1963).

41. Grade, ed., *Family Letters of Robert and Elinor Frost.*

42. See *Bibliography* under Biography.

43. Sutton, ed., *Newdick's Season of Frost.*

44. Ibid., p. 371.

45. Smythe, *Robert Frost Speaks.*

46. Thompson, *Robert Frost: The Early Years,* pp. 483–84, 521.

47. Louis Mertins, *Robert Frost: Life and Talks-Walking* (Norman, Okla., 1965).

48. Lesley Frost, *New Hampshire's Child: The Derry Journals of Lesley Frost* (Albany: State University of New York Press, 1969).

49. Robert Francis, ed., *Frost: A Time to Talk. Conversations & Indiscretions Recorded by Robert Francis* (Amherst, 1972).

50. Reginald L. Cook, *Robert Frost: A Living Voice* (Amherst, 1972).

51. Reuben A. Brower, *The Poetry of Robert Frost: Constellations of Intention* (New York, 1963).

52. Lentricchia, *Robert Frost: Modern Poetics* . . . .

53. Ibid., p. xii.

54. Richard Poirier, *Robert Frost: The Work of Knowing* (New York, 1977).

55. Kemp, *Robert Frost and New England*.

56. Ibid., p. 196.

57. Jac L. Tharpe, ed., *Frost Centennial Essays* (Jackson, Miss., 1974); *Frost Centennial Essays II* (Jackson, Miss., 1976); *Frost Centennial Essays III* (Jackson, Miss., 1978).

58. Wagner, *Robert Frost: The Critical Reception*.

59. Peter Van Egmond, *The Critical Reception of Robert Frost* (Boston, 1974).

60. Frank Lentricchia and Melissa Christensen Lentricchia, *Robert Frost: A Bibliography, 1913–1974* (Metuchen, N. J., 1976).

61. Donald J. Greiner, *Robert Frost: The Poet and His Critics* (Urbana, Ill., 1974).

62. Kathryn Gibbs Harris, ed., *Robert Frost: Studies of The Poetry* (Boston, 1979).

63. Peter Davison, *Half Remembered: A Personal History* (New York, 1973), pp. 206–13; Donald Hall, "Vanity, Fame, Love, and Robert Frost," *Remembering Poets: Reminiscences and Opinions* (New York, 1979), pp. 39–75; Alfred Kazin, *New York Jew* (New York, 1978), pp. 228–35.

# Selected Bibliography

## PRIMARY SOURCES

### 1. Poetry

*A Boy's Will.* London: Nutt, 1913; New York: Holt, 1915.
*North of Boston.* London: Nutt, 1914; New York: Holt, 1915.
*Mountain Interval.* New York: Holt, 1916.
*New Hampshire: A Poem with Notes and Grace Notes.* New York: Holt, 1923.
*West-Running Brook.* New York: Holt, 1928.
*A Further Range.* New York: Holt, 1936.
*A Witness Tree.* New York: Holt, 1942.
*A Masque of Reason.* New York: Holt, 1945.
*Steeple Bush.* New York: Holt, 1947.
*A Masque of Mercy.* New York: Holt, 1947.
*Complete Poems of Robert Frost.* New York: Holt, 1949.
*In the Clearing.* New York: Holt, Rinehart and Winston, 1962.
*The Poetry of Robert Frost.* New York: Holt, Rinehart and Winston, 1969.
    Edited by Edward Connery Lathem. Considered to be the definitive
    edition of Frost's poems.

### 2. Prose

*Selected Prose of Robert Frost.* New York: Holt, Rinehart and Winston, 1966.
    Edited by Hyde Cox and Edward Connery Lathem. Contains Robert
    Frost's most important essays concerning poetry and poets.
*Robert Frost on Writing.* New Brunswick, N. J.: Rutgers University Press,
    1973. Edited by Elaine Barry, with interpretive essays. A selection of
    letters, prefaces, reviews, lectures, interviews, parodies, and mar-
    ginalia in which Robert Frost speaks of writing and writers.

### 3. Interviews

*Interviews with Robert Frost.* New York: Holt, Rinehart and Winston, 1966.
    Edited by Edward Connery Lathem. A selection of fifty-four interviews
    originally published between 1915 and 1962.

## 4. Letters

*Family Letters of Robert and Elinor Frost.* Edited by Arnold Grade. Albany: State University of New York Press, 1972.

*The Letters of Robert Frost to Louis Untermeyer.* Edited by Louis Untermeyer. New York: Holt, Rinehart and Winston, 1963.

*Robert Frost and John Bartlett: The Record of a Friendship.* Edited by Margaret Bartlett Anderson. New York: Holt, Rinehart and Winston, 1963.

*Selected Letters of Robert Frost.* Edited by Lawrance Thompson. New York: Holt, Rinehart and Winston, 1964.

## SECONDARY SOURCES

### 1. Bibliography, books

Greiner, Donald J. *Robert Frost: The Poet and His Critics.* Chicago: American Library Association, 1974. A selective bibliography, aiming not at completeness but at listing the most important works about Robert Frost. The heart of the book is Greiner's valuable appraisal of the criticism.

Lentricchia, Frank, and Christensen, Melissa. *Robert Frost: A Bibliography, 1913–1974.* Metuchen, N. J.: Scarecrow Press, Inc., 1976. Attempts a "nearly exhaustive" list of works by and about Robert Frost, including data concerning his uncollected poems.

Van Egmond, Peter. *The Critical Reception of Robert Frost.* Boston: G. K. Hall & Co., 1974. An annotated bibliography chiefly of works about Robert Frost, 1913–1973.

### 2. Biography, books

Sergeant, Elizabeth Shepley. *Robert Frost: The Trial by Existence.* New York: Holt, Rinehart and Winston, 1960. The most comprehensive biography published prior to Thompson, highly personalized by the author's long-time friendship with Frost.

Sutton, William A., ed. *Newdick's Season of Frost.* Albany: State University of New York Press, 1976. Efforts toward a life of Robert Frost by Robert S. Newdick, originally selected as his official biographer by Frost. Includes a valuable commentary on the Frost-Newdick relationship by Sutton.

Thompson, Lawrance. *Robert Frost: The Early Years, 1874–1915.* New York: Holt, Rinehart and Winston, 1966.

————. *Robert Frost: The Years of Triumph, 1915–1938*. New York: Holt, Rinehart and Winston, 1970.

————and R. H. Winnick. *Robert Frost: The Later Years, 1938–1963*. New York: Holt, Rinehart and Winston, 1976. The standard biography of Robert Frost, who selected Thompson as his biographer and shared information with him for twenty-four years prior to his death in 1963.

3. Memoirs, books

Cook, Reginald L. *Robert Frost: A Living Voice*. Amherst, Mass.: University of Massachusetts Press, 1974. A record of the author's association with Robert Frost 1925–1963, consisting primarily of records of conversations plus transcriptions of tape recordings, supplemented by Cook's commentary regarding the occasions represented.

Cox, Sidney. *A Swinger of Birches*. New York: New York University Press, 1960. A highly personal account of various aspects of Frost's life and activities, written by a close personal friend whose subjectivity is never cloaked.

Francis, Robert. *Frost: A Time to Talk*. Amherst, Mass.: University of Massachusetts Press, 1972. Francis's records of conversations with Robert Frost during the 1930s and the 1950s, accompanied by Francis's running commentary on the two men's talks together.

Mertins, Louis. *Robert Frost: Life and Talks-Walking*. Norman: University of Oklahoma Press, 1965. Reminiscences taken from diary notes recorded since 1932 when Robert Frost first met Mertins, a collector and admirer.

Reeve, F. D. *Robert Frost in Russia*. Boston: Little, Brown and Co., 1964. Contains a comprehensive record and interpretation of the poet's 1962 trip to the Soviet Union, perhaps overly detailed in relation to the importance of the event itself.

Smythe, Daniel. *Robert Frost Speaks*. New York: Twayne Publishers, 1964. A unique work based upon the author's sporadic contacts with Robert Frost over a twenty-five-year span and containing many of the poet's remarks not recorded elsewhere.

4. Memoirs, parts of books

Davison, Peter. *Half Remembered: A Personal History*. New York: Harper and Row, 1973, pp. 206–213. Davison came to know Frost intimately in Cambridge during the eighteen years after 1945, was the recipient of Frost's kind attention, and thought him America's greatest poet and "the greatest of my teachers."

Hall, Donald. "Vanity, Fame, Love, and Robert Frost." *Remembering Poets: Reminiscences and Opinions*. New York: Harper and Row, 1978, pp. 39–75. Hall was sixteen when he first met Frost at Bread Loaf. Later they met at Harvard, Stanford, Ann Arbor, and finally in Vermont in 1962. Hall found that "over the years Frost changed for me, from a monument to a public fraud to something more human and complicated than either praise or blame could deal with."

Kazin, Alfred. *New York Jew*. New York: Alfred A. Knopf, 1978, pp. 228–35. Teaching at Amherst in 1957–58 while Frost was on campus there, Kazin found the poet "a raging battlefield of ambition, competitiveness, guilt," consumed with resentment toward his rivals and hungry for adulation.

Morrison, Kathleen. *Robert Frost: A Pictorial Chronicle*. New York: Holt, Rinehart and Winston, 1974. The title is misleading, as the photographs are balanced by the detailed reminiscences of Mrs. Morrison, who served as Robert Frost's secretary and manager from 1938, when Elinor Frost died, until 1963.

Untermeyer, Louis. "The Northeast Corner." *From Another World*. New York: Harcourt, Brace, 1939, pp. 206–28. Untermeyer tells of his early encounters with Frost and his poetry, drawing judiciously from Frost's correspondence but without revealing much of the unpleasant aspect of Frost's personality which would become apparent in the *Letters*.

5. Collections of criticism, books

*Frost: Centennial Essays*. Edited by Jac L. Tharpe. Jackson: University Press of Mississippi, 1974. Forty-one essays upon a variety of topics by Frost friends, admirers, and scholars.

*Frost: Centennial Essays II*. Edited by Jac L. Tharpe. Jackson: University Press of Mississippi, 1976. Twenty-two essays by Frost scholars.

*Frost: Centennial Essays III*. Edited by Jac L. Tharpe. Jackson: University Press of Mississippi, 1978. Third in a series. Thirteen new essays, chiefly biographical.

*Recognition of Robert Frost*. Edited by Richard Thornton. New York: Holt, 1937. A sampler of Frost criticism published during the twenty-five years since publication of *A Boy's Will*. Representative of attitudes toward Frost and his poetry but excludes negative criticism.

*Robert Frost: A Collection of Critical Essays*. Edited by James M. Cox. Englewood Cliffs, N. J.: Prentice-Hall, 1962. A superior and representative selection of major essays on Robert Frost and his poetry.

*Robert Frost: The Critical Reception.* Edited by Linda W. Wagner. New York: Burt Franklin, 1977. Collects the major newspaper and periodical reviews of Frost's books. A valuable aid for the student.

*Robert Frost: An Introduction.* Edited by Robert A. Greenberg and James G. Hepburn. New York: Holt, Rinehart and Winston, 1961. Collected essays and excerpts from essays on Robert Frost by a variety of critics.

*Robert Frost: Studies of the Poetry.* Edited by Kathryn Gibbs Harris. Boston: G. K. Hall, 1979. Fifteen new essays by Frost scholars upon a variety of topics.

*Saturday Review* (Feb. 23, 1963). Memorial Edition, including articles by Charles R. Anderson, John S. Dickey, John Frederick Nims, and an editorial by John Ciardi.

*Southern Review* (Oct. 1966). Issue devoted to critical views and reminiscences by a variety of Frost scholars and friends.

6. Criticism, books

Barry, Elaine. *Robert Frost.* New York: Frederick Ungar, 1973. A brief introduction to Frost's poetry, concentrating upon the lyrics, the dramatic narratives, and the sonnets.

Brower, Reuben A. *The Poetry of Robert Frost: Constellations of Intention.* New York: Oxford University Press, 1963. A reading of Frost's verse for form and theme, made particularly valuable for Brower's comparisons of Frost's work with the poetry of Wordsworth and Emerson.

Cook, Reginald L. *The Dimensions of Robert Frost.* New York: Rinehart, 1958. A fine study of Frost as man and poet based upon firsthand experience by a friend and great admirer.

Doyle, John Robert, Jr. *The Poetry of Robert Frost.* New York: Hafner, 1962. Devoted primarily to an incisive analysis of several dozen poems categorized according to type and theme.

Isaacs, Elizabeth. *An Introduction to Robert Frost.* Denver: Alan Swallow, 1962. One of the best of the comprehensive treatments of Robert Frost and his career.

Kemp, John C. *Robert Frost and New England.* Princeton: Princeton University Press, 1979. An in-depth examination of the New England farmer-poet myth, including Frost's invention and embrace of it, his later ambiguities concerning it, and the problems which maintaining it posed for his later poetry. Kemp includes a valuable bibliography 1913–77 of reviews and essays on the topic.

Lentricchia, Frank. *Robert Frost: Modern Poetics and the Landscapes of Self.* Durham, N. C.: Duke University Press, 1975. A readable and persuasive reply to George Nitchie and other critics who would deny Frost's claim to greatness on the basis of philosophical deficiencies. Lentricchia analyzes Frost's poems and their central symbols in the context of a continuing tension between imagination and environment, concluding that the separateness of society and nature prevades all of Frost's work.

Lynen, John F. *The Pastoral Art of Robert Frost.* New Haven: Yale University Press, 1960. Lynen presents Robert Frost as a conscious artist. In no sense a rustic, Frost adopts the pastoral mode and employs it and New England as sophisticated symbols through which the modern world is depicted.

Nitchie, George W. *Human Values in the Poetry of Robert Frost.* Durham: Duke University Press, 1960. Nitchie argues that Frost, while selecting the relationship between man and nature as a major theme, is reluctant to probe deeply into that complex subject. Compared with the treatment of nature by such poets as Wordsworth, Emerson, and Jeffers, Frost's poetry suffers.

Poirier, Richard. *Robert Frost: The Work of Knowing.* New York: Oxford University Press, 1977. A major study in support of Frost's greatness which includes an exhaustive examination of Frost's many-faceted concept of "home." A provocative reading of the poems, with many surprises, including severe judgments on poems ordinarily considered to be among Frost's finest.

Squires, Radcliffe. *The Major Themes of Robert Frost.* Ann Arbor: University of Michigan Press, 1963. A brief and extremely well written discussion of Frost's major ideas.

7. Criticism, parts of books

Aldridge, John W. "The Other Frost." *The Devil in the Fire: Retrospective Essays on American Literature and Culture, 1951–1971,* pp. 134–41. Essentially a review of the second volume of the Thompson biography. The darker image of Frost Aldridge finds "profoundly unpleasant," and yet it is to be preferred over "the Grant Wood-Mount Rushmore stereotype in which Frost's memory is reverently entombed." Thompson has performed a service, for it is now possible to approach Frost "with some real objectivity and candor."

Bogan, Louise. *Achievement in American Poetry 1900–1950.* Chicago: Henry Regnery, 1951, pp. 47–51. An admirer of Frost in his earlier phases, Bogan believes that his later poems never capitalized upon "the tragic power that *North of Boston* promised." Instead, by emphasizing affirmations, Frost ultimately became a poet of "romantic nostalgia."

Boynton, Percy H. "Robert Frost." *Some Contemporary Americans: The Personal Equation in Literature.* Chicago: University of Chicago Press, 1924, pp. 33–49. Emphasizes Frost's good fortune in locating a happy compromise in form between the demands of the spoken word and the conventions of verse patterns. Frost's philosophy is that of "a cheerful, persistent man of hard-headed common sense."

Braithwaite, William Stanley. *Anthology of Magazine Verse for 1915.* New York: Gomme & Marshall, 1915.

————. *Anthology of Magazine Verse for 1917.* Boston: Small, Maynard, 1917.

————. *Anthology of Magazine Verse for 1918.* Boston: Small, Maynard, 1918. These anthologies reprint Frost's poems which have appeared in periodicals during the given year, also critical reviews and a comprehensive report on the poetry situation. Valuable for comments on the contemporary literary scene.

Cowley, Malcolm. "Robert Frost: A Dissenting Opinion." *A Many-Windowed House.* Carbondale: Southern Illinois University Press, 1970, pp. 201–12. In his well-argued essay Cowley evaluates Robert Frost as a relatively minor writer when compared with the great figures of the New England tradition; "he does not strike far inward into the wilderness of human nature . . . lost in space, he manages to overlook the misfortunes under his eyes."

Dickey, James. "Robert Frost." *Babel to Byzantium: Poets & Poetry Now.* New York: Farrar, Straus and Giroux, 1968, pp. 200–209. Essentially a review of the first volume of Thompson's life of Frost, this article blames the Frost myth for the poet's having become a very misread writer. Dickey places the "real" Frost considerably nearer to "Trilling's Frost of darkness and terror."

Eberhart, Richard. "Robert Frost: His Personality." *Of Poets and Poetry.* Urbana: University of Illinois Press, 1979, pp. 179–201. An appreciation of Frost as a poet with a personality totally integrated with the life of his times, his nation, and with nature. "He teaches us courage in the face of the enigmas of existence. We feel that he wears no mask and speaks the truth directly."

Garnett, Edward. "Robert Frost's 'North of Boston.'" *Friday Nights: Literary Criticism and Appreciations.* London: Jonathan Cape, 1922, pp. 221–42. This essay, which first appeared in *Atlantic Monthly,* finds Frost "destined to take a permanent place in American literature." Garnett praises Frost as a fresh creative force, an original voice, and a master of blank verse.

Gregory, Horace, and Zaturenska, Marya. "*The Horatian Serenity of Robert Frost.*" *A History of American Poetry 1900–1940.* New York: Harcourt,

Brace, 1946, pp. 150–62. A resume of Frost's life and work in which Gregory agrees with Harriet Monroe that Frost's virtues are "of a consistently traditional order."

Howe, Irving. "Robert Frost: A Momentary Stay." *A World More Attractive.* New York: Horizon, 1963, pp. 144–57. Howe applies the strictest critical standards to Frost's verse and judges that he wrote a great deal of second-rate poetry, probably as a concession to the taste of his extremely wide audience. However, Frost did produce at least fifteen or twenty first-rate lyrics on which his future will depend.

Jarrell, Randall. "The Other Frost" and "To the Laodiceans." *Poetry and the Age.* New York: Alfred A. Knopf, 1953, pp. 28–36, 37–69. Two discerning and well-crafted essays by one of Frost's most steadfast admirers.

Jones, Llewellyn. "Robert Frost." *First Impressions.* New York: Alfred A. Knopf, 1925, pp. 37–52. An early appraisal which praises Frost's ability to make his verse "speak in human tones." While Jones finds Frost to be a romanticist, he is never one in "the cheap sense of the word."

Kreymborg, Alfred. "The Fire and Ice of Robert Frost." *Our Singing Strength.* New York: Coward-McCann, 1929, pp. 316–32. A review of Frost's career and poetry to 1929 within the context of the history of the modern verse movement. Kreymborg finds Frost's lyrics to be first-rate, his other poems of lesser quality. As an artist, Frost's "integrity with himself is absolute; he listens to no other voice."

Lewisohn, Ludwig. *Expression in America.* New York: Harpers, 1932, pp. 497–501. Lewisohn considers Frost in company with the Naturalists, but his revolt against convention is undertaken in order to return "from fashions to nature . . . to recover the freshness of the permanent." At the heart of Frost's poetry are his admission of the force of human passion and his acceptance of life as tragic.

Lowell, Amy. *A Critical Fable.* Boston: Houghton Mifflin, 1922, pp. 21–25. Lowell's praise and criticism of Frost put into rhyming couplets in a long satirical poem reminiscent of James Russell Lowell's "A Fable for Critics."

————. "Robert Frost." *Tendencies in Modern American Poetry.* New York: Macmillan, 1917, pp. 77–136. The first appreciation of Frost in book form. Lowell discusses primarily the poems in *North of Boston* and finds Frost centering his attention upon the sadness of New England decay: "His people are leftovers of the old stock, morbid, pursued by phantoms, slowly sinking to insanity."

Martin, Jay. "Robert Frost: The Two Roads." *Harvests of Change: American Literature 1865–1914.* Englewood Cliffs, N. J.: Prentice-Hall, 1967, pp. 159–64. Martin presents Frost as an artist who chose to work within the stereotyped themes of New England regional writing, but who revitalized his subject matter, taking from it an extreme implication for the isolation of man which is highly relevant to the alienated condition of man in the modern world.

Monroe, Harriet, and Henderson, Alice Corbin. *The New Poetry.* New York: Macmillan, 1919, revised 1923. The poems collected here, as well as the comments of the editors, are of historical significance in tracing the establishment of Frost's fame.

Pearce, Roy Harvey. "Frost." *The Continuity of American Poetry.* Princeton: Princeton University Press, 1961, pp. 271–83. Pearce stresses Robert Frost's limitations as a poet. Although he allies himself with Emerson, Frost is a lesser individual—and a lesser poet—than he might be were he truly like Emerson, a man who considered himself above all to be a "contemporary" poet.

Rexroth, Kenneth. *American Poetry in the Twentieth Century.* New York: Herder and Herder, 1971, pp. 30–31. In this brief passage Rexroth rejects Frost as a modern poet, declaring that he (and Robinson) instead revived the main tradition of the nineteenth century. Rexroth suggests that Frost is a minor poet whose work quite rightly "enjoys no intellectual prestige."

Rosenthal, M. L. "Robinson and Frost." *The Modern Poets: An Introduction.* New York: Oxford University Press, 1960, pp. 104–13. Rosenthal emphasizes Frost's dark speculations upon the life of woman, believes that Frost's New England world has for most of his readers "the charm of the completely exotic," and regrets the absence of formal daring in poems whose conventionality eventually produces tedium in the reader.

Sergeant, Elizabeth Shepley. "Robert Frost, Good Greek out of New England." *Fire Under the Andes.* New York: Alfred A. Knopf, 1927, pp. 285–303. A fine, and typical, example of appreciation from the 1920s, aimed at the deification of Robert Frost: ". . . the homespun background, the bucolic detail, is transformed and sublimated by a kind of abstract beauty and detachment, like the abstract quality of Frost's sculptured head as rendered in Du Chêne's fine bust."

Thompson, Lawrance. "Robert Frost." *Seven Modern American Poets: An Introduction.* Edited by Leonard Ungar. Minneapolis: University of Minnesota Press, 1967, pp. 9–44. Thompson here surveys Frost's life and poetry, centering upon the thesis that Frost is primarily a subjective lyric poet whose verses are strong in both thematic affirmations and negations.

Untermeyer, Louis. *Modern American Poetry*. New York: Harcourt, Brace, 1919; revised 1921, 1925. Relates Robert Frost to his contemporaries within the new verse movement. Significant in establishing the poet's early fame.

————. "Robert Frost." *The New Era in American Poetry*. New York: Holt, 1919, pp. 15–39. An appreciation that was instrumental in establishing Frost's reputation. Untermeyer finds Frost to be the natural inheritor of Whitman in being wholly American and "the one living poet who has never padded a phrase, never larruped an emotion."

Van Doren, Carl. "The Soil of the Puritans." *Many Minds*. New York: Alfred A. Knopf, 1924, pp. 50–66. Van Doren finds Frost's New England connection to be his chief strength: "If Robert Frost talks as becomes a Yankee poet, so does he think as becomes one." In his poems Frost emerges as neither a cynic nor a philanthropist, but as "a good neighbor" of consummate common sense.

Warren, Robert Penn. "The Themes of Robert Frost." *Selected Essays*. New York: Random House, 1958, pp. 118–36. Warren uses a group of Frost poems to illustrate his thesis that the poet's chief themes revolve around sets of oppositions such as "the world of nature and the world of the ideal, the heaven and the earth, the human and the non-human."

Weirick, Bruce. "The Note of Futility: New England and New York." *From Whitman to Sandburg in American Poetry*. New York: Macmillan, 1924, pp. 177–192. Considers Frost in company with E. A. Robinson: "Curiously enough a note of futility rather than any great national or spiritual hope is their bond of union."

Whipple, T. K. "Robert Frost." *Spokesmen*. New York: Appleton, 1928, pp. 94–114. An excellent critical appraisal of Frost which despite its relatively early date remains among the most perceptive studies.

Winters, Yvor. "Robert Frost: Or, The Spiritual Drifter as Poet." *The Function of Criticism*. Denver: Swallow, 1957, pp. 157–88. An important item in the negative criticism on Robert Frost. Winters finds Frost to be "in no sense a great poet, but he is at times a distinguished and valuable poet."

Wood, Clement. "Robert Frost: The Twilight of New England." *Poets of America*. New York: Dutton, 1925, pp. 142–62. Praises Frost's ability to bring to modern poetry "the speech that falls from the lips of living man" and emphasizes Frost's obsession with "this diminished thing, New England."

8. Criticism, periodicals

Adams, J. Donald. "Speaking of Books." *New York Times Book Review,* April 12, 1959, p. 2. A reaction to Lionel Trilling's description of Frost as a "terrifying" poet; emphasizes the influence of Emerson rather than Freud upon Frost.

Baym, Nina. "An Approach to Robert Frost's Nature Poetry." *American Quarterly,* Winter, 1965, pp. 713–23. Baym rejects the notion that Frost is Emersonian in his approach to nature, substituting instead the older concept of mutability as his guide. Frost's link with science shows in his acceptance of an entropic universe, constantly winding down and rendering all existence temporary, a principle which man is driven to resist in particular instances even while he accepts it as fact generally.

Beach, Joseph Warren. "Robert Frost." *Yale Review,* December, 1953, pp. 204–17. A personal memoir/appreciation written when Frost was seventy-eight. Treats Emerson's influence; "Self-Reliance" may have been "Frost's Bible."

Coursen, Herbert R., Jr. "The Ghost of Christmas Past: 'Stopping by Woods on a Snowy Evening.'" *College English,* December, 1962, pp. 236–38. A witty spoof of the overly abundant critical interpretations of Frost's best-known lyric.

Cowley, Malcolm. "The Case Against Mr. Frost." *The New Republic,* September 11, 1944, pp. 312–13; September 18, 1944, pp. 345–47. A provocative discussion of the limitations that keep Frost from achieving true greatness, chiefly concerning the poet's timidity and his ties to the past.

Cox, James. "Robert Frost and the Edge of the Clearing." *Virginia Quarterly Review,* Winter, 1959, pp. 73–88. Frost is called an "American literary man as public entertainer." Discusses the ironies of Frost's poems.

Dabbs, J. McBride. "Robert Frost and the Dark Woods." *Yale Review,* Spring, 1934, pp. 514–20. A discerning essay on the woods image, applicable to Frost's work finished after 1934 as well.

DeVoto, Bernard. "The Critics and Robert Frost." *Saturday Review of Literature,* January 1, 1938, pp. 3–4, 14–15. Ostensibly a review of *Recognition of Robert Frost* in which DeVoto classes Frost's critics as acceptable or unacceptable. DeVoto's bias is clear: "I think of Frost as the finest American poet, living or dead."

Donoghue, Denis. "The Limitations of Robert Frost." *Twentieth Century,* July, 1959, pp. 13–22. Discusses Frost's style, finding it of a "middle" type. Criticizes Frost for dilution of his poetry.

Dougherty, James P. "Robert Frost's 'Directive' to the Wilderness." *American Quarterly*, Summer, 1966, pp. 208–19. Relates "Directive" to the myth of the wilderness; in the poem Frost retreats from the complexity of the present into a simpler and more manageable past.

Duvall, S. P. C. "Robert Frost's 'Directive' out of *Walden*." *American Literature*, January, 1960, pp. 482–88. Duvall relates "Directive" in considerable detail to *Walden* and suggests that Frost has a far greater affinity with Thoreau than with Emerson.

Ellsbree, Langdon. "Frost and the Isolation of Man." *Claremont Quarterly*, Summer, 1960, pp. 29–40. Ellsbree analyzes the formal structure of "A Servant to Servant," "Home Burial," and "The Death of the Hired Man" in order to demonstrate the manner in which the organization of the poems aids Frost in achieving memorable demonstrations of the pain and loneliness of human life.

Fitts, Dudley. Untitled review of *A Further Range*. *New England Quarterly*, September, 1963, pp. 519–21. Fitts credits Frost with art that conceals art, but finds fault with Frost's didactic streak and "ponderous kind of playfulness."

Gerber, Philip L. "'My Rising Contemptuaries': Robert Frost Amid His Peers." *Western Humanities Review*, Spring, 1966, pp. 135–141. In the cultivation of his career after 1915, Frost became preoccupied with his rivals, real or imagined, particularly Edgar Lee Masters and Amy Lowell.

Griffith, Clark. "Frost and the American View of Nature." *American Quarterly*, Spring, 1968, pp. 21–37. Griffith agrees that Frost holds with the older idea of nature as teacher, but argues that he also represents the more modern view of nature as an opaque, impersonal force and even as an antagonist.

Hepburn, James G. "Robert Frost and His Critics." *New England Quarterly*, September, 1962, pp. 367–76. Treats the various critical approaches to "Stopping by Woods on a Snowy Evening," concluding that the poem is one of undertones and overtones rather than of explicit meaning.

Hicks, Granville. "The World of Robert Frost." *New Republic*, December 3, 1930, pp. 77–78. Hicks takes Frost to task for creating a world for himself which eliminates contemporary concerns; this for Hicks is a sign of Frost's lack of stature.

Humphries, Rolfe. "Verse Chronicle." *Nation*, July 23, 1949, pp. 92–93. A review of Frost's *Complete Poems*, crediting it as a first-rate achievement, yet lamenting that Frost has never fully realized his potential, being too eager to be "sane and wholesome."

Montgomery, Marion. "Robert Frost and His Use of Barriers: Man vs. Nature Toward God." *South Atlantic Quarterly,* Summer, 1958, pp. 339–53. Devoted to Frost's theme of man existing in an impersonal world where he preserves himself by erecting or destroying barriers.

Rosenthal, M. L. "The Robert Frost Controversy." *Nation,* June 20, 1959, pp. 559–61. A defense of Lionel Trilling's description of Frost as a "terrifying poet."

Ryan, Alvan S. "Frost and Emerson: Voice and Vision." *Massachusetts Review,* October, 1959, pp. 5–23. Compares Frost with Emerson; finds superficial similarities and wide differences between the two, both as poets and as thinkers.

Schneider, Isador. "Robert Frost." *Nation,* January 28, 1931, pp. 101–2. A balanced estimate of Frost's achievement in *Collected Poems,* recounting not only Frost's considerable merits but also his lack of touch with his own time and his weakness in dealing with ideas.

Traschen, Isadore. "Robert Frost: Some Divisions in a Whole Man." *Yale Review,* Autumn, 1965, pp. 57–70. Frost takes too few risks with his poetry, examines too few of the deepest human experiences. His is a divided personality; for example, between the involved man and the detached observer.

Trilling, Lionel. "A Speech on Robert Frost: A Cultural Episode." *Partisan Review,* Summer, 1959, pp. 445–52. Trilling attempts to counteract the too generally accepted view of Frost as a poet of comfort and affirmation by emphasizing his sorties into the darker areas of human existence.

Van Doren, Mark. "The Permanence of Robert Frost." *American Scholar,* Spring, 1936, pp. 190–98. Hypothesizes upon the durability of Frost's fame, "the middle ground he occupies in the present poetical scene" as the best grounds for prophecy. Frost is likely to last precisely because he has managed to avoid poetical extremes.

Watts, Harold H. "Robert Frost and the Interrupted Dialogue." *American Literature,* March, 1955, pp. 69–87. Examines Frost's attitudes of skepticism and acceptance, particularly in reference to "A Masque of Mercy" and "A Masque of Reason."

Whicher, George F. "Frost at Seventy." *American Scholar,* Autumn, 1945, pp. 405–14. In appraising Frost's achievement and durability, this personal friend of the poet offers a lengthy rebuttal to Malcolm Cowley's case against Frost.

# Index